Remaking the Labour Party

Exploring the development of revisionist thought in the Labour Party in the postwar era, *Remaking the Labour Party* focuses on the most distinctive and controversial aspect of Labour's new thinking – its changed attitude towards public ownership and socialism, private ownership and the market economy.

Developing a challenging thesis about the historic role of public ownership as the central idea within Labour's 'socialist myth', Tudor Jones examines:

- the Clause IV controversy of 1959–60 and the uneasy compromise forged in its aftermath
- the period of ideological truce under Harold Wilson's leadership
- the bitter conflicts that resurfaced during the 1970s and early 1980s
- the ideological rethinking developed after 1983 under the leadership of Neil Kinnock
- the continuation of Labour's 'second-stage' revisionism under Tony Blair.

Drawing on the author's own interviews with some of the leading protagonists in the debate, including Harold Wilson, Neil Kinnock and Roy Jenkins, as well as on a wide range of primary and secondary sources, *Remaking the Labour Party* is a valuable work for those studying modern British politics and contemporary political thought.

Dr Tudor Jones is a senior lecturer in politics at Coventry University.

Remaking the Labour Party
From Gaitskell to Blair

Tudor Jones

London and New York

First published 1996
by Routledge
11 New Fetter Lane, London EC4P 4EE

Simultaneously published in the USA and Canada
by Routledge
29 West 35th Street, New York, NY 10001

© 1996 Tudor Jones

Typeset in Times by Keystroke,
Jacaranda Lodge, Wolverhampton
Printed and bound in Great Britain by
Clays Ltd, St Ives PLC

British Library Cataloguing in Publication Data
A catalogue record for this book is available from the British Library

Library of Congress Cataloguing in Publication Data
Jones, Tudor,
    Remaking the Labour Party : from Gaitskell to Blair / Tudor Jones.
        p.   cm.
    Includes bibliographical references and index.
    ISBN 0–415–12549–9 (hardcover). — ISBN 0–415–12550–2 (pbk.)
    1. Labour Party (Great Britain)—History. I. Title.
JL1129.L32J66   1996
324.24107—dc20   96–26319
                                            CIP

ISBN 0–415–12549–9 (hbk)
     0–415–12550–2 (pbk)

Contents

To my father and to the memory of my mother.

Preface

This book does not purport to be a general history of the British Labour Party over the last forty years. Rather, it aims to provide an historical study of revisionist thought in the Labour Party from the 1950s to the present day, spanning the period from the leadership of Hugh Gaitskell to that of Tony Blair. It develops an analysis of Labour revisionism, presented as a highly influential body of thought and set of policies within the Party during that period. Specifically, the focus of this study is upon the most distinctive and ideologically contentious aspect of the revisionist position – its attitude towards public ownership and socialism, private industry and the market economy. The book's broader concern is thus with the historical development of Labour's long-running ideological conflict, crystallized in the Clause IV disputes of 1959–60 and 1995–6, over the Party's traditional commitment, in terms of both policy and doctrine, to the public ownership of the means of production.

In analysing this conflict and the manner in which it was conducted between, first, 'revisionists' and 'fundamentalists' and, later, 'modernizers' and 'traditionalists' within Labour's ranks, the study consistently employs as a central explanatory concept the term 'political myth', which is treated throughout as a dominant, inspirational idea that motivates a political group, galvanizing its thought and actions. It is argued that since 1918 public ownership, as enshrined in Clause IV of the Party Constitution, had provided the central feature of Labour's socialist myth – of, that is, its inspiring vision of a future Socialist Commonwealth, a transformed economy and society.

Furthermore, the study maintains that this concept of socialist myth helps to explain not only the vehemence of reactions within the Party against revisionist attempts to demote public ownership and amend Clause IV, but also the enduring, widespread appeal, at once doctrinal and sentimental, of the idea of public ownership and hence of the original text of Clause IV, Part Four.

To a large extent, the methods of the historian of political thought are used throughout this study – including, in particular, detailed attention to such published sources as the books, pamphlets and periodicals which form, together with Party policy documents, the main receptacles of British democratic socialist thought during the period under review. The study also draws upon unpublished papers and diaries, as well as upon my own interviews with some of the leading protagonists in the ideological and policy debates of those years.

Chapter 1 explores the contentious question of the status of public ownership – as both a political idea and an issue of economic policy – within the Labour Party's ideology and programmes after 1900. It attempts to place the fierce doctrinal and policy debates surrounding that question within their historical and theoretical contexts.

Chapter 2 examines the emergence and refinement of Labour revisionism as a response to the completion of the Attlee Governments' programme and, in particular, to the perceived inadequacies of rival attitudes towards public ownership and socialism that were promoted within the Party in the wake of that programme. The chapter analyses the development of Labour revisionism, both as a body of thought and as a set of policies, from 1956 onwards. It considers how, in those years following Hugh Gaitskell's accession to the Party Leadership, revisionism acquired increasing prominence as an ideological influence within the Party. It demonstrates how during that period revisionist ideas on public ownership and economic strategy, together with the underlying revisionist conception of socialism, were thoroughly developed, particularly by Tony Crosland, and steadily incorporated into official Party policy statements.

Chapter 3 explores the deepening confrontation that arose from the revisionist thinking of Crosland, Gaitskell and others and culminated in Hugh Gaitskell's ill-fated attempts in 1959–60 to revise Clause IV of the Party Constitution. The course and significance of the Clause IV dispute are examined, and the merits and shortcomings of the uneasy compromise forged in its aftermath are assessed.

Chapter 4 considers the manner in which Labour's subsequent ideological truce was extended after 1963 by Harold Wilson's ambiguous style of Party Leadership. It maintains that the revisionist approach was diluted, while Labour's traditional commitment to public ownership was partially restored, at least in terms of rhetoric, as a result of Wilson's emphasis on the broadly defined, yet unifying, concept of the scientific and technological revolution.

Chapter 5 describes, and seeks to explain, the bitter ideological conflict which resurfaced in the Party after 1970, leading eventually to the Party split of 1981 and to the electoral disaster of 1983. The left's advance, on the levels of both policy and ideology, is charted from the early 1970s to the period of their temporary ascendancy from 1979 to 1983. At the same time, the declining influence and fading appeal of revisionist social democracy during those years are scrutinized.

Chapter 6 focuses on the ideological shift that accompanied the policy and organizational changes which Neil Kinnock instituted during the period of his Leadership from 1983, and particularly from 1987 to 1992. It examines and discusses the nature and significance of that process of ideological change, exploring the ways in which Labour's rethinking under Kinnock both upheld and diverged from central tenets of earlier revisionist social democracy.

Chapter 7 examines the continuation of Labour's 'second-stage' revisionism under the Leaderships of, first and briefly, John Smith and, second, Tony Blair. It charts the course of the Party's ideological revision, which ostensibly involved Labour's official conversion to a form of European social democracy, through to Blair's successful attempt to revise Clause IV in April 1995.

The study concludes by raising some problematic questions arising from the apparent completion of the original revisionist project – to demote public ownership as an idca and a policy and to endorse a market-oriented mixed economy – that was symbolically expressed in the undertaking to revise Clause IV. Such questions, it is suggested, may well pervade future debates both about the essential character of the Labour Party and about the nature and purpose of democratic socialism in Britain.

I would like to acknowledge my gratitude to those Labour politicians, past and present, who generously granted me interviews during the course of the academic study which shaped the content and analysis of this book. They included the late Lord Jay of Battersea; Lord Jenkins of Hillhead; the Rt Hon. Neil Kinnock; the late Ian Mikardo; Lord Rodgers of Quarry Bank; the Rt Hon. Peter Shore, MP; Dick Taverne, QC; and the late Lord Wilson of Rievaulx.

I would also like to express my thanks to Professor Roderick Martin, who supervised the doctoral thesis which provided some of the material on which the analysis and interpretation of this book are based. My thanks are extended, too, to Julie Davis and Sue Noonan who word-processed the manuscript of the book with efficiency and patience.

During the lengthy period in which this book was conceived, prepared and completed, my parents and Frances were constant sources of encouragement, support, and patient, at times humorous, understanding. So, too, were my old friends Roger Griffin, Sara Glennie, Guy Backus and Richard Evans. A debt of affectionate gratitude is owed to them all.

Parts of Chapters 1, 3 and 6 originally appeared in articles published in *Contemporary Record*, vol. 5, no. 3, 1991, and vol. 8, no. 3, 1994.

1 Labour, public ownership and socialist myth

I

During the course of the Labour Party's maturation as a political force, the idea of public ownership has been widely regarded as an enduring symbol of its socialist commitment. Nearly sixty years after Labour's foundation, Emanuel Shinwell, formerly Minister of Fuel and Power in its first majority government, could thus maintain, at the 1957 Labour Party Conference in Brighton, that he was defending 'the vital principles upon which this Party is based'.[1] These, he believed, were being threatened by some controversial proposals in *Industry and Society*, the new Party policy statement that was then under debate. In opposing those proposals, Shinwell claimed that he was reaffirming Labour's historic commitment to the public ownership of the means of production. Yet his firm conviction obscured a fundamental and contentious issue – the status of public ownership, both as an idea and as a policy, within the Party's ideology and programmes.

An examination of the period of the Labour Party's infancy – from 1900 until the First World War – provides, it must be said, only limited evidence in support of Shinwell's view of public ownership as a 'vital principle' of the Party. As a political idea it had, admittedly, become established in the 1880s and 1890s as a central strand of British socialist thought. Furthermore, as Morgan has maintained,

> At least as an aspiration, the public ownership of major industries, utilities and natural resources was inseparable from the socialist idea in Britain from the foundation of Keir Hardie's Independent Labour Party in 1893 down to the Second World War.[2]

Indeed, the ideal of widespread public ownership manifestly formed 'the jewel in the crown for dedicated socialists, Marxists and non-Marxists alike'.[3] The belief, however, that public ownership constituted a fundamental principle of the Party from its very foundation has usually involved ascribing to Labour, even in its infancy, a distinctively socialist character. In opposition to such an interpretation many political historians have concurred with Crick's observation that within Labour's loose coalition of ideas and interests,

> socialism itself, except in a very broad sense, is only one element in this coalition ... certainly subsidiary, in both electoral and historical terms, to the Labour Party as the representative of organized labour.[4]

Various traditions of political thought can certainly be identified as influences upon the early Labour Party – among them radical or social liberalism, Victorian ethical reformism, the evolutionary socialist ideas of the Fabian Society and the Independent Labour Party (ILP), and the attitudes of British labourism. All of these helped to shape the Party's policies, priorities and character. With some justification, therefore, Labour's political thought, throughout the course of its development, has been described as an intellectual stockpot,[5] with old and new ingredients mixed together in an often haphazard manner.

Any analysis of Labour's early character which attaches primary importance to the influence of socialist ideas consequently seems misconceived. Similarly flawed are historical accounts that seek to emphasize a set of fundamental socialist principles, clearly distinguishable from social liberal beliefs, to which Labour's earliest supporters were allegedly committed. For, partly as a result of enduring liberal influences, a climate existed in which, as Bealey observed, 'the socialist society of the future was not a keen matter of debate at official levels of the Labour Party before 1914'.[6]

As Labour gradually emerged from 1915 onwards as a distinct national party, Ramsay MacDonald's flexible form of socialism was assuming greater prominence.[7] But it was not until the movement towards parliamentary and electoral independence was well under way – that is, after 1918 – that socialist ideas such as public ownership occupied the central position in Labour thinking later accorded to them by their most fervent advocates.

Nevertheless, public ownership itself had still been regarded by a section of the pre-1914 Labour Party as a central tenet of socialism. Such a view was already entrenched in a long tradition of socialist thought. As Pelling has pointed out,

Socialists of the late nineteenth and early twentieth centuries have almost all been committed to the aim of public ownership, in one form or another, of the means of production, distribution and exchange.[8]

That aim had been pursued since the 1880s in a stream of books, pamphlets, articles and speeches. The Fabians in their programme of 1887 thus sought to achieve 'the reorganisation of Society by the emancipation of Land and Industrial Capital from individual and class ownership, and the vesting of them in the community for the general benefit'.[9] A few years later Sidney Webb restated the Fabian belief that 'the main principle of reform must be the substitution of Collective Ownership and Control for Individual Private Property in the means of production'.[10] These sentiments were endorsed by the Independent Labour Party at its inaugural conference in 1893 when it announced that its central objective was 'to secure the collective ownership of all the means of production, distribution and exchange'.[11]

On the level of policy-making public ownership had also been advocated during this period within the developing trade union movement. In 1887 Keir Hardie, then a Scottish miners' leader, had called for the nationalization of mines, railways, minerals and land.[12] His demands found widespread support at the Trade Union Congress (TUC), where, from the 1890s onwards, his list of suitable candidates for state ownership was defended and even extended in a series of resolutions. It was not, however, until 1908 that a specific policy commitment – involving the railways – was approved by the Labour Party Conference. Further commitments, concerning the waterways and coal mines, were undertaken by the Party in 1910 and 1912.

Closer scrutiny of this new policy orientation on Labour's part suggests a pragmatic rather than doctrinal motivation; for the most insistent pressures for public ownership of the railways and coal mines emanated from the railwaymen's and miners' unions. It was their demands for improved wages, hours and working conditions that intensified those pressures.[13] Viewed from this perspective, public ownership could be seen as another aspect of the early Labour Party's 'politics of interest'.[14] Its endorsement by the Party could thus be regarded as a development of the policy of redressing various trade union grievances that was sedulously pursued from 1906 to 1914.

Any interpretation, however, of Labour's early commitment to public ownership which overlooks doctrinal factors appears inadequate. While attitudes towards that policy were shaped from the start by hard practical considerations, they also reflected current trends in political thought. They could be broadly related, for instance, to New Liberal ideas, with their emphasis on a more interventionist, enabling State. They were connected, too, with arguments advanced by socialist trade unionists within the TUC. Indeed, in the specific case of the proposal to nationalize the coal mines, it has been argued that that policy was 'put forward in the early days as part and parcel of the general Socialist programme, and not on the ground that mining was in a special position in relation to the British economy'.[15]

But in spite of the growing force of socialist arguments within the Labour Party and the TUC, there seems little justification for interpreting this as firm evidence that before 1914 Labour was either abandoning social liberal ideas or embracing a coherent socialist ideology. In its infancy the Party continued to lack a distinctive socialist identity. It remained, in MacDonald's description, a 'socialistic' party, subject to strong social liberal and other non-socialist influences. Its early policy commitments and priorities were not, therefore, anchored to clearly articulated socialist ideas such as public ownership. That ideological link was not to be forged until the end of the Great War.

The year 1918 has been widely regarded as a watershed in the history of the Labour Party since it brought two major new developments. First, the Annual Conference adopted in February 1918 a new Party constitution and organizational structure. Second, a further Conference, held in June 1918, officially accepted a new policy statement, drafted by the leading Fabian theorist Sidney Webb and entitled *Labour and the New Social Order*.

The new Constitution contained among other things an outline of the 'Party Objects', which included a brief statement, again largely drafted by Webb, of Labour's general domestic purpose. Set out in what later became known as Clause IV, Part Four, this committed the Party

> To secure for the workers by hand or by brain the full fruits of their industry, and the most equitable distribution thereof that may be possible, upon the basis of the common ownership of the means of production and the best obtainable system of popular administration and control of each industry or service.[16]

The second innovation of 1918, the acceptance of *Labour and the New Social Order*, involved the publication of the Party's first extended statement of aims, including recommendations for minimum living standards (a 'National Minimum', in Webb's phrase) and for an expansion of social services to be financed through the combined effects of direct taxation and nationalization of industry.

The immediate political significance of 'Labour and the New Social Order' has aroused conflicting judgements.[17] Its ideological importance, however, as well as that of Clause IV of the new Constitution, has been widely recognized by political historians. Egon Wertheimer claimed that Labour's documents marked the Party's transition 'from social reform to socialism',[18] while, in G. D. H. Cole's view, they 'unequivocally committed the Labour Party to Socialist objectives in the sense in which Socialism had been advocated by the Fabian Society and by other "evolutionary" Socialists'.[19] Bealey pointed out that *Labour and the New Social Order* is 'usually regarded as the first official acceptance by the Labour Party that it was a Socialist party',[20] while Pelling maintained that Clause IV 'for the first time explicitly committed the party to a Socialist basis'.[21] In similar terms, Beer regarded the 1918 pronouncements as indications of 'a basic change in ideology' that involved a movement away from radical Liberalism towards acceptance of 'the comprehensive ideology of Socialism'.[22] Once those formal commitments had been made by the Party, it was thereafter 'accepted and official usage to say that its ultimate aim was a new social order, the Socialist Commonwealth'.[23] Even Miliband, who judged *Labour and the New Social Order* to be devoid of any serious socialist intent, acknowledged that the document at least served notice 'that Labour had finally done with its own version of Liberalism'.[24]

Labour and the New Social Order did indeed underline the Party's break with Liberal reformism, as well as its commitment to the transformation of British society. The document thus declared that 'what has to be reconstructed after the war is not this or that Government Department, or this or that piece of machinery, but, so far as Britain is concerned, society itself'.[25] One of the major instruments of social reconstruction and one of the central 'pillars' of the new society was identified as 'the Democratic Control of Industry'.[26] The new social order would be characterized by 'a genuinely scientific reorganization of the nation's industry, no longer deflected by industrial profiteering, on the basis of the Common Ownership of the Means of Production'.[27]

This vision of a transformed economy had also been projected in Clause IV of the new Party Constitution adopted in February 1918. Establishing public ownership at the forefront of Labour policy,

Clause IV provided the only specific reference to the Party's domestic aims to be found in the new Constitution. The Clause's prominence thereby conferred on itself ideological significance, providing a formal recognition of the socialist identity confirmed in *Labour and the New Social Order*.

The wider implications of this have, however, been questioned by McKibbin. Underplaying the role of socialist ideas in the wartime growth of the Labour Party, he has maintained that

> It is easy to be overimpressed with the socialist objective and to be unconcerned with the corpus of the 1918 constitution ... [which] embodied not an ideology but a system by which power in the Labour Party was distributed.[28]

In McKibbin's view, the trade unions, with their dominant influence within the Party, were prepared to accept 'the socialist objective' embodied in Clause IV 'partly because they had always been collectivist, partly because they had advocated nationalization of specific industries even before the war, partly to indulge the Fabians, and partly because they did not think it mattered very much'.[29] Furthermore, the unions' willingness to 'indulge' the Fabians led them to offer Clause IV, in Pimlott's words, 'as a consolation prize to socialists in a package of reform which actually reduced socialist influence in the higher Party echelons'.[30] For although the clause gave the Party 'an officially socialist colouring which had been rejected in 1900',[31] it formed part of a constitution that seriously weakened the political and organizational role of the ILP, the main vehicle of the Labour left since 1900.

In view of the marginal influence of socialist ideas, Clause IV was formally adopted, McKibbin argues, partly because it 'offered the electorate a doctrine differentiated from that of the other parties'.[32] The 'socialist objective' thus 'served the useful purpose ... of sharpening the break between the Labour and Liberal Parties'.[33] In addition, Clause IV, 'precisely because of its vagueness and lack of rigour, paradoxically had an umbrella function: it was an acceptable formula in a Party where there was otherwise little doctrinal agreement'.[34]

In this respect, at least, McKibbin's interpretation lends support to Beer's influential thesis that the events and declarations of 1918 had a functional as well as normative importance for the Labour Party. In Beer's view, they offered the means by which Labour for the first time asserted its electoral and parliamentary independence of the Liberals. He thus argued that 'The adoption of Socialism as an ideology was functional to this choice of political independence'.[35] It is against this background that Labour's adoption in 1918 of socialist commitments needs to be viewed; for in Beer's judgement, the Party's apparent ideological conversion was 'not so much a cause as an effect of the hardly avoidable break with the Liberals'.[36] Considered in these terms, Labour's acquisition of a new ideology, a distinctive set of values and beliefs, fulfilled at least three purposes. First, it served to underline the Party's special identity, differentiating it from the Liberals; second, it provided a stimulus and an inspiration for the Party's members and supporters; and, finally, it purported to explain the direction of social and economic forces in British society.

Arthur Henderson, the Party's Secretary, was well aware of the functional significance of Labour's newly embraced socialist ideology. He had, according to Cole, already decided by 1917 that 'some sort of Socialist faith was the necessary basis for the consolidation of the Labour Party into an effective national force'[37] when he turned to Sidney Webb for intellectual and literary assistance. An essential requirement of that 'Socialist faith' was that it should be broadly acceptable to the trade unionists who formed the backbone of the Party. Hence the new ideology would involve constitutional and gradualist methods and would be rooted in communitarian values of fellowship and solidarity.

But Labour's new ideology was also designed to display at its very heart the socialist idea of public ownership. Henderson himself, a firm believer in extensive public ownership, later asked Sidney Webb 'to draft a complete scheme for "socialising industry" – the whole of industry' and to 'show that the principle of socialisation was applicable to all industries'.[38] It was left to Sidney and Beatrice Webb to point out to Henderson the various practical difficulties inherent in such a comprehensive undertaking.[39] None the less, in an earlier pamphlet which formed the basis of *Labour and the New Social Order*, Sidney Webb had already set the tone that Henderson desired by advocating 'the progressive elimination from industry of the private capitalist, individual or joint-stock; and the setting free of all who work, whether by hand or brain, for the service of the community and of the community alone'.[40]

By 1918 such socialist objectives appeared more palatable to British trade unionists, who before 1914 had supported public owner-ship for largely pragmatic reasons. The wartime extension of state control and planning to important areas of the economy – notably to the coal mines and railways – had ensured that public ownership seemed to trade unionists to be an even more practicable and realizable policy.[41] It had also created a climate in which the kinds of socialist arguments that had been advanced by Fabian and ILP theorists for the preceding thirty years at last began to command more serious attention within the unions.

The circumstances surrounding the acceptance of Labour's 1918 pronouncements appear, then, to underline their dual significance in being both normative and functional in character. This view was developed further by Winter, who, pointing to a complex of factors, emphasized the attempts of Sidney Webb and other socialists on the War Emergency Workers' Committee to work out a coherent and consistent wartime policy for the Labour movement.[42] Webb's eventual programme rested on 'an indictment of capitalism and offered a pledge to mitigate, if not to end, the inequality and deprivation it bred'.[43] Its underlying purpose was 'to make the choice among the parties one of conviction rather than just a comparison of personalities'.[44]

The statements formulated and refined by Webb, though shaped by the pressures of wartime austerity and by the needs of electoral politics, thus sprang, too, from his Fabian socialist beliefs. Moreover, Labour's formal adoption of socialist aims was itself the product of an ideological age, taking place 'in the heady days after the Bolshevik Revolution when the scent of radical change was in the air throughout Europe'.[45] Indeed, the Party's socialist conversion had also been prompted by Henderson's conviction, born of his experiences in Russia, that Labour somehow needed to steer an ideological middle course between Liberalism, on the one hand, and revolutionary Marxism, on the other. Specifically, too, the contemporary ideological climate had fostered the idea of state control, one that held considerable appeal for the rising clerical and administrative middle classes in Britain, including, not least, the 65,000 government officials who by 1918 were employed in the Ministry of Munitions.[46]

Both practical and doctrinal factors, then, inspired Labour's 1918 pronouncements. R. H. Tawney even suggested later that a fair measure of wishful thinking lay behind them, observing that 'In 1918 the Labour Party finally declared itself to be a Socialist Party. It supposed, and supposes, that it thereby became one. It is mistaken. It recorded a wish, that is all; the wish has not been fulfilled'.[47] Nevertheless, the Party's acceptance of Clause IV of the new Constitution, along with *Labour and the New Social Order*, did at least signal some kind of official socialist commitment, regardless of the various motives and purposes that inspired it.

II

The preceding discussion has indicated the limitations of a purely ideological interpretation of the developments of 1918. In broader terms, Drucker has underlined the shortcomings of a purely doctrinal view of the Labour's Party's ideology. By regarding the Party 'as if it were a machine for the creation and propagation of socialist doctrine and the translation of that doctrine into policy, legislation and prac- tice'[48] one is in danger, he argues, of overlooking another dimension of its ideology – namely, its 'ethos', that is, its characteristic values and traditions derived from British working-class experience. Labour's organizational and financial procedures, its attitude towards its leaders, even the personal style displayed by its politicians – all these, in Drucker's view, are reflections of the Party's distinctive working-class ethos.[49]

Furthermore, Labour's ethos 'emanates from a specific past',[50] since its characteristic values arose from a collective experience of exploitation and from the gradual construction of defensive organi- zations in response to that condition. The Party has thus become imbued, Drucker points out, with a strong sense both of its own past and of the past of the wider Labour movement that nurtured it. Indeed, Labour's sense of it past is 'so central to its ethos that it plays a crucial role in defining what the party is about to those in it'.[51] Labour is therefore 'a party which exists, as a result of certain remembered past actions, to do a particular job now and in the future'.[52]

Broadly in line with Drucker's thesis, Barker has suggested that the events of 1918 contained an additional dimension – that of 'political myth', which he regards as another aspect of Labour's ideology, sharing 'some of this quality of ethos'.[53] For one of the main functions of the accounts of the Party's socialism represented by the 1918 pronouncements was 'to describe the history of society, both past and future, in a manner which would justify and encourage the actions of the party, give its members a sense of identity, and provide a context for unity in a body which in terms of interest, aspirations and principles, was far from united.'[54] *Labour and the New Social Order*, along with Clause IV of the new Constitution, thus provided 'the necessary political myth' – that is, an inspiring account of Labour's development and purpose – 'for a party which was slowly gaining a sense of identity and direction, and which needed an ultimate, non- rational basis for this achievement'.[55]

The term 'political myth' is being applied here 'to a particular series of events and to the character and role of a particular political party'.[56] It seems appropriate, therefore, at this stage to attempt to provide a more general definition of a concept which is clearly not being used in the commonplace sense of any belief that is fictitious or illusory. Instead, I would follow Henry Tudor's view of a myth as 'by definition, a story, that is, a narrative of events in dramatic form which has a protagonist and . . . has a plot with a beginning, a middle and an end'.[57] Such a story is not a piece of pure fiction since it derives from actual events. As Tudor explains:

> A myth . . . is an interpretation of what the myth-maker (rightly or wrongly) takes to be hard fact. It is a device men adopt in order to come to grips with reality; and we can tell that a given account is a myth, not by the amount of truth it contains, but by the fact that it is believed to be true and, above all, by the dramatic form into which it is cast.[58]

These general characteristics of myth, Tudor notes, are shared by political myths. What distinguishes a political myth from other branches of mythology is simply its subject matter: it deals expressly with political events and phenomena.

Moreover, a political myth comprises a non-rational account of social and political events, for, as Leach observed, 'the non-rationality of myth is its very essence, requiring a demonstration of faith by the suspension of critical doubt'.[59] As an effect, too, of this non-rational character a political myth conveys a strong emotional force. Indeed, defining such a myth as 'the pattern of the basic political symbols current in a society', Lasswell and Kaplan identify as one of its main components what they term 'miranda', that is, 'symbols of sentiment and identification in the political myth',[60] the function of which is to strengthen the loyalties of particular groups, arousing their emotions and heightening their sense of collective identity. Cassirer, regarding myths as major symbolic forms, takes a similar but more unfavourable view of their emotional resonance. Considering them to be both traditional and illogical, he depicts them as enemies of Western civilization – to be resisted and opposed, not welcomed as a complement to reason.[61] Myths are at their most dangerous, in his view, when the other binding forces of social life – intellectual, artistic and ethical – lose their strength and their capacity for checking the power of myth. In his opposition to twentieth-century political myths, Cassirer under-lines, too, a significant change in the function of language from a logical to a manipulative use of words 'destined to produce certain effects and to stir up certain emotions'.[62] For myths are 'artificial things fabricated by very skilful and cunning artisans'.[63]

This emotional, non-rational essence of myths carries with it, therefore, the implication that they are fundamentally matters of faith. Indeed, this is the source of their strength. Their lack of specific proposals or of rational justification places them outside the testing-ground of rationalist thought. Consequently, as Sorel recognized 'People who are living in this world of "myths" are secure from all refutation'.[64] A political myth is also invariably the myth of a particular social group – whether it be a nation, race, tribe or class. As Durkheim observed, myths are collective representations: they contain ideas and beliefs shared by members of a group. They existed before any individual and will outlast any individual. Durkheim pointed out that 'The mythology of a group is the system of beliefs common to this group. The traditions whose memory it perpetuates express the way in which society represents man and the world'.[65] Similarly, Cassirer maintained that 'In mythical thought and imagination we do not meet with individual confessions. Myth is an objectification of man's social experience, not of his individual experience'.[66]

Another important feature of political myths, linking them closely to ideologies, is their practical orientation. They contain particular views of society that seek to explain the circumstances in which those to whom they are addressed find themselves. They thereby render their audience's experience more coherent and intelligible, giving it shape and meaning. Political myths do not, however, just provide explanations and interpretations of social and political situations. They also offer either a critique or a defence of those situations, and, in doing so, aim to promote a particular course of action. For Sorel this mobilizing role of myth was of supreme importance since, in his view, myths were 'expressions of a determination to act'.[67] The Marxist myth of capitalist collapse, for example, had become a crucial 'source of non-rational motivation'.[68]

In addition to these general characteristics, a political myth has two distinct temporal dimensions. Looking back, it develops an account of the past; looking forward, it projects a vision of the future. The present, it suggests, can best be understood in the light of both retro-spective and futuristic considerations. Duverger underlined this point when, in discussing Sorel's notion of myths of action, he observed that 'one of the most effective ways of influencing a community is to give it concise and uncomplicated images of a fictitious future or a fabled past, which will polarize its passions and lead to action.[69]

In wider theoretical terms these two dimensions of myth relate to a significant distinction between foundation myths and eschatological myths. The former can be defined as a category 'by the fact that they explain the present in terms of a creative act that took place in the past', 'in most cases ... an actual and often quite recent historical event which has been dramatized for the purposes of political argument'.[70] Eschatological myths, on the other hand, are concerned with the termination or complete reversal of an existing set of circumstances. They look forward to the abolition of the old order and the birth of a new order, usually as a result of some cataclysmic future conflict.

As examples of foundation myths Tudor cites the Roman foundation myth, the Russian myth of the October Revolution and the American myth of the Founding Fathers,[71] all of which tell the story of how a particular political society came to be founded. They seek to explain the present in terms of some dramatized historical event.

By contrast, the very different, visionary dimension contained in eschatological myths was disclosed in a challenging manner by Sorel in his *Reflections on Violence*, in which he tackled the problematic question of why men engaged in violent struggles frequently display levels of courage and self-sacrifice that cannot be explained in terms of narrow self-interest. The main reason for their endurance, Sorel argued, is that such men are motivated by a great myth – a grand vision of the future, a great social movement or cause, which enables them to 'picture their coming action as a battle in which their cause is certain to triumph'.[72] As examples of such eschatological myths Sorel cited the Marxian expectation of a proletarian revolution, the syndicalist notion of a general strike and millennialist doctrines of the early Christian Church. As Tudor points out,

> The hallmark of a myth, as Sorel understands it, is that it provides a vision of the future which makes crude but practical sense of the present. ... Typically, each conflict in the present is seen as a prelude to the decisive battle destined to take place in the future.[73]

In general terms, then, a political myth can be defined as an emotive, non-rational account of social and political events, directed at a particular social or political group, and seeking to explain, justify or repudiate the condition of that group. It may be either retrospective or forward-looking, nostalgic or inspirational. As an account of the past, its main function is to strengthen the group's sense of collective loyalty and identity. As a vision of the future, its task is to galvanize the group itself, instilling in its members a firm sense of direction and purpose.

III

When one turns to consider the character of the Labour Party, many of these general features of political myths come into sharp focus. In the first place, the account of Labour's socialism provided by the 1918 statements amounted to a dramatic narrative of events. It clearly had a protagonist – the new Party itself – and a plot with a beginning, a middle and an end. Its beginning was the establishment by 1918 of a socialist party in the midst of a hostile capitalist society, whilst its middle phase involved the eventual emergence of Labour governments, fired by socialist principles to reform that society. Its envisaged end was the attainment of a Socialist Commonwealth, a new social order.

Labour's myth thus offered an emotive account of its development and purpose as a political organization and movement. The distinctive feature of that myth was the public, or common, ownership of the means of production, which since 1918 had been widely regarded within the Party as the necessary condition of the social and economic transformation described in the myth as Labour's ultimate goal. Clause IV of the Party Constitution provided the formal expression of Labour's myth and hence the official declaration of the Party's historic socialist purpose.

Furthermore, Labour's socialist myth was directed at a particular group – the members and supporters of the infant Party gradually stumbling towards adolescence. It was the shared possession of that group and performed the essential function of binding the Party together as a mass organization. It imbued its members with a sense of collective identity and common purpose, thereby providing a firm basis for Party unity. In such ways it fulfilled that crucial mobilizing role emphasized by Sorel. All these benefits were reinforced, too, by the sense of legitimate authority conveyed by the myth. For the general socialist principles invoked in 1918 served to legitimize the specific social and industrial demands of the youthful Party. As Barker observed, 'The account of socialism given to the party in 1918 provided the authority for social reform and collectivism, by propounding in elevated but vague terms an alternative social order'.[74]

While the mythic element in Labour's socialism found its formal recognition in the events of 1918, it had already developed in a gradual, tentative manner. In Barker's view, Ramsay MacDonald was the most active contributor to that process, 'the single most important cultivator of the myth'[75] that unified and sustained the Party. In a succession of writings and speeches in the years stretching from 1905 to 1918 he thus assumed his role as Labour's 'principal propagandist and mythologist',[76] persuasively employing socialist rhetoric and symbolism to enhance the Party's sense of identity, direction and purpose. In MacDonald's hands, Labour's myth was tailored more to meet these ends than to produce any precise doctrine or programme.

As well as providing, therefore, an account of the Party's past development, Labour's socialist myth, cultivated by MacDonald and others, projected an inspiring vision of its possible future – of a new social order, a Socialist Commonwealth, destined to be created in the years and decades ahead. As Drucker points out, in 1918 Labour stated its 'project', announced in Clause IV and involving 'a will for the replacement of the present order of things, which embodies a conception of the new order'.[77] The Party's political myth was thus developed partly for the purpose of encouraging its supporters to hasten the advent of the new society.

Moreover, as both a narrative account of unfolding events and a vision of the future, the socialist myth enabled the Party's current predicament to be regarded as just an episode in a long-running political drama. Each political and industrial conflict in the present could be seen as a prelude to decisive battles in the future. Every extension of public ownership could be viewed as a further step down the long and winding road to a Socialist Commonwealth. Conversely, every rejection of public ownership could be regarded as a retreat from that ultimate socialist goal.

Viewed from this perspective, then, Labour's visionary account of socialism can be interpreted as containing elements of an eschatological myth. It depicted as its *eschaton* a complete reversal of the condition of British society, that is, the abolition of the old capitalist system and the gradual emergence of a new socialist order. Like many other eschatological myths, Labour's myth was addressed to a social group distancing itself from established capitalist society, viewing it with distaste. In particular, it displayed two distinctive features of this category of myth: first, a concern with the task of achieving a just social order;[78] and, second, the idea of revolutionary change. At the outset a future society was envisaged in which social need would be recognized and merit justly rewarded. The new social order was to be based 'on a deliberately planned cooperation in production and

distribution for the benefit of all who participate by hand or by brain
... on a systematic approach towards a healthy equality of material
circumstances for every person born into the world'.[79]

The emergence of this new order could be seen, too, as a revolutionary upheaval in so far as it involved the gradual transformation
of the old, unacceptable capitalist system. As Beer observed, 'If the
implication of sudden and violent change is extracted from the term
'revolution', it is correct to say that the meaning of Socialism to the
Labour Party was a commitment to ultimate social revolution'.[80]
Indeed, Labour was 'utopian in its ultimate aspirations', Beer argues,
since 'the millenary emotions that animated large sections of the
party were not fixed simply on the redress of a grievance' but were
'matched on the intellectual plane by the vision of a radically new and
different world'.[81] The 'new view of society', the 'new social order',
the 'Socialist Commonwealth' – these were all symbolic expressions
of powerful 'millenary emotions'.

Although many political historians have stressed this mystical
aspect of Labour's origins and early development, both Beer and
Hobsbawm have rejected the simplistic view of twentieth-century
British socialism as an outgrowth of nineteenth-century evangelism,
pointing instead to its secular aspects and non-religious traditions.[82]
Nevertheless, it is worth emphasizing that the pioneers of the
Independent Labour Party gave a central place to the language and
theology of contemporary religion. As Pimlott has pointed out, 'the
Socialist Commonwealth was more than merely analogous to the
Second Coming: in the imagination of speakers and audiences there
was a blurring and a merging of the two'.[83] The ILP pioneers' vision
of socialism as an earthly realization of the New Jerusalem, a vision
that had inspired Edward Carpenter and Robert Blatchford, had
bequeathed to the early Labour Party an intense, quasi-religious
fervour. Philip Snowden had delivered lectures on 'The Christ That
is to Be', while Bruce Glasier had declared that socialism would come
'as the very breath of April, full of sweetness and strength'.[84]
To many in the ILP, socialism appeared to be 'in the fullest sense
a secular religion – a rationalist equivalent of Christianity'.[85] Shaw
Desmond, a popular ILP orator in its early days, was later to comment ruefully, 'We had but to blow our trumpets seven times outside
the walls of the capitalist Jericho, and lo! the walls would fall and it
would be transformed into the New Jerusalem with streets of shining
gold'.[86] In Desmond's view, the 'spirit of religion' pervading the early
Labour movement had made it 'essentially a "faith" rather than a
"politic", a movement which in its beginnings seemed to form the

natural refuge of those who had gone out from the temples of dogmatic religion'.[87]

Labour's depiction of the Socialist Commonwealth as the New Jerusalem thus reflected in a secularized manner the eschatological aspect of its myth of socialism. Just as its account of the past had helped to reinforce its socialist identity, so its vision of the future inspired its ultimate socialist purpose. The old capitalist system would be dismantled, gradually and peacefully, and the new socialist society – a morally, economically and socially superior alternative – would be constructed in its place. A major act of social transformation would thereby be accomplished.

From 1918 onwards, therefore, the Labour Party's socialist myth of a new social order, with public ownership as its centrepiece, provided both an emotive account of its past and an inspiring vision of its future. These two characteristic features were really interrelated, for Labour's 'project', its drive to transform the social order, was 'at once cautiously forward-looking but rooted in a particular past'.[88] The Party's hopes and expectations for the future were constantly rekindled by an acute sense of its past achievements. The shared recollections of early struggles and of gradual development thus formed the secure common ground from which its future progress could be charted.

IV

Whether recalling past travail or envisaging future advances, Labour's socialist myth clearly rested on one dominant idea – that of a transformed economy and society, a Socialist Commonwealth. That goal both embodied the traditional aspirations of the Party's members and supporters and inspired their thought and actions. As the prerequisite of the transformation which they desired, public ownership of the means of production was inseparable from Labour's most potent vision. Its mythic importance – both as an idea and as a policy – was in turn reflected in the ideological pronouncements of 1918.

The question is therefore raised of the relationship between Labour's myth and its declared ideological commitment. Without embarking on an extended general discussion of the term 'ideology', I would endorse here Eccleshall's view that political ideologies exhibit two principal characteristics: first, specific images of society which seek to render it intelligible from a particular point of view and, second, radiating from those images, distinctive programmes of action which offer 'prescriptions of what ought to be done to ensure that social ideal and actual reality coincide'.[89] A socialist image of society portrays ideality and reality as fundamentally inconsistent and consequently gives rise to recommendations for 'drastic surgery to reconstruct the political order'.[90]

Viewed in this light, political ideologies appear to display some of the characteristic features of political myth. They project vivid images of a desired society, and they prescribe or seek to instigate certain courses of action in pursuit of that ultimate goal. The distinction, however, between ideology and myth can perhaps be drawn most clearly in terms of degrees of rationality. Duverger, for example, considered that ideologies may be defined as 'collections of rationalized and systemized beliefs' whereas myths are 'vaguer, less rational, less carefully thought out'.[91] He also maintained that 'myths are simplified ideologies, or rather ideologies reduced to brief and brutal themes or images'.[92] Developing this point with a different emphasis, Sorel argued that 'ideologies have only been translations of . . . myths within abstract forms'.[93] In his view, an ideology could be regarded as a myth that had been elaborated and rationalized and thereby made available for discussion and analysis.

Sorel's position here suggests a fruitful approach towards understanding the relationship between Labour's socialist myth and the ideology which it formally adopted in 1918. That ideology provided the means of translating – into both programmatic and theoretical terms – the Party's vision of a Socialist Commonwealth. By establishing particular proposals as agreed Party policy and by developing a theoretical justification for that process, Labour politicians and intellectuals in the interwar years gradually fashioned a distinctive ideological garment. In doing so, they gave systematic expression to their Party's leading, visionary idea.

Each part of this undertaking therefore began with a renewed commitment to Labour's goal of a future socialist society. The Party's major policy statements, for instance, underlined its concern with the task of social and economic transformation rather than with mere piecemeal reform. The documents displayed a predilection for what Beer called 'system thinking'[94] – a tendency to view the principal issues of the day in terms of a clash between capitalism and socialism as distinct and antithetical economic systems.

This approach, already evident in *Labour and the New Social Order*, was favoured, too, in the 1928 statement *Labour and the Nation*, largely written by Tawney. In a foreword to the document MacDonald, from his elevated position as Party leader, insisted that

'The Labour Party, unlike other parties, is not concerned with patching the rents in a bad system, but with transforming Capitalism into Socialism'.[95] Endorsing this grand objective, *Labour and the Nation* advocated

> the organization of industry, and the administration of the wealth which industry produces, in the interest not of the small minority . . . who own the greater part of the land, the plant, and the equipment . . . , but of all who bring their contribution of useful service to the common stock.[96]

The next major policy document, *For Socialism and Peace*, published in 1934, shared the 'system thinking' of previous documents. In terms that echoed MacDonald's earlier pronouncement, it claimed that 'the choice before the nation is either a vain attempt to patch up the superstructure of a capitalist society in decay at its very foundations, or a rapid advance to a socialist reconstruction of the national life'.[97] Moreover, it stressed its conviction that the tension between capitalism and socialism could never be resolved, since

> There is no halfway house between a society based on private ownership of the means of the production with the profit of the few as the measure of success, and a society where public ownership of those means enables the resources of the nation to be deliberately planned for attaining the maximum of general well-being.[98]

Finally, Labour's supreme domestic goal was restated in *Let Us Face the Future*, the Party's major policy statement and manifesto for the 1945 General Election. Bringing together the dominant themes of Labour's series of programmes since 1918, the document declared that 'The Labour Party is a Socialist Party, and proud of it. Its ultimate purpose at home is the establishment of the Socialist Commonwealth of Great Britain'.[99]

All these policy statements reflected, therefore, the visionary force of Labour's socialist myth. But they were also designed to give practical, programmatic substance to that myth by means of commitments to public ownership. As the Party's fundamental reform, it was that policy, above all others, which lay at the heart of successive programmes designed to fulfil the ideal of the Socialist Commonwealth. *Labour and the New Social Order*, officially endorsed in 1918, had thus put forward proposals for the national ownership of essential public utilities – including the railways, coal mines, electric power, canals, harbours and steamship lines. In 1928 and 1934 *Labour and the Nation* and *For Socialism and Peace* had maintained this emphasis. The former document proposed public ownership and control of urban and agricultural land, coal, power, communications and transport, stressing that these basic necessities were simply 'too vital to the welfare of the nation to be organized and exploited for private profit'.[100] Labour would therefore aim to 'vest their ownership in the nation and their administration in authorities acting on the nation's behalf'.[101]

For Socialism and Peace went further, calling in 1934 for 'drastic reorganization', involving 'for the most part nothing short of immediate public ownership and control' of a long list of major industries and services which included transport, water, coal, electricity, gas, agricultural land, steel, shipbuilding, engineering, textiles, chemicals, banking and insurance.[102] This unprecedently extensive set of proposals formed the basis of Labour's 1935 Election programme.[103] Significantly, too, the 1934 document firmly established the public corporation as the favoured method of extending public ownership into those industrial areas. This model had been promoted by Herbert Morrison – on both practical and theoretical levels – since the early 1930s as the suitable organizational structure for the nationalization of British industry.[104]

Morrison's approach to public ownership had many critics within the Party, who, pointing to the bureaucratic and paternalistic tendencies inherent in the public corporation, called instead for a revival of the older notion, derived from Guild Socialist theory, of public ownership as 'socialization', with effective control of each industry exercised by the workers themselves.[105] By 1934, however, it had become clear that the Party's preference, with regard to both policy and strategy, lay with the Morrisonian position. This was to be underlined in 1945 by the commitments of *Let Us Face the Future* and, more concretely, by the Attlee Governments' subsequent legislative programme.

The prominence accorded to the public corporation was reinforced, too, by the increasingly influential idea of central economic planning – another distinctive feature of *For Socialism and Peace*. Anticipated in 1931 by Labour's election commitment to work for 'the substitution of coordinated planning for the anarchy of individualistic enterprise',[106] *For Socialism and Peace* reaffirmed that objective, stressing, in Webbian terms, the need for 'the foundations of the national industrial system' to be 'planned scientifically'.[107] Such a task would in turn require, the document stressed, a substantial extension of public ownership and control to be achieved through the proliferation of nationalized boards.

From 1934 onwards, therefore, the idea of national economic planning and the policy of public ownership, in its new guise of the public corporation, became intimately connected. Indeed, as Morgan has observed, 'the vogue for planning in the 1930s gave public ownership a new credibility'.[108] The latter was increasingly viewed as an instrument of state planning and control, while the Morrisonian model of the public corporation was promoted as the suitable vehicle for such planning. This dual approach was to be applied to what later came to be referred to as a 'shopping list' of industries and services considered ripe for nationalization.

Each of these elements in Labour's policy synthesis was evident in the proposals set out in the Party's 1945 Election programme, which committed the next Labour government to nationalize, by means of newly created public corporations, the main public utilities. These included coal, gas, electricity, railways, road transport, civil aviation and the Bank of England. In addition, and more controversially, the document contained a commitment to bring the iron and steel industry, a cornerstone of the British economy, into public ownership.[109]

In the wake of Labour's sweeping victory at the 1945 Election, Clement Attlee's Governments proceeded to translate these manifesto pledges into a coherent legislative programme that took the form of seven major statutes.[110] This political achievement had been assisted by a recent wartime climate favourable to central planning and to public control of essential industries. It had been legitimized, too, by technical arguments, advanced by a number of investigative and advisory committees,[111] for nationalization on grounds of efficiency, coordination and modernization.

But above all, the Labour Governments' legislation appeared to its supporters as a realization of long-standing commitments of principle and policy and hence as a partial fulfilment of deep-seated aspirations. It was widely perceived as the first, necessary stage in pursuing the Party's supreme goal of economic and social transformation, in furthering what *Let Us Face the Future* had described as Labour's 'ultimate purpose at home ... the establishment of the Socialist Commonwealth of Great Britain'.[112]

V

In the period, then, stretching from 1918 to the fall of the second Attlee Government in 1951, Labour's goal of a transformed economy and society was continually promoted through major programmatic statements. It was also justified in the interwar years by sustained theoretical argument and analysis. R. H. Tawney's elegant political writings, for instance, developed his own conception of the Socialist Commonwealth, depicting it as nothing less than 'a classless society, which does not mean a society without differentiated groups, but one in which varieties of individual endowment, not contrasts of property, income and access to education, are the basis of differentiation'.[113] The fulfilment of that ideal, Tawney believed, would require a programme of action based on public control of the economy. If Labour were to seize its opportunity to become 'an instrument for the establishment of a Socialist Commonwealth', then its main function should be 'to carry through at home the large measures of economic and social reconstruction which . . . have been too long postponed, and with that object to secure that the key positions of the economic system are under public control'.[114] This would involve liberating industry 'from the domination of proprietary interests', thereby 'making economic, as well as political, power responsible to authorities acting for the nation'.[115] Such a major task would entail, he argued, 'a significant change of ownership', 'a genuine and decisive transference of economic sovereignty', in short, 'the transference of property to public hands'.[116]

Public ownership of the means of production was therefore judged by Tawney to be an essential step in building the Socialist Commonwealth. In advancing that view, he was deploying some traditional socialist arguments for public ownership. Most notably, he was clearly reaffirming the belief that it constituted a necessary means of securing public control over private economic power. He was also implicitly commending public ownership as a means of realizing the socialist objective of production for social use or public service rather than for private profit. Each of these positions underpinned his conviction that the nation's essential industries and services should be publicly owned for the common good, ensuring their accountability to the community as a whole.

In the years that followed the formal commitments of 1918 other doctrinal arguments, too, were regularly supported within the Party to justify its enduring attachment to public ownership. Foremost among these was the egalitarian case for it – 'the oldest (even pre-Marxist) argument for public ownership',[117] as Anthony Crosland later put it. This advocated the extension of public ownership, and nationalization in particular, as a means of achieving a fairer distribution of wealth by eliminating unearned private income derived from profits and dividends.

Public ownership was also widely regarded throughout the Labour movement as an important means of redistributing power within industry. This argument was prominent in the Guild Socialist advocacy of economic democracy and in subsequent demands in the 1930s for the 'socialization' of major industries. After 1931, too, public ownership was increasingly promoted within the Party as an essential instrument of state economic planning, designed to maintain central control and direction over national economic activity and to further major policy objectives such as full employment. All these socialist arguments, the last in particular, were often reinforced by more practical considerations – about, for instance, increasing the productive efficiency of industries or about curbing or replacing private monopolies.

This blend of theoretical and programmatic prescription gradually produced what Taylor has referred to as 'a mainstream democratic socialist ideology'[118] within the Labour Party. Revealed in the declarations of 1918, that ideology was drawn from the 'mainstream' in the sense that it embodied those 'ideas and practices most generally subscribed to within the Party'.[119] Shaped both by the character of British trade unionism and by the parliamentary and collectivist commitments of the Fabian Society and the ILP, it had become established by the 1920s as a gradualist, reformist and statist form of socialism.

This notion of a 'mainstream' socialist ideology clearly presupposes a high degree of ideological consensus within the Party – or at least the absence of fundamental disagreement about its desired economic and social goals. The very real debate about methods, about means, was thus, according to this view, destined to be conducted within a broad framework of shared ideals and common purposes.

The classic statement of such a view has been expressed by Beer.[120] Underlying the central goal of a Socialist Commonwealth, he maintains, lay a unique combination of a set of communitarian values – fellowship, mutuality, cooperation, solidarity – with an explanatory theory of society that traced all major social and economic ills to one root cause: the capitalist system and hence the private ownership of the means of production. Conversely, that theory of society prescribed as the only true remedy for such ills is nothing less than a new social order, suffused with the spirit of fellowship and based on the structural foundation of common or public ownership.

In Beer's view, this fusion of attitudes resulted in 'something that can be called an orthodoxy, a unified doctrine ... which not only pervades the party, but also ... persists without fundamental change through the interwar period and into the years after 1945'.[121] The formal commitments of 1918 could thus be regarded as the starting point of a 'Socialist generation', lasting for over thirty years and during which Labour was 'an ideological and programmatic Socialist party based primarily upon the organized working class'.[122] This was a period, he argues, in which 'there was a broad consensus in the party on ideology, programme and strategy'[123] – a consensus reflected in the succession of writings, speeches and policy statements that appeared during the interwar years and beyond.

For Beer the 1918 policy document, in particular, therefore performed a unifying function and profoundly affected subsequent Party policy and strategy. This view has been widely shared by political historians.[124] Miliband, for example, ascribed this long-term influence to the seductively promising tone of *Labour and the New Social Order*, contending that

> It is because the document held this promise that it reconciled so many socialists to its limitations and created a basis of agreement between socialists and social reformers in the Labour Party. In fact, it was only in the fifties that this basis of agreement really began to crack.[125]

This broad consensus was forged, then, by the official pronouncements of a party that was at last acquiring political maturity. It was sustained by the ideas of Labour's most influential thinkers in the interwar period – notably by Tawney in his seminal political writings *The Acquisitive Society* and *Equality*.[126] The practical effect of these influences was the establishment, by the 1930s, of certain broad but persistent themes and lines of policy, of what David Coates called 'a democratic socialist trinity: of public ownership, planning, and universal social welfare'.[127] Through the use of those three instruments of policy an interwar socialist generation sought to fulfil its 'commitment to capitalist transformation'.[128]

Public ownership thus remained a central bonding feature that secured Labour's increasingly firm internal agreement. For as 'the ancient orthodoxy of Socialism',[129] that policy idea was still widely regarded as nothing less than, in Beer's words, 'an indispensable condition and a major expression of a radically transformed economy, society and culture'.[130] It was 'stressed consistently . . . not merely as one among many features of the Socialist society, but as the basic and governing reform'.[131]

This commitment to public ownership was inspired by the simple conception – 'the soul of the party in the 1920s and 1930s'[132] – of an economic system and social order radically different from, and ultimately incompatible with, capitalism. Moreover, such beliefs provided the vital means of political identification and unity, for, as Tomlinson has pointed out,

> Since at least the First World War nationalization and public ownership have been the touchstone of socialist positions in Britain. . . . With all the multifarious groupings, ideologies and politics grouped under its banner, perhaps only the commitment to nationalization has served to unite British socialism.[133]

Binding together, then, Labour's loose coalition of ideas and interests was the shared conviction that 'whatever else socialism might be about, it is irredeemably about nationalization and public ownership'.[134] That view by no means implied complete agreement about the form or purpose of public ownership. But it did spring from the widespread assumption that public ownership itself was intimately connected with the achievement of all major socialist objectives. Throughout the Party it was perceived as 'a crucial part of how the goal of socialism is defined, and therefore, at the same time, a crucial part of what is seen as defining socialist politics as clearly distinct from all others'.[135]

Public ownership had acquired this central importance – as the major doctrinal strand in Labour's mainstream socialist ideology – largely, as we have seen, as a result of the formal commitments of 1918. The official acceptance of *Labour and the New Social Order* and of Clause IV had raised a leading idea to the status of Party orthodoxy. But the pre-eminence of that idea in turn reflected its mythic force, its revered status both as a symbol of Labour's socialist identity and as the cornerstone of a future Socialist Commonwealth.

2 The emergence and refinement of Labour revisionism, 1951-9

I

During the 1950s Labour's broad ideological consensus, which since 1918 had rested to a large extent on the idea and policy of public ownership, gradually started to crumble. Signs of this process were apparent after the fall of the Attlee Government in 1951. By the mid-1950s the growing fragmentation, and resulting discord, became more marked and more serious with the advent of Labour revisionism.

The term 'revisionism' itself is descriptively imprecise. Originally applied at the end of the nineteenth century to Eduard Bernstein's attempts to re-examine certain basic Marxian tenets, its use and abuse has, as Labedz observed, 'a long history'. It has been employed in the twentieth century to refer 'not only to social-democratic reformists, or to disillusioned young communists, but also to leaders of the Communist establishment'.[1] Nevertheless, Greenleaf has offered a useful general definition of the term in his view of revisionism as 'synonymous with some form of reinterpretation of doctrine so critical as to amount (in the eyes of orthodoxy) to heresy or deviation'.[2]

Bernstein's revisionism had involved a reappraisal of social, economic and political problems in the light of major changes within European capitalism. Greenleaf suggests that in Britain during the 1950s a similar approach was evident in the

> tendency in the Labour Party to accept that the capitalist enemy is not what it was a couple of generations ago, that the economic and social state of affairs has been so altered since the beginning of the century that it is no good continuing to apply automatically perceptions based on the old analysis but necessary rather to think out a new programme relevant to the radically changed circumstances.[3]

Revisionism as an ideological tendency within the Labour Party during the 1950s and early 1960s attempted, therefore, to do just that. It sought to reformulate socialist principles and to revise Labour policies through a new analysis of the changed economic and social conditions of post-1945 British society. As it was developed throughout the 1950s it steadily acquired its distinctiveness both as a body of theory and as a set of policies.

First outlined in 1952 in the Fabian publication *New Fabian Essays*, Labour revisionism was most thoroughly and coherently expressed in Anthony Crosland's major work *The Future of Socialism*, published in 1956. The period from 1956 onwards, following Hugh Gaitskell's accession to the Party leadership, witnessed the increasing prominence of revisionism as a major ideological influence within the Party. This marked the beginning of what Minkin has called Labour's apparent 'revisionist metamorphosis',[4] during which revisionist ideas on public ownership and on economic strategy were widely propagated and steadily incorporated into official Party policy statements.

Labour revisionism can be examined most clearly in the ideas and writings of two distinct but connected groups – first, the parliamentary friends and supporters of Hugh Gaitskell, and, second, the organization Socialist Union[5] and its related periodical *Socialist Commentary*. Revisionism manifestly became a 'Gaitskellite' position from 1956 to 1963, since the Party leader was strongly committed to revisionist ideas, with their leading exponents, in the main, his friends and allies. Gaitskell himself had become a central figure in Friends of Socialist Commentary, a body which forged links between the two main revisionist groupings.[6] He was thus very much the focus of revisionist thinking and policy-making. To describe, however, the revisionist outlook simply as 'Gaitskellism' or 'Gaitskellite' would be to overpersonalize a coherent body of ideas. That would be particularly misleading since it was Crosland rather than Gaitskell who provided the main intellectual thrust behind this new political influence.

The forerunners of Labour revisionism have been widely cited as a group of mainly Oxford-educated and London-based intellectuals meeting in the 1930s.[7] Centred on initially the New Fabian Bureau, founded in 1931 by G. D. H. Cole, the group developed ideas for Labour's National Executive policy subcommittees, which throughout the 1930s were dominated by Hugh Dalton and Herbert Morrison.[8] Its leading members – Evan Durbin, Hugh Gaitskell and Douglas Jay – were concerned in general with redefining democratic socialist principles and policies. Specifically, they were eager to introduce into the Labour Party recently formulated Keynesian ideas on macroeconomic intervention.[9] Jay in particular was concerned to shift the main emphasis of socialist strategy away from public ownership towards the taxation of income and wealth. It was his belief that socialists had been 'mistaken in making ownership of the means of production instead of ownership of inherited property the test of socialization'.[10]

The tensions between revisionist arguments – anticipated by views such as this – and more traditional socialist attitudes were not to surface in any overt form until the 1950s. The completion of the Attlee Governments' programme and Labour's election defeat in 1951 created the climate in which revisionist positions could be systematically developed – notably by Crosland, Gaitskell and Jay.

The body of ideas that subsequently took shape in the 1950s involved two major, highly controversial deviations from accepted Labour orthodoxies. First, revisionism repudiated the traditional view that socialism could be adequately defined as, or at least identified with, the public ownership of the means of production. It thereby questioned the established Labour commitment to extensive public ownership as a precondition of achieving all major socialist objectives. It firmly rejected the fundamentalist reverence for public ownership as, in Beer's words, 'an indispensable condition and a major expression of a radically transformed economy, society and culture'[11] Instead, revisionists agreed with Crosland 'that the ownership of the means of production has ceased to be the key factor which imparts to a society its essential character'.[12]

Second, revisionism diverged from orthodox Party thinking by presenting a distinctive ethical reinterpretation of socialism – in terms of values and ideals such as personal liberty, social welfare and social equality. Public ownership was consequently viewed as one important means among several others of realizing these socialist values. It was not to be considered the central aspect of some finite socialist goal.

II

The formulation of the revisionist view of public ownership can best be understood as a response to the completion of the Attlee Governments' nationalization programme and to the perceived inadequacies of rival attitudes towards public ownership – those held by 'fundamentalists' and 'consolidators' – which arose in the wake of that programme. The 'fundamentalists', as they have often been called,[13] consisting mainly of the Bevanite left, interpreted the completed programme of 1945–9 as the necessary first stage in the gradual but deliberate advance towards a socialized economy. Their key strategic objective was therefore to extend, rather than merely consolidate, the Labour Governments' achievements. That meant expanding the frontiers of the public sector and accelerating the pace of advance towards their ultimate socialist goal. To that end they therefore advocated a substantial extension of public ownership through the nationalization of a series of individual industries, identified on a 'shopping list' of specific proposals. In their view, there was no alternative to this process, for, as Aneurin Bevan, their leading, charismatic advocate, asked rhetorically, in a resonant declaration of faith in public ownership that conveyed its mythic force,

> Are we seriously as Socialists going to be told that in 1952 we have discovered some royal road, some ingenious way of trying to achieve our socialist purposes which would not lead us through the old hard agony of public ownership? There is no royal road.[14]

But to the 'consolidators' – that is, mainly Herbert Morrison, chief architect of the nationalization programme, and his supporters – Labour's record in office seemed well worth defending for its own sake. In contrast, the prospect of further large-scale nationalization appeared to them increasingly uninviting.[15] They therefore adhered to Morrison's view, first advanced by him in 1948, that, before contemplating further nationalization measures, Labour should first seek to consolidate its recent achievements in office, devising practical methods for developing and making more efficient the existing nationalized industries.[16] In policy-making terms this meant abandoning the left's expansionist, 'shopping-list' approach to nationalization and replacing it with a more pragmatic emphasis on certain 'broad criteria' for any future extensions of public ownership.[17]

The debate between 'consolidators' and 'fundamentalists' in the early 1950s was accompanied by the emergence of a third viewpoint which challenged both schools of thought. This position gradually became characterized, by its champions and detractors alike, as a 'revisionist' one. It was concerned not just with reviewing existing Labour policy but also with a critical reinterpretation of traditional socialist doctrine.

The publication, in 1952, of *New Fabian Essays* provided the occasion for such a reappraisal. Edited by Richard Crossman, the *Essays* outlined positions that were later to become central to the revisionist outlook during the 1950s and early 1960s. They also contained contributions from some of the most prolific revisionist writers of that period – notably Anthony Crosland and Roy Jenkins.

New Fabian Essays made it clear at the outset that their overriding purpose was to produce 'a new analysis of the political, economic and social scene as a basis for reformulating socialist principles'.[18] The most thorough attempt in the volume to achieve that end was made by Crosland in his essay 'The Transition from Capitalism', in which he argued that classical capitalism had been transformed by a number of important developments in the post-1945 period. These included the growth in size and scale of joint-stock companies, involving more widely dispersed shareholdings, and the increasing divorce between legal ownership and managerial control within private industry. The consequence of such changes was that 'the propertied class had thus lost its traditional capitalist function – the exploitation with its own capital of the techniques of production – and as the function disappears, so the power slips away'[19]

Crosland refined his examination of the transformation of post-1945 capitalism in his major work *The Future of Socialism*. Published in 1956, this highly influential book constituted the most ambitious and systematic expression of British revisionist thought to appear since 1945. Rejecting in its pages 'the predominantly Marxist analysis'[20] which, in his view, still underlay so much British socialist thought, his own unorthodox economic analysis provided the intellectual foundation of the first part of the revisionist project – the repudiation of the traditional identification of socialism with public ownership.[21]

Crosland maintained in *The Future of Socialism* that a substantial change in the pattern of economic power had taken place in postwar Britain. This involved, in his view, a transfer of economic power away from the prewar capitalist class in three directions – toward the state, towards organized labour and towards salaried managers within private industry.

Crosland thus drew attention to the greater economic power and functions of the state – evident not just in the large nationalized sector but also in the increasingly prominent role of government in national economic management. He emphasized, too, the shift of industrial power in Britain – largely as a result of full or near-full employment – from the propertied business class to the trade unions.

In the final and most controversial part of his analysis, he pointed to major structural changes within private industry which amounted

to a transfer of power from the capitalist class to a salaried managerial class. Here he developed points raised in his 1952 essay, thereby
elaborating a thesis which had first been advanced by Berle
and Means in 1932[22] and then popularized by James Burnham in his
influential book *The Managerial Revolution*.[23]

In this area of change Crosland stressed, above all, the growing
divorce between legal ownership and managerial control resulting
from the increased scale, complexity and technicality of modern
industry. Such conditions had produced a steady growth in the
number of virtually functionless shareholders who played no significant part in the day-to-day running of private industry. At the same
time a burgeoning class of salaried managers and technicians, who in
the main did not own major shareholdings, increasingly took the
important specialist decisions within industry. Furthermore, this
managerial class had become, in Crosland's view, more socially
responsible, more sensitive to the public interest, than their capitalist
forebears. He was thus offering a 'benign interpretation of the
managerial revolution'.[24]

Crosland's thesis profoundly affected the entire revisionist
approach to public ownership. For if the ownership and control of
industry were no longer to be considered inseparable, it was hard to
regard public ownership as an indispensable part of socialist policy
and strategy. Other methods of achieving socialist ends – government
controls or fiscal measures, for instance – might well be deemed
equally useful.

The empirical basis of this managerialist thesis has since been
subjected to severe critical scrutiny.[25] Nevertheless, it was accepted at
the time by other revisionist writers[26] and, most notably, from outside
the revisionist camp by John Strachey.[27] It was endorsed, too, albeit
in more qualified and less commendatory terms, in the controversial
and influential 1957 Party policy statement, *Industry and Society*.[28]
Its ideological implications were far-reaching since it described
major internal changes within British capitalism which, in Crosland's
view, were paving the way for a new post-capitalist order. For as a
result of the transformation, 'the economic power of the capitalist
(i.e. industrial property-owning) class is enormously less than a
generation ago; while even that of the managerial business class is
significantly restricted by the new economic activism of governments,
and the greater strength of organised labour'.[29] This new, 'quite
different configuration of economic power'[30] had coincided, too, with
the achievement of rapid and sustained economic growth. Taken
together, these two developments had not only transformed classical

capitalism but also thereby 'rendered obsolete' the established 'intellectual framework within which most pre-war socalist discussion was conducted'[31] – built as it had been around the twin Marxist assumptions of acute and deepening class conflict and imminent capitalist collapse.

Crosland's conception of this post-capitalist society, in which the ownership of the means of production had become an increasingly irrelevant question, drew him towards a major, highly contentious conclusion – namely, that the traditional association of socialism with the public ownership of the means of production embodied in Clause IV of Labour's Constitution was both obsolete and inadequate. It made no sense, he argued, to continue to regard socialism as a distinct form of economic organization based on a particular pattern of ownership, a factor of declining importance.

Such views disturbed large sections of the Labour Party. They shared the conviction expressed in 1956 by Strachey, at that time by no means a fundamentalist, that 'the social ownership of the decisive parts of the means of production is the only permanent basis for a Socialist, classless society'.[32] Many agreed, too, with Strachey's belief that, if socialists were to abandon their commitment to public owner-ship, 'they will cease, in a very real sense, to be Socialists at all: they will subside into the role of well-intentioned, amiable, rootless, drifting social reformers'.[33]

Crosland, however, did not attempt to disguise the iconoclastic nature of the revisionist exercise. In view of the economic transfor-mation which he had been examining, he was convinced that 'most pre-war analyses have lost their relevance and the much-thumbed guidebooks of the past must now be thrown away'.[34]

His own analysis, and the irreverent conclusion to which it led, in turn helped to shape the major features of the revisionist approach to public ownership. For abandonment of the orthodox identification of socialism with public ownership entailed an erosion of the traditional argument for both public ownership and nationalization, its most commonly practised form, as means of redistributing wealth through the appropriation of capitalists' property incomes. This, 'the oldest (even pre-Marxist) argument for public ownership', as Crosland described it,[35] was exposed to particularly heavy criticism by revi-sionists. Both Crosland and Gaitskell[36] pointed out that, in view of the payment of full compensation to shareholders, the transfer of industries to the state had a strictly limited effect on the distribution of income. The flow of unearned income simply continued in the form of interest rather than profits or dividends.[37]

This revisionist critique acquired greater force through an increased awareness of the practical shortcomings of nationalization. Strong reservations on this score had already been voiced in the early 1950s – both by revisionists[38] and by some of their Bevanite opponents.[39] After 1956 such doubts were expressed with a greater insistency. The practical reality of nationalization, Crosland observed, had 'proved rather different from the blueprints'.[40] In particular, the unsuitability of the traditional form of nationalization – the centralized state monopoly – for competitive manufacturing industry was clearly recognized.[41] Other defects inherent in the nationalized boards were also underlined. These included their lack of accountability – to Parliament, employees or consumers[42] – as well as their over-centralized, bureaucratic and hierarchical structures.

Dissatisfaction with nationalization bred a desire to explore other forms of public ownership. Among these the most distinctive and innovative proposals to emerge revolved around the ideas of competitive public enterprise and state shareholdings in private industry. The former had first been advocated by Douglas Jay and was favoured by such diverse Party figures as Mikardo, Crossman and Jenkins.[43] This method of extending public ownership would involve the state, as Crosland explained, either in taking over individual firms rather than entire industries or in setting up government-owned plants to compete with existing private firms.[44]

The second policy option, state shareholdings, which, again, had first been commended by Jay[45] and which turned out to be ideologically contentious, was envisaged as a form of partial public ownership without public control. Jay had been 'advocating state holding of equity shares from 1945 onwards in discussions generally with Labour Party colleagues'.[46] By the 1950s this proposal had evolved in his mind, partly as a result of his studying the experience of countries such as Italy and France, 'into the idea of a national finance corporation or national enterprise board'.[47] By 1957 he was proposing this particular innovation, which was designed to 'own some of the shares of many firms'.[48] He discussed the idea with Gaitskell and, more broadly, 'argued in favour of public participation rather than 100% ownership'.[49]

Gaitskell himself, as Jay later recalled, 'evidently sympathized'.[50] In fact, he strongly supported the main thrust of Jay's unorthodox proposal, arguing in his own writings that the state might either take in death duties equity shares rather than cash or bonds, or else use the proceeds of a budget surplus to purchase equity shares. In such ways it could extend its ownership of industrial and commercial property without exercising detailed control over individual companies or industries.[51] The effect of this process was designed to be redistributive, with the state replacing the passive shareholder and thereby receiving dividends and reaping capital gains on behalf of the community.

These innovative policy ideas had been discussed 'a good deal' during this period by Jay, Gaitskell and Crosland, the leading revisionist thinkers on economic affairs.[52] They were advanced as practicable methods both of raising the productive efficiency of a mixed economy and of reducing inequalities of wealth. As such, they were presented by their advocates as contributions to a strategy of social amelioration, not as means of transforming British capitalism.

For precisely that reason, however, Jay's state-shareholding proposal, in particular, was viewed by many observers with deep suspicion. Although in 1957 it was advocated in the Party policy document *Industry and Society*, the very idea that it embodied – partial public ownership of private industry without public control – was regarded by its traditionalist critics as an unprincipled accommodation, or even a direct partnership, with the capitalist system. Emanuel Shinwell, for example, considered that the proposal, if implemented, would involve taking 'the capitalist way'.[53] By abandoning outright nationalization in such a manner, Labour's policy-makers would, he believed, be violating 'the fundamental principles of this Policy'.[54] Maurice Edelman, too, argued that by accepting 'the pernicious principle of state investment in capitalist industry', Labour would soon become 'a hostage bound hand and foot to the capitalist system'.[55] In similar vein, Barbara Castle declared that she was 'not interested in the state acquiring a few shares here and there in order to share the capitalist swag'.[56]

Such statements clearly indicated the degree of ideological controversy which the revisionist proposal had generated. Its unashamedly reformist approach was implicit, too, in the promotion of other policy instruments which might even supplant public ownership itself. Special attention was focused here on fiscal measures, which for Crosland meant a series of taxes on capital – a gifts tax, stiffer death duties, capital gains and corporate taxes, and, possibly, an annual wealth tax.[57]

The revisionists' advocacy of such measures sprang from their assault on the traditional egalitarian case for nationalization. For if, in the light of fair compensation, that policy had become a blunt instrument of redistribution, then, as Jay had long argued, taxation ought to assume a more prominent role in socialist strategy.[58]

Jay's emphasis on fiscal policy as an alternative to public ownership soon developed into another matter of doctrinal controversy.[59] Even more sharply contested was the favourable view of the mixed economy which underlay this and other revisionist proposals. In *The Future of Socialism* Crosland invited charges of heresy by declaring that:

> The ideal (or at least my ideal) is a society with a diverse, diffused, pluralist and heterogeneous pattern of ownership, with the State, the nationalised industries, the Co-operatives, the Unions, Government financial institutions, pension funds, foundations, and millions of private families all participating.[60]

Socialist Union, in its publication *Twentieth Century Socialism*, drafted by Rita Hinden and Allan Flanders, joined in this defence of the mixed economy, even arguing that the continuance of private ownership was a precondition of political freedom.[61] In a socialist economy, which was depicted as 'a mixed economy, part private, part public, and mixed in all its aspects', private industry would have 'a legitimate and indeed a necessary function to perform',[62] a view that Gaitskell also embraced.[63]

It was this attitude, above all, that was widely resented within the Party. Support for the mixed economy was a logical consequence of the revisionists' attempt to remove the intimate link between socialism and public ownership – their first major challenge to orthodox Labour thinking – and hence to transcend the traditional antithesis between socialism and capitalism. Yet to their critics this meant discarding Labour's doctrinal commitment to the goal of a mainly socialized economy.[64]

III

The revisionists' second major divergence from Party orthodoxy was less sharp, but significant all the same. It involved their restating socialist aims in terms of certain ethical values – with a particular emphasis on social equality. This undertaking implicitly challenged any view of socialism as a distinct form of economic organization to be achieved through the gradual socialization of industry.

Gaitskell strongly favoured this ethical approach, declaring that, in his view, socialism consisted of 'a collection of ideals towards which we hope to advance'. He considered 'the central socialist ideal' to be equality, which for him meant not equality of incomes or uniformity of tastes and habits but rather 'a classless society . . . one in which though there are differences between individuals, there are no feelings or attitudes of superiority or inferiority between groups'.[65]

From the same ideological standpoint Crosland, in *The Future of Socialism*, followed up his examination of structural changes within capitalism with a reappraisal of the fundamental aims of British socialism. He acknowledged the absence in British political thought of any 'single constant and consistent body of socialist doctrine'.[66] British socialist thought had always been highly variable, with different theories and doctrines prevailing at different historical periods. Moreover, the Labour Party had consistently maintained an antidoctrinal and antitheoretical bias. He recognized, too, that the word 'socialism' had no precise, descriptive meaning, for it did 'not describe any present or past society, which can be empirically observed, and so furnish unimpeachable evidence for what is or is not "socialism"'.[67]

Nevertheless, Crosland identified certain enduring ideals and aspirations – shared by the various schools of socialist thought – which sprang from 'a vision of a just, cooperative and classless society'.[68] It was these, he stressed, that represented 'the only logically and historically permissible meaning of the word socialism'.[69] The most important of them included 'a wider concern for "social welfare" – for the interests of those in need, or oppressed, or unfortunate', 'a belief in equality and the "classless society"' and 'an ideal of fraternity and co-operation'.[70] Of these, Crosland placed special emphasis on the first and second, regarding the cooperative ideal as less relevant in contemporary conditions.[71] The welfare ideal implied 'an acceptance of collective responsibility and an extremely high priority for the relief of social distress or misfortune'.[72] The ideal of social equality in turn implied the goal of 'a distribution of rewards, status and privileges egalitarian enough to minimise social resentment, to secure justice between individuals, and to equalise opportunities'.[73] Furthermore, this belief in greater equality had been, Crosland maintained, 'the strongest ethical inspiration of virtually every socialist doctrine' and still remained 'the most characteristic feature of socialist thought today'.[74]

Crosland's restatement of socialism was thus, like Gaitskell's, unmistakably ethical in tone. As he later confirmed, his conviction was that 'it is these ideals, and not some particular economic theory or arid dogma, which constitute the essence of democratic Socialism'.[75] Such a belief, which was shared by Rita Hinden of Socialist Union,[76] had important theoretical implications. First, it indicated a clear distinction between socialist ends and means, between certain values and ideals and the practical methods of fulfilling them. This had to be stressed, revisionists argued, because too often socialist ends and means had been confused. Crosland, for example, pointed out that the word 'socialism' 'generally . . . came to be applied to policies for the economic and institutional transformation of society, instead of the ultimate social purposes which that transformation was intended to achieve'.[77]

Second, the revisionist emphasis on socialist ideals and values led to a pragmatic and instrumental view of public ownership. The latter was to be regarded merely as a useful technique or method, not as the supreme goal of socialism. Gaitskell had long viewed public ownership in this way, treating it as a means of pursuing his 'central socialist ideal' of equality and offering some practical illustrations of his approach.[78] Jenkins, too, at this time argued that any extension of public ownership should be justified on the grounds that it was 'an essential prerequisite of equality of earned incomes and an inevitable concomitant of greater equality in the ownership of property'.[79]

Finally, this revisionist insistence on the primacy of socialist ends even brought about both the demotion of public ownership to a secondary status in Labour policy and strategy and the consequent elevation of fiscal and social policy measures – strongly commended in the writings of Crosland and Jay – as the chosen methods of attaining those ends.

The ethical view of socialism that underlay these attitudes can, it is true, be considered not particularly 'revisionist'. It was, after all, in harmony with a British socialist tradition which had been, in Tawney's words, 'obstinately and unashamedly ethical'.[80] Yet in the past the ethical and economic aspects of British socialism had been indissolubly linked. Labour's overriding aim had been the gradual replacement of capitalism by an alternative system that was economically, socially and morally superior. Tawney himself, whom Gaitskell described as 'the democratic socialist *par excellence*',[81] had recognized in the interwar years that the building of the Socialist Commonwealth would entail 'large measures of economic and social reconstruction'.[82] These, in turn, would require 'a significant change of ownership . . . the transference of property to public hands'.[83] The public ownership of industry, while not an end in itself, was thus, in Tawney's view, intimately connected with the realization of the socialist ideals of equality, liberty and fellowship.

In rejecting this notion of the interdependence of ethical and economic concerns, revisionist writers were departing from mainstream Labour thinking. While reaffirming the value of a long ethical socialist tradition, they appeared – Crosland in particular – to be separating socialist ideals from the supporting framework of a socialist economic analysis and from the programmatic implications of such an analysis. Labour revisionists were, in fact, developing an ethical approach to socialism that did not imply systematic opposition to British capitalism.[84] Indeed, in Crosland's view the most distinctive socialist ideals, namely social welfare and equality, could be fulfilled within the context of a state-regulated yet market-oriented mixed economy and through the interventions in such an economy of a benevolent state.

IV

The revisionists' dual undertaking – the rejection of the traditional identification of socialism with wholesale public ownership and the ethical reformulation of socialist aims – provided, therefore, the essential features of what gradually became identified as the social-democratic model or paradigm. These were reinforced by a policy commitment to sustained economic growth and full employment. On that basis high social expenditure and redistributive taxation were in turn commended as the necessary practical means both of promoting social welfare and of pursuing greater equality of wealth and resources. Keynesian interventionist techniques thus became the accepted economic foundation of the revisionist social-democratic project.

The ideological position that bore these characteristics was designed to be both intellectually coherent and electorally attractive. This did not mean that such a position was purely pragmatic and non-doctrinal. Beer observed that, like their fundamentalist adversaries, revisionists shared in the 'compulsive ideologism'[85] of the Labour Party. They were concerned, after all, as Crosland had stressed, 'to decide what precise meaning is to be attached to the word "Socialism"'.[86] Nevertheless, the revisionist project did entail the promotion of a view of the role of public ownership which, if not exclusively pragmatic, was uncompromisingly rationalistic. For that view rested on an attempt to demythologize public ownership, that is, to disregard the visionary force of a dominant political idea.

Each part of the revisionists' task of reappraisal – their repudiation of an ownership-based definition of socialism as well as their ethical restatement of its ultimate purposes – involved them in this icono-clastic exercise. Their efforts to refute those traditional arguments which had upheld public ownership as, in Strachey's phrase, 'the fundamental part of Socialism'[87] thus indicated an indifference to the mythic significance of that idea. Similarly, their ethical perspective revealed a dispassionate view of public ownership as an instrument of social reform rather than as an agent of economic and social transformation.

The effect of this demythologizing process gradually became apparent in the main arenas of Party debate – at the Annual Party Conference, for instance, and in the pages of socialist journals. There the revisionists' undervaluation of the doctrinal status of public ownership was viewed with suspicion and mistrust. Certainly that was the widespread response to their critique of the traditional case for nationalization, to their highly cautious view of the strategic importance of public ownership and, above all, to their favourable references to private industry and the mixed economy.[88]

All these revisionist stances were supported by rational arguments and by an impressive theoretical analysis. Yet for all their strengths, the result of their advancement throughout the 1950s was a disruption of that ideological consensus which for so long had bound Labour's loose coalition together. This was evident in two main respects. First, revisionist ideas – whether expressed in the form of theoretical or policy statements – sharpened differences over Labour's future direction and ultimate destination. They depicted the mixed economy not as some provisional expedient but rather as a stable environment in which to pursue both economic growth and social reform. By contrast, an older generation of Labour leaders, although cautious and moderate in their policy recommendations, had always, as Miliband observed, 'held out to their followers the promise that accommodation with capitalism was a temporary halt, however prolonged, on the journey to the Socialist Commonwealth'.[89] Outwardly at least, their dispute with the left had been 'about the pace of advance, not about the ultimate desirability of advance itself'.[90] But the revisionists were openly questioning both the practicality and the desirability of advancing towards a socialist economy based on widespread public ownership of the means of production.

In addition, revisionist ideas were disturbing because they appeared to their critics to be undermining Labour's socialist identity, to be betraying fundamental values and beliefs. For that reason revisionist approval of the mixed economy was considered deeply suspect. More specifically, it was from such a perspective that Jay's state-shareholdings proposal, presented in the 1957 policy document *Industry and Society*, had been fiercely denounced, by Shinwell and others, as a violation of traditional socialist principles and as a form of 'direct partnership with capitalism'.[91]

As a result of this ideological turbulence, Labour was beginning to acquire by the late 1950s the appearance of a coalition of inconsistent and perhaps even incompatible elements. Large sections of the Party – and not just the left – remained committed, for both doctrinal and sentimental reasons, to the traditional goal of a Socialist Commonwealth founded on public ownership. The mixed economy was accepted by them only grudgingly as a staging post on that road. In sharp contrast, Labour revisionists willingly embraced the mixed economy, including a vigorous private sector, as an established framework within which their desired social and economic goals could be pursued.

Labour's ideological conflict was, however, partially contained in the late 1950s. There were several reasons for this. In the first place, the Party's theoretical and policy debate in the period stretching from 1956 to the 1959 General Election, while conducted with passion and at times bitterness, was not marked by the degree of ferocity that was later to become so evident. This was due partly to Bevan's accommodation with Gaitskell in 1957[92] and partly to the pressure of external events such as the Suez crisis and the mounting nuclear arms controversy, which, in their political impact, tended to eclipse domestic disputes.

Another significant factor during this period was the manner in which Harold Wilson, operating from outside the revisionist camp but within Labour's Shadow Cabinet, played an important mediating role. In the Party debate he helped, in particular, to restore the link in Labour policy between public ownership and economic planning – an association that stretched back to the mid-1930s.[93] He made this contribution against the current of national economic thinking, which had yet to accord a major role to planning techniques or agencies.[94] Yet, by doing so he broadened the appeal of public ownership throughout the Party, presenting it as an instrument of economic growth and modernization. He skilfully employed, too, traditional socialist rhetoric in support of pragmatic or even revisionist policy proposals – for instance, whilst defending *Industry and Society* in 1957. In all these respects Wilson was offering pointers to a later course of reconciliation within the Party.

Ultimately, too, these forces of mediation or diversion were in time strengthened by the realities of electoral politics, for sharp differences over the role of public ownership and the ultimate purposes of democratic socialism were eroded by a growing desire for

Party unity as the 1959 General Election drew closer. By such means, then, were the ideological tensions that had been raised by the revisionists' theoretical and policy initiatives gradually lowered during the late 1950s. They were to reappear, however, in dramatic form, in the period following Labour's third successive election defeat in 1959.

3 The climax of revisionism:

Gaitskell and the Clause IV dispute

I

Labour's heavy defeat at the 1959 General Election soon gave rise to a fierce internal debate characterized by a sustained intensity which had been less evident in the Party's previous, more overtly theoretical disputes of the mid- to late 1950s. With the pre-election pressures for Party unity lifted, deepening divisions and tensions became more starkly apparent.

The debate itself, conducted against a background of mounting pessimism, centred around three main areas of controversy. These concerned, first, the question of the Party leadership, with Hugh Gaitskell an increasingly beleaguered figure; second, the future direction of Labour policy; and, third, fundamental aspects of socialist doctrine. In the wake of electoral defeat a revisionist initiative soon emerged in the second and third of those areas. Initially, this took the form of a series of articles and essays by Gaitskell's supporter Douglas Jay which directly challenged the role of nationalization within Labour policy and doctrine. Subsequently, it took the more dramatic form of a proposal by Gaitskell to amend Clause IV of the Party Constitution – the formal expression of Labour's socialist myth.

The starting point for this initiative has been located by some observers[1] in a farewell party for Hugh Dalton at Gaitskell's house in Hampstead, London, barely forty-eight hours after the General Election results were known.[2] On that occasion Jay in particular spoke out on the lessons to be learned from Labour's defeat. He made a number of controversial suggestions – including dropping further nationalization proposals, loosening the party's links with the trade unions, exploring the possibility of agreements with the Liberals, and even altering the name of the Party.[3]

Suggestions of this kind encouraged suspicion on the Labour left that this Hampstead meeting of Gaitskell and his friends had, in Foot's words, provided 'the level which helped to let . . . loose' a deliberate revisionist strategy.[4] Jay, however, later claimed that such a suspicion was groundless and constituted 'a classic example of that common political phenomenon: an elaborate and sinister conspiracy being detected in what was really a series of accidents'.[5]

Nevertheless, the left's fears of a Hampstead conspiracy were inflamed by the publication in the revisionist journal *Forward* a few days later of an article by Jay in which he amplified some of his earlier recommendations. He argued that Labour's future electoral success would hinge on the removal of two 'fatal handicaps' – namely, the Party's unmistakably working-class image and what he called 'the myth of nationalisation'.[6] In his judgement, that 'myth' had been based on two misconceptions – first, the confusion between nationalization and public ownership as a whole and, second, the widespread belief that Labour 'intended to "nationalise" anything and everything.'[7]

In order to destroy this damaging presentation of nationalization it was essential, Jay believed, for Labour to make plain 'that we believe in social ownership through the Co-operative Movement, municipal enterprise and public investment; but that we do not believe in the extension of the public monopoly to manufacturing industry or distribution'.[8] The publication of such views eight days after the General Election was regarded by many on the left as the launching stage of a deliberate strategy conceived at Gaitskell's gathering of friends. Foot, for example, claimed that it was Jay's article 'in the semi-official *Forward* which gave a semi-official stamp to the post-election revisionist *démarche*,' with the overriding aim thus being 'to seize the moment to carry forward the revisionist ideas of recent years no longer by relentless pressure, but by a *coup d'état*'.[9] Yet there appears to be little evidence in favour of this view of events. For according to Williams, Gaitskell 'did not suggest the article, or see the text, or agree with the content',[10] while Jay himself later stated that his article derived not from any suggestion of Gaitskell's but rather from his own party workers' canvassing experience in Battersea, south London, during the election campaign.[11] Jay recalled, too, that Gaitskell was at first 'a bit perturbed'[12] by his article but had later written to him saying that, while he did not agree with all its suggestions, he nonetheless admired Jay's courage.[13] Crosland had also written to Jay 'expressing almost entire agreement with the article, but surprise at my candour'.[14]

But in spite of the absence of any organized conspiracy or planned revisionist strategy, Jay's *Forward* article did have the effect of provoking conflict within the Party in the weeks following the Election. The deeper implications of his proposals – that by calling for a halt to nationalization he was thereby challenging its doctrinal significance – were recognized by Hugh Dalton. In the throes of Labour's post-election inquest Dalton told Gaitskell that Jay's article really 'gave it all a bad start, and struck the tuning-fork for all the Gregorian Chants of the Old Believers'.[15] Such fears were confirmed by critical reactions to Jay's views. In the pages of both *Tribune* and the *New Statesman* fundamentalists and traditionalists in the Party expressed their grave concern.[16] To them Jay seemed to have disregarded the role of both nationalization and public ownership as the foundations of an alternative, non-capitalist economic system and social order. The strictly limited role assigned by him to nationalization, together with his presentation of public ownership in purely pragmatic and reformist terms, thus appeared, in their view, to threaten Labour's socialist identity and purpose.

II

Jay's pronouncements had revived the long-running debate within the Party both over the nature and purpose of nationalization and public ownership and over their future role in Labour policy, strategy and ideology. The stage was now set for an intensification of that debate at the two-day Party Conference held at Blackpool on 28 and 29 November 1959.

The revisionist initiative launched, albeit unsystematically, after the Election by Jay's articles was sustained at that Conference by Hugh Gaitskell in a keynote speech delivered on 28 November. Whereas Jay's main task – to limit the future scope of nationalization and to broaden Labour's conception of public ownership – had been a practical yet highly controversial one, Gaitskell's contribution turned out to be even more contentious and far-reaching in its implications. For the object of the Leader's attention was to be not just nationalization and public ownership but also the document that had enshrined them for forty years – the Party Constitution itself.

Gaitskell's Conference speech, which concentrated on the issue of nationalization, had been prompted to a large extent by Labour's official post-election inquest. The report of the Party's General Secretary, Morgan Phillips, had emphasized the electoral damage caused by the Party's ambiguous proposals for leading private-sector companies. Gaitskell himself had no doubt that widespread fears of 'backdoor nationalization' had, as the report indicated, lost Labour votes.[17] He therefore sought to focus attention upon the place which nationalization should occupy within the Party's broad strategy and philosophy. At that time, in autumn 1959, his own attitude towards nationalization and public ownership remained both pragmatic and generally favourable. He maintained that 'One must argue for nationalization instance by instance, showing what had to be done, why it had to be done, how public ownership could help, and why it was necessary'.[18] Labour's inquest into its election defeat seemed to present Gaitskell with the opportunity for advocating this kind of hard-headed approach. Acutely aware of the Party's electoral difficulties, he had thus come to believe that the time had come to reconsider Clause IV, Part Four, of the Party Constitution, which had stated that Labour's central domestic aim was

> To secure for the workers by hand or by brain the full fruit of their industry, and the most equitable distribution thereof that may be possible, upon the basis of the common ownership of the means of production, distribution and exchange, and the best obtainable system of popular administration and control of each industry and service.[19]

In his various writings on nationalization and public ownership throughout the 1950s Gaitskell had consistently upheld the revisionist view of public ownership as a means and not an end, while making it clear that for him the pursuit of equality was the supreme socialist goal. Shortly before becoming Party leader he had confirmed these attitudes when he observed that, since Clause IV 'speaks of obtaining for the worker the full fruits of his labour, the emphasis is really on equality'.[20]

However, he also believed, as his statements during the post-1959 period were to indicate clearly, that Clause IV, as it stood, was a source of misunderstanding and misinterpretation. For to many observers it suggested, he thought, that Labour was committed to the public ownership of the whole – or at least the bulk – of the British economy. By 1959 he had therefore reached the conclusion that, in order both to emphasize that this was not in fact Labour's overriding objective and to clarify the Party's broader socialist aims, it would be necessary to amend or revise Clause IV of the Party Constitution.

Just as the left had suspected that Douglas Jay's original, controversial article in *Forward* had been the first stage of a carefully planned revisionist strategy, so there developed, as Jay himself has recalled, a 'legend' that Gaitskell's Conference speech at Blackpool 'represented the supporting offensive in the campaign started by my *Forward* article'.[21] But here again there seems to be little empirical evidence in support of such a belief. Instead, it would appear that Gaitskell's decision to raise the issue of Clause IV was a solitary one, made largely without advice or encouragement from his friends or supporters.[22]

Certainly his proposal, as Williams stressed, 'was not concocted by the "Hampstead set"'.[23] Jay, for example, had made no mention of Clause IV in his post-election articles and later recalled that 'I doubt if I was even aware of Clause Four. It was the last thing on my mind at the time'.[24] Furthermore, he 'knew nothing about Gaitskell's idea of mentioning Clause IV, or about any of the contents of his speech'[25] until the night before at Blackpool. Crosland, however, did have fore-knowledge of Gaitskell's proposal, but strongly advised him against it.[26] The Miners' leader Sam Watson also warned Gaitskell not to proceed along these lines since he considered such a move to be 'misjudged and unnecessary'.[27] One of the few encouraging responses came from Hugh Dalton, who pointed out that Arthur Henderson, the original co-author of the 1918 document, had remarked in 1927 that the wording of Clause IV was in need of reconsideration since it dated from 1892.[28]

But support of this kind was in short supply. The predominant reaction among Gaitskell's associates was one of considerable unease. In spite of this, the Party leader remained determined to put forward his views on Clause IV in his Conference speech. The symbolic importance of this – the fact that he was proposing to challenge the formal expression of Labour's socialist myth – was evident in a conversation (one of several on the subject) which he held before-hand with Jim Griffiths, the retiring Deputy leader. Griffiths later recalled that

> He knew that I belonged to the old tradition in socialist thought and practice, and that Clause Four was an article of faith to me and my generation. When I reminded him of this he replied sternly: 'Maybe, but you know that we do not intend, any of us, to implement Clause Four fully, and I regard it as my duty to say so to the Party and the country'.[29]

Gaitskell accordingly presented his speech to Conference on 28 November 1959 as his own contribution to the 'post mortem' on Labour's election defeat. He began by examining what he called 'a significant change in the economic and social background of politics'[30] in Britain. The changing character of the working population, reduced unemployment, the welfare state, improved living standards and higher consumer expenditure – these were all major economic and social changes which seemed to be working against Labour electorally. Such changes even led Gaitskell to deduce, as Crosland had done in *The Future of Socialism*, that 'capitalism has significantly changed'.[31]

In the face of these developments it was essential, Gaitskell argued, for Labour to adapt itself and 'to be in touch always with ordinary people, to avoid becoming small cliques of isolated doctrine-ridden fanatics, out of touch with the main stream of social life in our time'.[32] Such adjustments ought not, however, to require some of the 'rather desperate remedies'[33] recently prescribed – such as a pact with the Liberals, or changing the Party's name or cutting Labour's links with the trade unions. He thus rejected without hesitation some of Jay's earlier recommendations.

Turning eventually to consider nationalization and public ownership, Gaitskell maintained that most people involved in the 1959 Election were agreed that nationalization had been a vote-losing issue for Labour – apparently for two reasons. First, some of the existing nationalized industries were clearly unpopular. To a large extent this was the result of circumstances – inadequate investment in the railways, for instance – which had nothing to do with nationalization per se. It was consequently essential to improve the performance of those industries since 'Our fellow-citizens are more likely to judge the value of the public sector by their experience of it than from theoretical arguments in speeches or Labour Party pamphlets'.[34]

The second damaging factor for Labour lay in 'the confusion in the public mind about our future policy'[35] on nationalization. This situation had largely arisen from gross misrepresentation of the Party's policy proposals by its political opponents. As a result, countless voters had been persuaded 'to think that we intended to nationalise any and every private firm, however efficiently it might be operating . . . to suppose we were going to take over everything indiscriminately . . . simply out of a doctrinaire belief in public ownership'.[36] But such misunderstanding sprang too, Gaitskell added, from a lack of precision in Labour policy itself – concerning both its objectives and its underlying rationale.

In this difficult area Gaitskell was anxious to find a middle way between 'two extreme points of view'[37] – between, first, the complacent suggestion that the existing frontiers between the public and private sectors should remain fixed and unchanged; and, second, the fundamentalist belief that 'nationalisation or even public ownership is the be-all and end-all, the ultimate first principle and aim of socialism'.[38] Such a belief had itself arisen, he believed, from 'a complete confusion about the fundamental meaning of socialism and, in particular, a misunderstanding about ends and means'.[39]

In order to dispel this confusion Gaitskell set out what he considered to be 'the basic first principles of British democratic socialism'.[40] These included a concern for the disadvantaged and oppressed; a belief in social justice, involving an equitable distribution of wealth; the ideal of a 'classless society' without snobbery, privilege or restrictive social barriers; a belief in human relations based on fellowship and cooperation; an insistence that the public interest should override private interests; and an underlying commitment to freedom and democratic self-government.

This was certainly a wide-ranging list of egalitarian and humanitarian ideals. Michael Foot later argued that it was expressed in such generalized terms as to call into question its distinctive socialist character.[41] Yet in the Party debate it served two revisionist purposes. First, it provided, from the lips of the Party leader himself, a broad restatement of an ethical, rather than ownership-based, approach to socialism. Second, it helped to re-emphasize the distinction between enduring ends and flexible, expedient means. Public ownership was to be regarded, in Gaitskell's view, as merely a 'means to realising these principles in practice'.[42]

On the basis of these reflections Gaitskell concluded that Labour needed to make two points clear to the country: first, 'that we have no intention of abandoning public ownership and accepting for all time the present frontiers of the public sector' and, second, 'that we regard public ownership not as an end in itself but as a means – and not necessarily the only or most important one – to certain ends – such as full employment, greater equality and higher productivity'.[43] This instrumental approach towards public ownership necessarily precluded any commitment to indiscriminate, wholesale nationalization. For as Gaitskell insisted,

> We do not aim to nationalise every private firm or to create an endless series of State monopolies. While we shall certainly wish to extend social ownership, in particular directions, as circumstances warrant, our goal is not 100 per cent State ownership. Our goal is a society in which Socialist ideals are realised.[44]

Gaitskell believed that it was necessary to 'clear our minds on these fundamental issues'[45] and for Labour to restate its basic aims and principles in a simple and comprehensive fashion. The only official document that embodied such an undertaking was the forty-year-old Party Constitution. In the view of the Party leader this now had to be brought up to date since it omitted any references to, for instance, colonial freedom, race relations, disarmaments, full employment or planning. Furthermore, its only specific reference to Labour's domestic objectives was contained in its celebrated Clause IV, concerning which Gaitskell argued:

> Standing as it does on its own, this cannot possibly be regarded as adequate. It lays us open to continual misrepresentation. It implies that the only precise object we have is nationalisation, whereas in fact we have many other Socialist objectives. It implies that we propose to nationalise everything, but do we? Everything? – the whole of light industry, the whole of agriculture, all the shops – every little pub and garage? Of course not. We have long ago come to accept . . . , for the foreseeable future, at least in some form, a mixed economy; in which case, if this is our view – as I believe it to be of 90 per cent of the Labour Party – had we better not say so instead of going out of our way to court misrepresentation.[46]

He acknowledged the fact that his comments on this subject would not be palatable to everyone in the Party. Yet in his own defence he declared:

> I am sure that the Webbs and Arthur Henderson who largely drafted the Constitution would have been amazed and horrified had they thought that their words were to be treated as sacrosanct 40 years later in utterly changed conditions.[47]

Insisting that Labour needed to be a forward-looking Party, with a broad appeal to all age groups, and that there was 'no use waving the banners of a bygone age',[48] he hoped, therefore, that Labour's National Executive would, over the next few months, 'try to work out and state the fundamental principles of British democratic socialism as we see and as we feel it today, in 1959, not 1918'.[49]

Gaitskell's Conference speech thus provided a clear expression of his revisionist approach to public ownership. His principal argument, reinforced by contemporary sociological and economic evidence, drew heavily upon the theoretical analysis which Crosland, Jay and he himself had developed during the 1950s. It welded together a number of revisionist social-democratic themes – scepticism about nationalization, support for alternative forms of public ownership, an emphasis on public ownership as a means and not an end, and a positive acceptance of the mixed economy.

The promotion of such ideas had acquired greater urgency in the light of increasing awareness of the electoral unpopularity of nationalization. The main recommendation at the heart of Gaitskell's speech – the revision or amendment of Clause IV – was therefore the logical development of an argument based on both theoretical and practical considerations. It was presented to Conference as part of a necessary process of ideological adaptation which Labour, in Gaitskell's view, now had to undergo.

At Blackpool, however, the widespread response to the leader's address was a vehement defence of traditional socialist attitudes. To a large extent such a mood had already been anticipated from the platform by Barbara Castle,[50] who poured scorn on the revisionist notions of reforming and civilizing capitalism, of abandoning plans for further nationalization and of using public ownership 'merely to ensure that the community gets a cut of the capitalist cake'.[51] In place of Labour's subjection to the 'commercialised society' and 'the windfall state', Castle advanced the orthodox socialist case for public ownership, what she called 'the real case for public ownership' – that the community as a whole rather than a few private interests should be in control of the economy, taking over industries not just to make them more efficient but also 'to make them responsible to us all'.[52]

Castle's response underlined the sharp differences that existed between the Party leader and his Conference critics. He did, admittedly, receive unequivocal support from Douglas Jay and Dick Taverne.[53] Jay, for instance, restated his emphasis on the need to move beyond nationalization in its established form in order to explore 'non-monopoly rather than monopoly forms of public ownership'.[54] Taverne, who later recalled that he was 'Gaitskell's most forthright defender'[55] on the question of amending Clause IV, went so far as to lend support to that controversial proposal. In his judgment, that was the 'only . . . way in which we can make clear that we as a party . . . do not stand for the nationalisation of all the means of production, distribution and exchange'.[56]

But these were isolated voices in a Conference debate in which most other speakers took an openly hostile view of Gaitskell's position, regarding it as another major example of dangerous revisionist thinking. His ideas were widely viewed as undermining Labour's sense of common direction and purpose, as well as eroding its socialist identity. Michael Foot, for example, rejected Gaitskell's attempt to distinguish between socialist ends and means on the ground that

Many of the ends Hugh Gaitskell described at the end of his speech are in such general terms that the Tories could agree with them, too ... it is a fallacy to try to separate the ends and the means because socialism ... is a doctrine which reveals how only by mobilising the resources of the community can you achieve the ends.[57]

In the face of such deep-seated unease it was left finally to Aneurin Bevan, closing the debate from the platform, to attempt to retrieve the situation. His initial reaction to Gaitskell's speech had been one of angry disapproval, even though he had expressed no objection when shown the text on the night before.[58] Pressed by some of his supporters to stage a 'coup' against Gaitskell and to make his own bid for the leadership,[59] he decided against this course at the last minute, presenting himself in the role of conciliator.

In his Conference speech Bevan therefore made an appeal for Party unity, while strongly upholding traditional socialist commitments. In his view the central socialist case remained 'that in modern complex society it is impossible to get rational order by leaving things to private economic adventure. Therefore, I am a Socialist. I believe in public ownership'.[60] Yet this clear expression of socialist principle was qualified by a statement of aversion, which he shared with Gaitskell, to wholesale state ownership. As he explained to Conference:

I agreed with Hugh Gaitskell yesterday: I do not believe in a monolithic society. I do not believe that public ownership should reach down into every piece of economic activity, because that would be asking for a monolithic society.[61]

Bevan's speech was certainly a timely one since it was delivered in response to a contribution from the Party leader which many found deeply disturbing for at least two reasons. First, Gaitskell's comments, following on from Jay's writings[62] and, more broadly, from a coherent body of theory and policy, appeared to give an official stamp to the revisionist view of public ownership and nationalization. Second, his proposal concerning Clause IV directly challenged the status of a revered document which had placed public ownership at the very centre of Labour thinking. Bevan's achievement lay, therefore, in lowering the tensions raised by Gaitskell's initiative. At the end of a stormy debate, as Jay later recalled, 'the great Welsh orator, in a way nobody else could have done, soothed the explosive passions which were simmering not far below the surface'.[63]

Nevertheless, Bevan himself, in spite of his conciliatory approach, continued to share the deep suspicions of Gaitskell's critics. In the week following the Conference he fiercely attacked Gaitskell and his views at a *Tribune* board meeting in London, telling Foot at the time that: 'We are living in the presence of a conspiracy'.[64] Moreover, in his only published comment on Blackpool, Bevan wrote of the dangers of Labour spurning its vision of a socialist future. The Party should never forget, he stressed, that it had been 'nurtured in the belief that its *raison d'être* is a transformation of society'. In his view, the current controversy was really 'between those who want the mainsprings of economic power transferred to the community, and those who believe that private enterprise should still remain supreme but that its worst characteristics should be modified by liberal ideas of justice and equality'.[65]

III

By early 1960 Gaitskell had begun to receive a number of warnings about likely reactions throughout the Labour movement to his undertaking to amend Clause IV. Jennie Lee, in particular, impressed upon him Bevan's wish that nothing should be done to undermine Party unity by abandoning the clause.[66] But in spite of such warnings and in the face, too, of the misgivings of half of his Shadow Cabinet colleagues,[67] Gaitskell remained determined to press ahead. In February he therefore delivered a major speech, largely written by Crosland, at Nottingham,[68] in which he restated his view that Clause IV was both too narrow, in so far as it omitted many of Labour's fundamental aims, and too broad, since it implied a commitment to wholesale nationalization.

In the light of a broadly favourable response to his speech, even in the pages of *Tribune*,[69] Gaitskell's position seemed more secure, with support for his plans increasing among several leading Party and trade union figures.[70] Nevertheless, the atmosphere within the Party at this time, reflecting 'the worst mood of bitterness and suspicion since the war',[71] compelled him to retreat from his original desired objective of removing Clause IV and replacing it with a new statement of Labour's aims[72] towards a compromise arrangement. The latter would leave Clause IV as it stood, while augmenting it with a new statement setting out the Party's fundamental principles and aims in more contemporary terms. Under pressure from George Brown and Charlie Pannell, the main leaders of the trade union group of MPs, Gaitskell thus embraced the idea of adopting both statements, which soon became distinguished as the 'Old and New Testaments'. The decision, however, to accept the 'New Testament' as an accompaniment to Clause IV rather than as its replacement was taken by Gaitskell 'as a necessary compromise rather than as his preferred solution'.[73]

Gaitskell's 'New Testament' – a twelve-point statement of Labour's aims which largely reaffirmed those 'basic first principles of British democratic socialism'[74] set out by him at Blackpool – was presented to the Party's National Executive Committee (NEC) at a special meeting in March 1960. Its Section J, which was to prove the most controversial part of the document, confirmed the need for an extension of public ownership, but qualified that position with two revisionist emphases: first, the view that public ownership ought to assume a variety of forms and, second, firm acceptance of a mixed economy, in which both public and private enterprise had a recognized place. At the NEC meeting, however, Gaitskell readily accepted an addition to Section J proposed by Jennie Lee – involving the insertion of Bevan's celebrated reference to 'the commanding heights of the economy'. He also agreed to the proposal that in the preamble to the document it should be pointed out that the 1960 statement 'reaffirms, amplifies and clarifies' the Party Objects of the 1918 Constitution.[75]

Duly modified in these ways, Gaitskell's statement received the approval of the NEC. Section J eventually read as follows:

It [the Labour Party] is convinced that these social and economic objectives can be achieved only through an expansion of common ownership substantial enough to give the community power over the commanding heights of the economy. Common ownership takes varying forms, including state-owned industries and firms, producer and consumer co-operation, municipal ownership and public participation in private concerns. Recognising that both public and private enterprise have a place in the economy it believes that further extension of common ownership should be decided from time to time in the light of these objectives and according to circumstances, with due regard for the views of the workers and consumers concerned.[76]

The significance of the NEC's acceptance of Gaitskell's statement has been interpreted in conflicting terms. According to Williams, Gaitskell himself was reasonably satisfied, inasmuch as he had fulfilled his Blackpool undertaking of clarifying and amplifying Clause IV. From his point of view, 'at the very worst, the result looked like a draw'.[77] Goodman, however, maintained that by the end of the NEC meeting Gaitskell's draft was 'left in a battered and almost absurd state'. For the inclusion of Bevan's crucial phrase in Section J had arguably 'strengthened rather than weakened the attachment to public ownership'.[78] Moreover, in Crossman's opinion the adoption of the word 'reaffirms' in the preamble meant not only that Gaitskell had failed to remove Clause IV but also that 'there would now be a New Testament and an Old Testament and every justification for the Tories asking which we believed in'.[79]

In spite of these textual amendments Gaitskell's controversial plans for Clause IV remained at the centre of Party debate throughout the spring of 1960. They gained greater credibility from the publication of fresh evidence concerning the unpopularity of nationalization. This took the form of an opinion survey, carried out under the direction of Mark Abrams, which appeared to confirm the main findings of Morgan Phillips's earlier post-election inquest. Abrams's work soon caught the attention of the Party leader. 'Needless to say', Gaitskell wrote to Rita Hinden, editor of *Socialist Commentary*, 'I have also read Mark's survey with intense interest'.[80] Published in *Socialist Commentary* between May and July 1960,[81] it pointed to Labour's public identification with nationalization as, along with its class image and divided leadership, a major reason for its electoral unpopularity.

This view was firmly held, too, by Crosland, who, in a trenchant Fabian pamphlet published in May 1960, argued that Labour's perceived association with nationalization was 'without doubt a liability; for all polls show that a majority of the electorate . . . and indeed even of Labour voters, are opposed to further large-scale nationalization'.[82] Yet elsewhere he also made clear that he was well aware of the emotional and symbolic appeal of public ownership and nationalization and hence of their central role in Labour's socialist myth. He acknowledged the fact that

> The older party stalwart, brought up in the inter-war years to equate Socialism with the nationalisation of the means of production, feels lost and bewildered if deprived of this familiar mental sheet-anchor. The dogma of nationalisation informed and symbolised his early years of struggle; if he is asked to give it up, he feels that he is being asked to say that his whole political life, to which he sacrificed so much, was pointless and wasted.[83]

In defending Gaitskell's revisionist project, Crosland emphasized, too, its international dimension. Nearly all Western European socialist parties, he pointed out – among them those of Austria, West Germany, Sweden, the Netherlands and Switzerland – were currently revising their programmes in the light of contemporary social and economic developments. That process entailed their adopting revisionist positions such as a repudiation of the traditional definition of socialism as the public ownership of the means of production, an explicit acceptance of the mixed economy, and a view of nationalization as a means and not an end. Crosland was confident that this movement pointed the right way forward for democratic socialism. Indeed, his attendance at a recent international socialist conference in the Netherlands had convinced him that 'a spectre is haunting Europe – the spectre of Revisionism'.[84]

Vigorous support of this kind, together with Abrams's survey evidence, had thus reinforced Gaitskell's view that nationalization was an electorally damaging issue for Labour and that Clause IV, by implying a commitment to wholesale nationalization, was badly in need of amendment. The leader's position was summed up with admirable clarity by another of his close associates, Patrick Gordon Walker. Defending Gaitskell from the charge made by Foot, Crossman and others that he had misinterpreted Clause IV, Gordon Walker maintained that

> Whatever the originally intended meaning of Clause IV, it had in time lost its meaning. Partly because of the misrepresentation of our opponents, but mainly because of the gloss put on the Clause within our own ranks, 'common ownership' came to be identified with 'nationalization'; and the word 'all' came to be assumed before the means of production, distribution and exchange.[85]

IV

Viewed from the standpoint of Gaitskell and his supporters, Clause IV remained a constant source of confusion and misunderstanding which could be removed only through the acceptance of a more up-to-date statement of Labour's aims. By the summer of 1960, however, it had become increasingly clear that such acceptance would be extremely hard to achieve within the Party as a whole. The mandates, for instance, of affiliated trade unions had begun to swing against the idea of any amendment of Clause IV. Four out of the six major unions – namely, the Engineers, Transport Workers, Miners and Railwaymen – passed resolutions at their conferences opposing any change in the Party Constitution. Only two major unions – the

Shopworkers and General and Municipal Workers – were prepared to see Gaitskell's 'New Testament' formally inserted into the Constitution.[86]

To some extent this withdrawal of support from Gaitskell could be explained in terms of the growing interaction throughout 1960 of the Clause IV and nuclear defence issues. A clear trend had developed since the spring of that year for trade unions to link opposition to nuclear weapons with an aversion to any interference with Clause IV.[87] Three out of the big six unions – namely, the Engineers, Transport Workers and Railwaymen – had thus declared their support for a unilateralist defence policy whilst at the same time opposing Gaitskell on Clause IV.

For many trade unionists this defence of the Party Constitution might well have involved, as *New Left Review* alleged, 'acknowledging – rather guiltily – past loyalties, rather than affirming present principles'.[88] But at any rate, the widespread indignant reaction to Gaitskell's proposal throughout the Labour movement did nothing to help stem the rising unilateralist tide. Nor did it assist in any way the cause of Gaitskell's allies among trade union leaders who found themselves, as Labour's two crucial issues converged, reluctant to fight on two fronts.

The result of this movement of opposition to Gaitskell was that by the summer of 1960 it seemed virtually certain that he would be heavily defeated at the forthcoming Party Conference if he continued to press for a constitutional amendment. In July the Party's National Executive therefore decided 'not to proceed with any amendment or addition to Clause IV', declaring that the new statement adopted in March was 'a valuable expression of the aims of the Labour Party in the second half of the twentieth century',[89] which was accordingly commended to Conference. This officially accepted formula thus involved both the demotion of Gaitskell's 'New Testament' to a lower status and the retention of Clause IV in the Constitution. It was an outcome which led Gaitskell to confess privately that, if he could have foreseen the extent of opposition to his proposal, he would never have raised the issue of Clause IV in the first place.[90]

Gaitskell's retreat on that issue, together with the prospect of his imminent defeat by unilateralists on defence policy, created a climate in which the Campaign for Democratic Socialism (CDS) gradually emerged in 1960. Among the architects of this organization, which sought to preserve Gaitskell's leadership in the face of these pressures, were Bill Rodgers, then General Secretary of the Fabian Society, Dick Taverne, a parliamentary candidate at the 1959

Election, and Tony Crosland. CDS was formed in response to the need for a more organized centre-right in the Party at both parliamentary and constituency levels and counted among its supporters forty-five Labour MPs, including four members of the Shadow Cabinet – Brown, Callaghan, Healey and Gordon Walker – and several trade union leaders.[91] The organization soon became active in constituency parties, trade union branches and the parliamentary party.

While preoccupied with the immediate crisis over defence and, following the 1960 Party Conference, with attempts to reverse unilateralist policy decisions, CDS was, as Dick Taverne later recalled, 'just as concerned with Clause Four – which was ideologically more important – as with the defence question'. For the fear in the minds of the founders of the organization was that 'Labour was becoming entrenched as an old-style, fundamentalist socialist party'.[92] Bill Rodgers, too, emphasized this point, maintaining both that 'C.D.S. was far more concerned with the overall position of the Party than with just the defence issue,' and that 'in a sense, the aim of the Campaign was to make the Party revisionist'.[93]

Certainly it was the case that the principles and policies upheld by CDS were unmistakably revisionist and very much in harmony with Gaitskell's attitudes, though he himself was never formally associated with the organization. It could therefore fairly be said that CDS 'possessed, and was seen to possess, all the qualities of organized Gaitskellism; with the express purpose of working for a new-style Labour Party on the lines suggested by the Leader himself'.[94] To that end the Campaign even published a manifesto in October 1960, soon after Gaitskell's anti-unilateralist Conference speech at Scarborough. Drafted mainly by Philip Williams, with some assistance from Crosland,[95] the document presented a concise statement of revisionist views and, on the question of public ownership, largely reproduced Section J of Gaitskell's 'New Testament'.[96]

Fortified by such support, Gaitskell eventually defended his own statement of *Labour's Aims* at the 1960 Party Conference. He freely admitted that he had misjudged the mood of the Party over Clause IV, acknowledging the fact that during the controversy

> it became obvious that there were throughout the Party and the movement very strong feelings about the 1918 constitution. It might be misleading to call them sentimental, and if I used a term of that kind it would not be in any derogatory sense; but there was an attachment to that constitution.[97]

He and his colleagues on the National Executive had therefore 'felt bound to take note of the obvious feelings that existed'.[98] Yet while recognizing the emotional force of Clause IV, he again seemed insensitive to its deeper significance as an expression of Labour's socialist myth. He did not consider that his original undertaking had raised 'a great issue of principle on which there were clear divisions in the Party'. In his view, the clarification of the clause was in fact 'never an issue of principle; it was an issue of presentation'.[99]

The desire for Party unity, reinforced by his own rationalistic approach, was therefore leading Gaitskell to underestimate the degree of tension and acrimony underlying this continuing debate. He did, however, make it clear that tactical considerations, as well as a respect for Party sentiment, had prompted the decision not to proceed with a revision of the Constitution. It had been apparent, he explained, that 'we were going to have a major division over defence, and we did not want to add to the divisions in the Party unnecessarily'.[100] Somewhat late in the day he was realizing the difficulties of fighting on two fronts.

In October 1960 Gaitskell's new statement of *Labour's Aims* was none the less endorsed by Conference with a clear majority in its favour. The Party had thus approved Gaitskell's 'New Testament' in its relegated status as 'a valuable expression of the aims of the Labour Party in the second half of the 20th century'. It could be reasonably argued, however, that the statement had really been accepted 'only on terms which gave it little constitutional legitimacy'.[101] After all, it had not been moved as an amendment or addendum to the 1918 Constitution, but merely commended to Conference as a 'valuable' declaration.

Gaitskell's enforced retreat from his original objective to an acceptance of this inadequate compromise was, in the circumstances, an elaborate but necessary face-saving exercise designed to enable him to escape from a humiliating Conference defeat. Nevertheless, the end result was unquestionably a setback for him since the Party Constitution and Clause IV were to remain completely unchanged. In this respect, the entire episode indicated, as Williams observed, that 'though Gaitskell's face was saved, he had lost the battle over Clause IV after all, because of a sudden change in the dynamics of the political conflict'.[102]

Moreover, in the light of that reverse, Gaitskell's 'compromise for the sake of unity looked to some like a retreat, encouraging to his enemies and demoralising to his friends'.[103] Some of his supporters in the Campaign for Democratic Socialism were 'actually quite critical of him for conceding too much and not fighting to the last ditch'[104] in order to include his new statement of aims in the Party Constitution. Faced by the hostility of the left and by the indignation of the trade unionist centre, and caught up in a gathering onslaught against his defence policy, he had finally been compelled to abandon any attempt to amend, let alone remove, Labour's article of faith.

V

Gaitskell's attempt to amend Clause IV has often been strongly criticized – both by political historians and commentators and by his own contemporaries. R. T. McKenzie, for example, described it as 'one of the most maladroit operations in the modern history of party politics', while David Wood regarded it as 'perhaps the worst misjudgment' that Gaitskell made in party management.[105] Harold Wilson, the successor to the Party leadership, later considered the undertaking to have been 'misconceived both tactically and strategically'.[106]

It would certainly appear that Gaitskell's campaign was tactically mishandled in a number of important respects. At the outset the profound disappointment of Labour's heavy election defeat drove him and his supporters into a series of hasty and ill-considered actions. Allowing themselves little time for recuperation after the election, they committed, as Roy Jenkins later recalled, 'serious tactical mistakes during the ensuing weeks'.[107] Williams identified a whole sequence of such errors on Gaitskell's part[108] – the fact that at first he withheld his own views on Clause IV, that he arranged for no direction to be given on the issue by the National Executive and that he allowed friends such as Jay to make unpopular suggestions. Indeed, recalling those events, Bill Rodgers later characterized Gaitskell's plan as 'an ill-prepared initiative which had been launched too much in his name by the Hampstead Set'.[109]

In particular, the tactical imprudence of Gaitskell's proposal has been perceived on two levels. First, by raising the Clause IV issue he had thereby drawn public attention to something which very few voters or even Conservative activists were aware of.[110] In the opinion of many critical observers, the effect of this was to alarm the electorate and to weaken the Labour Party by handing to the Tories a powerful weapon. Iain Macleod could scarcely understand why Labour 'should load us with such golden gifts',[111] while Michael Foot commented bitterly that 'only eagles could foul their own nests on a scale so alarming'.[112]

Second, Gaitskell's conduct clearly antagonized the trade unionist centre of the Labour Party, which for some time had provided much of his power base. His plans infuriated both the trade union leaders who had backed him as leader and the trade unionist groups of MPs who supported his annual re-election by the Parliamentary Labour Party (PLP). He underestimated, as Shinwell recalled, the extent to which his views would 'upset the conservative mentality of trade union veterans' who cherished Clause IV as 'a sentimental memento of the past'.[113] For these Party traditionalists were well aware of the symbolic importance of public ownership, of its central role in the story of Labour's long struggle. Their support for Clause IV was reinforced, too, by the fact that many unions retained a similar clause in their own constitutions and rule books.

This alienation of trade union leaders and MPs was particularly damaging in view of Gaitskell's pressing need for their support in the imminent battle over defence policy. Their resentment instead gave rise to a political situation that was the very opposite of what he desired. By the summer of 1960 he had succeeded in unwittingly forging a novel and temporary alliance – in defence of Clause IV – between the conservatives of the Party's centre and the fundamentalists of the Bevanite left.

But if Gaitskell's undertaking was tactically mishandled in these ways, to what extent was it also misconceived strategically? Here, in his defence, it can be argued that Labour did suffer, as the available evidence indicated, from an electorally damaging reputation for seeking wholesale nationalization. Gaitskell believed that revising Clause IV would therefore make Labour's real intentions clearer to voters and Party members alike. From this standpoint the battle commenced at Blackpool in 1959 seemed to be one which, in Jenkins's words, simply 'had to be fought'.[114] For the revisionists were convinced that a harmful ambiguity characterized the Party's entire approach to public ownership since its comparatively recent, official acceptance of the mixed economy coexisted uneasily with its historic commitment, embodied in Clause IV, to large-scale collectivization.

Furthermore, even if the clause was not regarded by all Labour supporters as implying such a commitment and was valued by some merely as 'a memento of the past', it none the less 'remained on record both as a point of reference for opportunistic campaigns by the Labour Left and as an ammunition dump for political opponents'.[115] To Gaitskell and his followers, then, it appeared irrational for Labour to retain, in an unqualified form, a theoretical attachment to a mainly collectivized economy. Such a position was considered incompatible with the practical requirements of both future policy-making and electoral success.

Some observers have even suggested that this last factor lay at the heart of Gaitskell's whole campaign. Mikardo, for example, describing the leader's proposal as 'a rationalization of the desire to avoid electoral liability', later maintained that 'Gaitskell thought that amending Clause Four would be electorally advantageous',[116] while Wilson, too, expressed the view that Gaitskell believed his proposal 'would win votes'.[117]

For all these reasons Gaitskell had reached the firm conclusion, as Jay recalled, that 'Clause Four was an albatross one had to get rid of'.[118] Yet in the view of his critics, his undertaking was marred by serious strategic errors. In the first place, his plans seemed to many in the centre of the Party to jeopardize a valuable arrangement by which Labour had succeeded, throughout the 1950s, in reconciling apparently incompatible objectives. After all, the Party had combined pragmatic economic and industrial policies which implied acceptance of a mixed economy with a constitutional clause that signified a commitment to wholesale public ownership. What, then, many asked, was to be gained from removing a useful piece of ambiguity which had helped to keep a broadly based party together? Crosland later made this point by citing the example of the Swedish Social Democratic Party. Looking back on the Clause IV dispute, he wrote:

> it was foolish to go for the doctrinal element in the party constitution. We should have taken a lesson from the Swedish Socialists, who have only been perfectly contented under a Monarchy, who still have as No. 1 article in their basic constitution a commitment to Republicanism.[119]

A second, related criticism of Gaitskell's strategy was that, by opening up the Clause IV issue and unleashing such fierce opposition, he had thereby precluded the possibility of any discreet demotion of further nationalization in Labour policy-making. As a consequence he found himself under fire not just from the left but also from pragmatists of the centre. The latter took the view, as Williams put it, that 'any squabble over "theology" should have been avoided by silence in opposition until the same ends could be attained, still silently, in practice after coming into power'. They were thus committed to submitting the Party to a process of 'adaptation by stealth'.[120]

This alternative course was subsequently favoured by one of Labour's leading pragmatists, Harold Wilson, who later maintained that he 'got the same results as Hugh – without splitting the Party'.[121]

For Wilson this, in a sense, involved holding up the banner of nationalization while at the same time leading Labour away from it, just as,
in his view, Macmillan had once used the 'banner of Suez' in his own
party.[122] In Jay's view, however, such an approach was 'regarded as
altogether too cynical by Gaitskell, who firmly believed that leaders
should lead intellectually as well as tactically'.[123]

But Gaitskell's principled stance was undermined by a strategic
defect more serious than either his allegedly imprudent desire to
remove doctrinal ambiguity or his readiness to adopt a confrontational style. For above all, his conduct over Clause IV revealed
an insensitivity to the mythic significance for Labour of the idea of
public ownership. The text's importance in this respect had been re-
emphasized throughout 1960 by *Tribune*. It was still, the journal
insisted, widely viewed on the left as the official declaration of
Labour's supreme socialist purpose – the economic and social transformation of capitalist society. Its practical fulfilment would mean that
'The commanding heights would have been conquered. The public
sector of the economy would have been made dominant. The whole
motive power and nature of society would have been changed'.[124]

Public ownership was therefore considered fundamental both to
Labour's ultimate purpose and to the socialist myth, expressed in
Clause IV, which described that purpose. While such a conviction was
held most strongly on the left of the Party, the sentiments underlying
it pervaded the Labour movement as a whole. It was this powerful
appeal of public ownership, and hence of Clause IV, that Gaitskell's
rationalistic view of the matter tended to overlook. That was all the
more surprising in the light of his earlier indignant reaction to any
idea of changing the Party's name, 'with all its emotional links to the
romantic attachments and moral commitments of his own youth'.[125]
Such a response ought, as Williams observed, to 'have made him
sensitive and sympathetic to the emotional freight carried by the
concept of public ownership'.[126]

Gaitskell thus committed a grave error in failing to foresee that
Party activists would react with bewilderment and outrage to his plans
for revising Clause IV, to his proposal for, in Williams's words, 'taking
down the signpost to the promised land'.[127] Biblical language and
imagery of this kind in fact pervaded the entire controversy, underlining its mythic implications. Charles Pannell, for example, warned
Gaitskell not to tamper with 'the Tablets of Stone', while Attlee tried
to dissuade him from interfering with 'the 39 Articles'.[128] Earlier, too,
as we have seen, Griffiths had told Gaitskell privately that Clause IV
was 'an article of faith' to him and his generation. In similar vein,

Crossman maintained that the Party's debate was touching on 'the central tenet of its creed',[129] while the *New Statesman* deplored the 'public abandonment of the ark of Labour's covenant'.[130] As Harold Wilson, well aware of the symbolic significance of Gaitskell's challenge, recalled, 'we were being asked to take Genesis out of the Bible; you don't have to be a fundamentalist in your religious approach to say that Genesis is part of the Bible'.[131] He therefore opposed Gaitskell's plans, as he later explained, 'on the grounds that to tell the Labour Party member that his political bible has been torn up is like telling a Christadelphian that there is no God'.[132]

By underestimating the potency of such symbolism Gaitskell had thus alienated not just the left but also those in the centre of the Party, with their sentimental attachment to Clause IV. To a large extent that feeling probably stemmed from a protective attitude towards a revered document, one that reflected the close association between socialism and public ownership which they had formed in their early, formative years of Party activity. But in addition, for some leading figures of the centre – notably Wilson and Crossman – traditional symbolism appeared as a useful instrument to be employed in the service of Party unity. This essentially functional view is evident, for instance, in Crossman's significant warning at the height of the controversy that

> Leaders seek to change the inmost nature of their parties at dire peril. The Labour Party was founded as a movement of moral protest, which denounced the capitalist 'status quo' and preached the need for a Socialist transformation of society. To tell our party workers that the need for a Socialist transformation has been eliminated, and that the leadership must now show it can manage a mixed economy as well as the Tories, will destroy the morale of the rank and file without regaining the confidence of the electorate.[133]

The symbolic value of Clause IV was widely perceived throughout the Party, as Drucker has noted, in that 'continuous tradition of opposition to capitalism'[134] which the Constitution had bequeathed in 1918 – that tradition which Crossman had recognized so clearly. The retention of Clause IV within the Constitution therefore held Labour 'true to its past, true to what its originators wanted it to be: for labour and against capital'.[135] It served to protect and reinforce the Party's distinctive ethos; for the commitment which the clause secured was, as *Tribune* had stressed, as much a part of Labour's socialist heritage 'as the memory of Keir Hardie'.[136]

The major strategic flaw, then, in Gaitskell's undertaking was his underestimation of the force of public ownership as a central feature of Labour's socialist myth and of the appeal of Clause IV as the formal expression of that myth. The largely hostile reactions within the Party to his attempts to amend the clause were further expressions of concern about the threats to Labour's socialist character and purpose which his revisionist approach was widely thought to pose. To these deep-seated anxieties Gaitskell's overtly rationalistic conduct had thus added the new fear that the Party leader himself seemed unaware of either the attraction or the usefulness of the symbolism through which Labour's socialist vision of a new social order found its vivid expression. Clause IV, the Party's rallying point and central 'article of faith', had for forty years embodied and preserved that myth. It had thereby provided Labour supporters with a strong sense of collective identity and direction which, in their view, Gaitskell's revisionist initiative was perceived to be placing in jeopardy.

Viewed from this perspective, therefore, Gaitskell, in acting as he did over Clause IV, appeared to have, in Jenkins's words, 'overestimated the rationality of political movements'.[137] For the leader's decision, which he had considered both reasonable and timely, 'to seize the standard and grind it in the dust', meant to many in the Party, as Wilson later remarked, nothing less than 'breaking people's hearts'.[138] To that response Gaitskell had seemed insufficiently sensitive. But then, as Williams observed, ' . . . it was a weakness as well as a strength that his commitment to rational discourse sometimes blinded him to the likely emotional reactions of his followers'.[139]

During this turbulent episode Gaitskell's unyielding rationalism had rested on a pragmatic and entirely non-visionary conception of public ownership and, as a consequence, had spread unease and alarm throughout the Party. In his biography Williams recognized this point, without developing it in any detail, when he cited a passage from F. S. Oliver's *The Endless Adventure* – one that Gaitskell 'read . . . later, and regretted not having done so in time'.[140] While discussing the impact of 'idols and ideals' upon political activity, Oliver had maintained that 'idols', which he regarded as 'full-grown' ideals, were 'rarely harmful' forces 'until they have reached old age'.[141] Yet he warned that

> we can never make quite certain of their impotence; for even
> when they are so quiescent as to seem almost lifeless, they have a
> capacity for becoming suddenly and violently inflamed by casual

friction. . . . An astute politician will never meddle with an idol if he can help it. . . . No politician can hope to prosper unless he has a weather-sense that warns him in good time what to expect from each of these forces . . . an idol whose worshippers have taken alarm, may threaten him with disaster.[142]

Oliver was really describing here the emotive content of political myths – what Lassell and Kaplan referred to as 'miranda', those 'symbols of sentiment and identification'[143] which serve to strengthen the loyalties of particular groups, enhancing their sense of collective identity. The most potent of such symbols within Labour's socialist myth – the idea of public ownership as the expression of a transformed economy and society – was something which Gaitskell had consistently disregarded. By attempting to revise Clause IV he had dramatically underlined his rationalistic disdain. In Oliver's terms, he had disturbed the traditional worship of Labour's most revered idol and, in doing so, had appeared to deride the historic text which had codified and guided the worshippers' most cherished belief. By late 1960 it seemed to many observers that the result of such iconoclasm was that the Party leader had fractured Labour's broad ideological consensus, largely based on the symbolic appeal of public ownership and Clause IV, and had thereby perilously shaken the foundations of Party unity.

4 Revisionism diluted, 1960–70

I

In the aftermath of the Clause IV dispute a spirit of compromise began to spread in 1960 throughout various sections of the Party. In the centre – a substantial though loose grouping which then embraced such prominent figures as Wilson and Crossman – there was a determination to prevent Labour from falling apart during this critical period. It was recognized that such a task would involve reconciling the Party's warring factions. For, as Peter Shore has recalled, it was widely felt that there was 'a need to get out of the trenches of the battles of the '40s and '50s'.[1]

In this climate of reconciliation an interim Party policy statement, *Labour in the Sixties*, was published. Co-drafted by Shore and Morgan Phillips, this document appeared, in a somewhat coded manner, to shift Labour away from a revisionist approach. It did so by offering as a 'framework of principle' a distinctive socialist approach to the 'scientific revolution', which was emphasized as 'the central feature of our postwar capitalist society'.[2] Such an approach was considered fundamental not just to Labour's alternative set of policies but also to its vision of 'a different and better society'.[3] In practical terms this socialist view of the 'scientific revolution' was presented as justification for an extension both of public ownership and control and of central economic planning. Unlike the Tories, Labour believed that 'the great concentrations of economic power' should, in this new era, 'serve the interests of the community'.[4] The authors of the document were convinced that:

> our Socialist beliefs will be vindicated in the 1960s, as it is ever more clearly seen that the new postwar capitalism is creating its own insuperable problems and that, in the epoch of scientific revolution, democracy, if it is to survive, must plan its resources for the common good.[5]

These sentiments were echoed when *Labour in the Sixties* was even-tually commended to the 1960 Party Conference at Scarborough. In support of the document, Harold Wilson maintained that it really did represent, as Shinwell had earlier insisted, 'a return to Socialism'.[6] Its central purpose, Wilson explained, was 'to show the relevance for the 60s of our Socialist faith and to convince our fellow electors of it'.[7] Labour rejected 'the idea ... put forward in the Tory and Liberal press, and perhaps by some of our own comrades, that socialism and public ownership are out of date'.[8]

Underlining the theme of the scientific revolution, Wilson went on to declare, in broad but ambitious terms, that 'socialism must be harnessed to science and science to socialism'.[9] In many industries, he argued, 'the right scientific and technological approach' would require public ownership.[10] The machine-tools industry was a case in point. In general, Labour's 'message for the 60s' should be one of 'a Socialist-inspired scientific and technological revolution releasing energy on an enormous scale and deployed not for the destruction of mankind but for enriching mankind beyond our dreams'.[11]

This beguiling vision of a future society in which public ownership would once again assume central importance helped to persuade many on the left that *Labour in the Sixties* did indeed herald a socialist renaissance. *Tribune* declared that the 1960 Conference debate had 'formally buried revisionism',[12] while the *New Statesman* took the view that the new policy statement 'offers the Labour Party a clear restatement of its Socialist objective in modern terms'.[13] The Clause IV controversy had already underlined the fact that 'the vital dividing line in British politics' still lay 'between those who believe in a Socialist policy built around public ownership and those who do not'.[14]

The key, therefore, to the developing process of reconciliation within the Party from 1960 onwards lay in the manner in which *Labour in the Sixties* appeared both to depart from revisionist assumptions and to restore public ownership to a pivotal role in Labour policy, strategy and rhetoric. Wilson's distinctive contribu-tion, in particular, had adroitly promoted that dual approach with a blend of traditional socialist rhetoric and contemporary policy ideas.[15] Further advance was made in those directions in 1961 with the publication of the NEC policy statement *Signposts for the Sixties*. First drafted by Peter Shore and finally co-written by Gaitskell, Brown, Crossman and Wilson, *Signposts for the Sixties*, like its predecessor of 1960, argued the case for a contemporary application of well-tried socialist remedies. 'We live', it declared, 'in a scientific revolution' and in such an 'epoch of revolutionary change' ways had to be found of 'assuring that national resources are wisely allocated and community services humanely planned'.[16] To that end a future Labour government should seek 'firstly, to harness the forces released by science in the service of the community; secondly, to plan and supervise the balanced growth of the economy; and thirdly, to ensure that the ever-increasing wealth created by modern techniques of production is fairly shared'.[17]

Moreover, in its analysis of Britain's increasingly evident state of economic decline, *Signposts for the Sixties* identified as one of its major symptoms 'the growth of new forms of privilege and the rapid concentration of economic power' within a private sector 'still dominated by a small ruling caste'.[18] It drew attention, too, echoing Galbraith's then influential thesis, to 'the contrast between starved community services and extravagant consumption, summed up . . . in the phrase "private affluence and public squalor"'.[19]

The first of those developments posed nothing less than 'the greatest single problem of modern democracy . . . how to ensure that the handful of men who control these concentrations of power can be made responsive and responsible to the nation'.[20] In a tone conspicuously critical of private industry, the document argued that,

> With certain honourable exceptions, our finance and industry need a major shake-up at the top. Too many directors owe their position to family, school or political connections. If the dead wood were cut out of Britain's boardrooms and replaced by the keen young executives, production engineers and scientists who are at present denied their legitimate prospects of promotion, our production and export problems would be much more manageable.[21]

Signposts for the Sixties followed Wilson's lead in locating the solution to those problems in both a national plan for economic growth and, within that framework, an increased role for public ownership. Economic planning was considered vital for maintaining full employment, for developing social services and for improving living standards generally. It was one of the 'essential signposts to Britain's economic revival'.[22] As for public ownership, two particular areas were identified as suitable for its extension. First, the public sector should be expanded 'at the growing points of the British economy and in the new industries based on science'.[23] Second, public ownership should be introduced to those sections of private industry dependent upon state aid in its various forms, including loans, subsidies, government contracts and research and development grants.

Signposts for Sixties was concerned, therefore, to reaffirm the pre-eminence of public ownership in Labour policy and strategy, whilst restoring, as Wilson advocated, the historic link in Labour policy between public ownership and economic planning. It did so on the basis of a largely unfavourable view of private industry, highlighting its oligopolistic tendencies. It embellished, too, its main argument with traditional socialist rhetoric – apparent, for example, in its references to 'a small ruling caste' dominating the economy, or to 'vast concentrations of economic power' beyond public control, or to 'the capitalist begging-bowl'[24] increasingly filled with state assistance.

Some political historians and commentators have contended that Labour's 1961 policy statement merely presented revisionism in a new guise. The document has been regarded as 'fundamentally revisionist in content, although with a few symbolic concessions to the left'.[25] In its pages, it has been claimed, 'all the revisionist arguments were consolidated, in a rhetoric only made slightly more critical of private enterprise by the repeated stagnation of the economy under Macmillan and by Galbraith's newly introduced liberal attack on private affluence and public squalor'.[26] As for the distinctive idea of the 'scientific revolution', which provided *Signposts for the Sixties* with its main theoretical framework, this was later derided by Ian Mikardo, the document's sole critic on Labour's NEC, as 'disguised revisionism – revisionism in a more attractive guise'.[27] In broader strategic terms, too, the eventual acceptance by Conference of *Signposts for the Sixties* has been viewed as 'a triumph for Gaitskell and an important landmark in the campaign to make the Labour Party a revisionist party'.[28] Its endorsement marked another important stage in Labour's 'revisionist metamorphosis'[29] in the period from 1957 to 1962.

Some evidence can be cited in support of this interpretation. Revisionist elements are clearly discernible in the document's analysis and proposals. It put forward, for instance, a pragmatic and instrumental view of public ownership, regarding it as a useful means of achieving controlled economic expansion. It was also flexible in its actual proposals for public ownership, which appeared to involve, as its critics pointed out, a minimum of detailed and specific commitments. This was something which Crosland noted with relief. Welcoming the absence of some of the left's preferred options, he observed that the statement offered 'no blanket municipalisation, no 600 companies, fewer (though still some) vague threats'.[30]

Moreover, *Signposts for the Sixties* accepted the existence of a mixed economy – albeit a more efficient, more state-regulated, faster-growing mixed economy. Indeed, the document's left-wing detractors argued that its criticisms of private industry – as, for instance, in its much-quoted passage concerning the 'dead wood' in Britain's boardrooms – derived from 'the benign Crosland image of postwar capitalism'.[31] Its proposals were in turn based on 'the Crosland answer', according to which 'the problem isn't one of control; it is simply one of more efficient managership, of shoring up the inefficient gaps in the structure of the mixed economy'.[32]

However, this interpretation of *Signposts for the Sixties* as 'revisionism in a new guise' is, on closer examination, unconvincing. In the first place, it seriously understates the role which public ownership played in the document's main proposals, for Labour's 'ancient orthodoxy' assumed far greater prominence there than in the policy statements of the 1950s. As the *New Statesman* acknowledged, Labour's overriding commitment in 1961 to 'planning for expansion' entailed shifting the balance within the mixed economy 'from the private to the public sector', which thereby required 'a much greater degree of public ownership and state intervention'. It was largely for that reason that the journal commended *Signposts for the Sixties* for its 'Socialist sense of direction'.[33]

This restoration of public ownership to a central place in Labour policy had been underlined by Wilson in his introduction to the 1961 Conference debate, in which he had specified at least six ways in which *Signposts for the Sixties* proposed to widen the scope of public ownership – all of which were additional both to the renationalization of iron and steel ('the heart of the economy',[34] as the *New Statesman* described it) and road haulage and to the public ownership of the freehold of building land. All of this amounted, he stressed, to 'a substantial expansion of a public ownership at the points where it is most relevant to the fulfilment of our plan to expand'.[35]

As well as containing these clearly stated policy commitments, *Signposts for the Sixties* advanced the specific argument, which Barbara Castle had earlier deployed during the Clause IV debate,[36] that rapid technological change provided fresh grounds for a wide expansion of public ownership. That view was translated into the proposal to create new state enterprises in science-based industries, which was in itself, as Perry Anderson later argued, 'politically, a small masterpiece'[37] since it satisfied the left and right of the Party alike. It was a policy, after all, that promised incursions into advanced and profitable industries instead of backward and bankrupt ones, and it did so in a manner that appeared neither electorally damaging nor politically controversial. In broader terms, the proposal implied that a Labour government would build up an enlarged public sector alongside an intact private sector. The mixed economy would thus be preserved, yet reshaped in a socialist style, as Bevan had recommended in *In Place of Fear*.

In the Party's wider debate, the ideological significance of such policy recommendations was later acknowledged by Peter Shore, author of the document's first draft. Recalling that the statement itself sprang from a recognition of 'the need to relate socialist values to a changing society', Shore maintained that

> *Signposts for the Sixties* was a defeat for the revisionists. For the new relevance of public ownership was stressed. This was a major change. With the need for state intervention with regard to research and development, for new industrial development, and so on, the case for socialism was re-emerging very powerfully and genuinely.[38]

Anderson had earlier taken a similar view, arguing that, with the publication of *Signposts for the Sixties*, 'the hightide of the Right had receded'.[39] In his view, this 'final outcome of the ten-year battle over Labour's road to socialism'[40] had signalled a retreat from revisionism, which itself had been caused by two main factors: first, the declining performance of the national economy and, second, the social imbalance inherent in British capitalism, crystallized in Galbraith's dichotomy of 'private affluence and public squalor'. Both these weaknesses had already been emphasized by Crossman as grounds for a substantial expansion of the public sector.[41]

This conviction that developments in the early 1960s were leading Labour away from revisionist social democracy and in new socialist directions was fully shared by Shore. Defending *Signposts for the Sixties* from any left-wing doubts about its socialist credentials, he argued that

> The 'revisionism in a new guise' thesis misreads the whole course of events in the UK in the early '60s. For instance, by 1961 there was a major economic crisis. By 1962 there was the establishment of the NEDC [National Economic Development Council] and a new series of interventionist policy initiatives. The Galbraithian thesis, too, involving the wider activities of the state, was part of a

reviving collectivism. So with *Signposts for the Sixties* we caught the mood of the '60s.[42]

Signposts for the Sixties continued, therefore, that process by which, since 1960, revisionist influences within the Party had been curbed. The document had developed a highly critical view of current trends within private industry in-Britain. It was certainly reticent about those merits of the private sector which revisionist writers had been eager to recognize. It had firmly restated, too, the traditional socialist case for elevating the status of public ownership in Labour Party policy and strategy. In doing so it had restored the close link in British socialist thought between public ownership and state economic planning – a link which derived from the mid-1930s[43] and which Wilson in particular had re-emphasized in the new context of indicative planning initiatives. In addition, the document had advanced a compelling case for extending public ownership into the territories uncovered by the scientific revolution.

Moreover, these clear indications of the restoration of public ownership had been reinforced with rhetorical endorsements of the idea's mythic importance. This had been apparent in barbed phrases that conveyed either hostility or suspicion towards private industry,[44] as well as in stirring visions of a transformed society, of what Wilson called 'a climate and an environment of social justice'[45] that would emerge from 'an epoch of revolutionary change'.[46] Wilson had justi-fied, too, the linkage between public ownership, economic planning and the scientific revolution in terms that underlined his desire to give contemporary substance to Labour's socialist vision. *Signposts for the Sixties*, he had declared, was 'a statement of our basic Socialist principles and our faith in a manner directly relevant to the problems and the needs of the sixties'.[47]

By such means, then, *Signposts for the Sixties* furthered that course of compromise and reconciliation within the Party which had been steadily pursued since 1960. The document's adoption at the 1961 Party Conference even led *Socialist Commentary* to conclude that this event marked 'the final burial of the Clause IV controversy',[48] even though some on the left were, admittedly, less than enthusiastic about the outcome at Blackpool.[49] To many observers it did at least seem that the crisis of 1959–60 had finally been resolved, an impression that was further confirmed by Gaitskell's victory over the supporters of nuclear unilateralism at that same 1961 Conference.[50]

II

Signposts for the Sixties had helped to lower dangerous tensions
within the Party, since it was widely perceived as providing a firm
basis for a broad consensus on Labour's domestic policy and on the
public ownership issue in particular. It thus appeared acceptable
to centre-right opinion within Labour's ranks. In Jay's view, the
document offered 'a reasonable compromise in so far as it involved
a movement away from the state monopoly – though not from
public ownership itself'.[51] Crosland, too, viewed its publication in a
generally favourable light. The subsequent revisionist response, he
believed, should accordingly be one of tactical reticence on the
subject of both Clause IV and nationalization. As he wrote to his
colleagues in the Campaign for Democratic Socialism:

> Our policy now must be under no circumstances to re-open Clause
> 4 but to be completely silent on nationalisation and let it gradually
> become a forgotten issue, like the Swedish Socialists' commitment
> to republicanism. Then we must see what we can get away with
> when we come to the final Election Manifesto.[52]

This sanguine attitude was largely misplaced, for by 1961 the fierce
conflict over the public ownership issue had been mitigated only
through a compromise favourable in important respects to Party
traditionalists. Public ownership had been rehabilitated, albeit in a
modernized form, both as a leading political idea and as a major
instrument of policy. Revisionist attempts to assign to it a more
limited role within the Party's ideology and strategy had therefore
been countered.

Nevertheless, by 1962 this divisive issue, with all its ramifications,
appeared to be less prominent in the main arenas of Party debate.
This was due partly to the compromise on domestic policy forged by
Signposts for the Sixties and partly to the centrality of the European
Common Market issue as the year unfolded. During the course
of 1962, however, both Crosland and Jay produced books which
provided a restatement and clarification of revisionist attitudes
that were being increasingly challenged within the Party. In *The
Conservative Enemy*, which, in the author's words, was 'intended to
supplement *The Future of Socialism* in the light of recent developments',[53] Crosland unequivocally reaffirmed his earlier support
for the managerialist thesis,[54] an integral part of his revisionist
case, maintaining that 'The idea of the managerial revolution is now
widely accepted . . . in the majority of large firms the divorce between
ownership and control is virtually complete'.[55] From this confident

starting point he then set out to refute the principal arguments deployed by the 'new left' critics of that thesis.[56]

Crosland's restatement of the managerialist thesis in *The Conservative Enemy* thus implied continuing support for the revisionist view of the role of public ownership in democratic socialist strategy. A more detailed and wide-ranging defence of that approach appeared earlier in 1962 in Douglas Jay's book *Socialism in the New Society*. This work contained an extended exposition of revisionist ideas, including those developed by Jay in his *Forward* articles following the 1959 Election. Jay himself later recalled that his book 'followed on directly from the 1959 Clause Four controversy and sprang from the feeling that: "It's all got into a tangle."'[57] In general, it constituted 'an attempt to present the social-democratic case – in the Swedish sense of that term'.[58] Crosland, too, had described the scope of *The Conservative Enemy* in a similar manner, explaining that it outlined 'a programme of radical, social-democratic reform for the middle 1960s'.[59]

In *Socialism in the New Society* Jay defended major positions which revisionist writers had advanced in the 1950s. Like Crosland in *The Future of Socialism*,[60] he provided, for instance, philosophical arguments in support of the pragmatic view of public ownership as a means and not an end.[61] In his view public ownership was 'not some mystic symbol or revolutionary banner, but just one practical means among various others of achieving social justice, productive efficiency or social advance'.[62]

Like Crosland and Gaitskell,[63] Jay revealed a highly sceptical attitude towards public ownership as an instrument for redistributing wealth. It was possible, he maintained, to effect a massive transfer from private to public ownership without achieving any major redistribution of incomes or any significant advance towards social justice – 'as many employed in the British publicly-owned enterprises would now be the first to admit'.[64] However, 'a really radical approach to social justice' could 'unquestionably be achieved by direct fiscal redistribution of incomes and property'.[65] He was consequently in no doubt that 'Progressive direct taxation . . . is more effective and immediate in its redistributive power than the spread of public ownership'.[66] In *The Conservative Enemy* Crosland made it clear that he still shared that view.[67] Like Jay, he considered that the unequal distribution of wealth in Britain sprang largely from private inheritance rather than from ownership of the means of production.[68] Like Jay, too, and in accordance with his own earlier writings,[69] he insisted that such inequalities could be reduced most effectively not

by an extension of public ownership but rather by fiscal measures –
in particular, by a capital gains tax and extended death duties.

By arguing in these terms, both Crosland and Jay were demoting
public ownership in favour of taxation as a policy instrument capable
of redistributing wealth and income. In Crosland's view, public
ownership was also likely in many instances to take second place to
governmental controls of various kinds as a method of regulating
the economy.[70] Nevertheless, both writers stressed the need to
explore other forms of public ownership, with Jay providing a further
defence of his proposal, advanced in *Industry and Society*, for state
shareholdings in private industry.[71] In general, Crosland argued that
the overriding aim ought to be 'not an unending chain of public
monopolies, but a diverse, diffused, pluralist and heterogeneous
pattern of ownership',[72] which might well embrace not just state
shareholdings but also competitive public enterprise, municipal
ownership and cooperative enterprise.

The promotion of these varied forms of public ownership
sprang from a renewed concern to distinguish clearly between
nationalization and public ownership. Jay was therefore concerned
to re-emphasize that distinction, which had featured so prominently
in his writings of 1959,[73] observing that

> British historical accident has perhaps sometimes misled the post-
> 1945 generation into thinking of the monopoly public board as the
> only form of public ownership, and therefore attaching to public
> ownership as a whole virtues or vices which really only attach to
> these monopolies.[74]

Underlining the practical shortcomings of nationalization, he concluded that 'Socialists will thus be wise to recognise that the State
monopoly form was devised to suit an earlier age which British
manufacture and commerce have now largely outgrown'.[75] Finally,
both Jay and Crosland reinforced these views with the most controversial of revisionist attitudes – a positive acceptance of private
industry and hence of a mixed economy. In Jay's opinion, a complex
set of arrangements and reforms would, admittedly, need to be
established in order to steer the private sector on a socially
responsible course. To that end he called for a large public sector
controlling public utilities and natural monopolies, redistribution
of income through taxation and public services, state shareholdings
in private industry, worker participation by means of works councils
and election of directors by employees, and trade union pressure to
defend employees' rights. Once that elaborate framework had been

secured, however, Jay considered that 'it ought to be perfectly possible within a free society to ensure that private enterprise works according to the national interest; and when it does so work, it ought to be welcomed and complimented, not denounced.'[76] In similar vein, Crosland, too, reaffirmed his support for a mixed economy, remaining convinced that 'a thoroughly mixed-up, variegated pattern of ownership' would 'alone . . . guarantee personal liberty and the fragmentation of power'.[77]

In their works of 1962 Crosland and Jay provided, therefore, concise and confident restatements of the revisionist approach towards public ownership. More broadly, their arguments comprised the last major presentation of the revisionist case to appear before Gaitksell's unexpected death in January 1963. Yet at the time they provoked only a limited critical response on the British left.[78] The fresh, unifying theme of the 'scientific revolution', together with the Common Market controversy, had helped, by the close of 1962, to shift the focus of Party debate away from the revisionist challenge. This development was carried a stage further at the 1962 Party Conference in Brighton, where Gaitskell parted company with most of his closest supporters by opposing British membership of the European Economic Community. It thus came about, as Howell has commented, that 'ironically the great confrontationist's last major statement was one that blurred factional divisions'.[79]

Many political historians and commentators have maintained that by the end of 1962 Gaitskell's leadership was unchallenged, with his public and Party prestige at an unprecedented peak.[80] More contentiously, some have suggested that by this time revisionism was equally entrenched within his Party, with Labour 'broadly united behind a revisionist programme'.[81] There are, however, substantial grounds for disputing this interpretation of ideological change. For the course of reconciliation which Labour in opposition pursued from 1960 onwards involved both a revival of traditional socialist ideas in a contemporary form and a containment of revisionist influences. The Party's broad agreement on domestic policy, emerging with the acceptance of *Signposts for the Sixties*, had been fostered by the novel idea of the 'scientific revolution' and strengthened by the growing desire for electoral success. But it had been based, too, on the re-instatement of public ownership in Labour policy and strategy. Through the combined emphasis on 'planning for expansion' and on the need to develop new science-based industries, the 'central and historical doctrine of the party', as one traditionalist MP described it,[82] had acquired a fresh relevance and appeal.

In terms of practical policy Harold Wilson had been an important promoter of that development. Under his influence, too, the central role of public ownership in Labour's socialist myth of a transformed society was again recognized. The vision of the 'scientific revolution' invested that myth with a renewed potency. The restored link between public ownership and economic planning provided the means of fulfilling a long-standing desire to give the myth practical expression.

This rehabilitation of public ownership helped to repair the foundations of the ideological consensus which Labour revisionists had first challenged and then fractured. Such an operation required at the same time the dilution of revisionist ideas and policies. The doctrinal conflict within the Party, which had culminated in the Clause IV dispute, had thus been contained by a settlement established on terms congenial to those who reaffirmed, for various reasons, Labour's historic commitment to public ownership. That arrangement involved a deliberate compromise since revisionist positions were to be officially modified rather than abandoned. The emphasis, too, on the need for 'modernization' served to rebut any suggestion that Labour was merely turning back to its past. Yet the overall impression widely conveyed after 1960, in both Party policy and rhetoric, was that revisionism had been superseded in the light of important new developments and that traditional socialist concerns had consequently been restored and revived.

III

The ideological truce between revisionists and fundamentalists that was implicit in Labour's post-1960 settlement was, in important respects, both provisional and unsatisfactory. For it obscured major differences of opinion and principle by suspending and even concealing fundamental disagreements about the very nature and purpose of both public ownership and democratic socialism. Harold Wilson's accession to the Party leadership in 1963 consolidated that process. It also generated a coherent set of political ideas which appeared to dilute revisionism further by continuing Labour's rehabilitation of public ownership. Warde has suggested that such ideas amounted to a distinctive new ideological form, superseding revisionism, which he terms 'technocratic collectivism'.[83] Stressing the role of social engineers as well as the importance of effective state intervention, this approach offered 'a philosophy of expert dirigisme'.[84] It rested, above all, on the interconnected themes of the scientific revolution and national economic planning, which Wilson had already promoted whilst defending Labour's major policy statements of 1960 and 1961.

The central emphasis which Wilson placed on the idea of the scientific and technological revolution was evident in at least two respects. In the first place, this contemporary development was presented as the precondition for modernizing and revitalizing the British economy. It was also celebrated by him as the means of realizing a new socialist vision. The scientific revolution thus became, in Warde's words, 'the symbolic expression of a particular political strategy',[85] one which involved the purposeful and efficient direction by a meritocratic elite of a modern industrial economy and society.

In line with the key proposals of the 1961 policy document, *Signposts for the Sixties*, planning was emphasized as the second, and related, major theme of that strategy. It was commended as the instrument for achieving technological advance in the field of the new science-based, and in some cases, publicly-owned enterprises and industries. In broader policy terms it was advocated, too, as the means of raising levels of investment and productivity and hence of securing economic growth. Furthermore, as in his previous post-1960 pronouncements, Wilson depicted planning as the crucial ideological link between the notion of the scientific revolution and the British socialist tradition.

Under the influence of Crossman,[86] Wilson proceeded to make these pivotal ideas the central feature of his highly influential landmark speech at the 1963 Party Conference in Scarborough.[87] Maintaining that a future Labour government would ensure that new developments in science and technology would be introduced in a purposeful way through economic planning rather than through the haphazard interplay of unregulated market forces, he thereby sought to redefine Labour's socialist purpose in contemporary terms. He argued that

Since technological progress left to the mechanism of private industry and private purpose can lead only to high profits for a few, a high rate of employment for a few, and to mass redundancy for many, if there had never been a case for Socialism before, automation would have created it.[88]

As well as establishing this linkage between planning, science and socialism, Wilson stressed the related theme of modernization, by which he meant a major reconstruction of British society and institutions in order both to improve the nation's economic performance and to revive national esteem. In a series of speeches delivered in the first quarter of 1964 he made this his central concern, underlining the need to adapt to modern technological developments and social change.[89]

Wilson's ideological approach was clearly collectivist, since it attached great importance to the purposeful activity of an inter-ventionist state. This would involve a renewed and practical role for the traditional socialist ideas of both central economic planning and public ownership, rehabilitated in the form of state-owned enterprises in the new science-based industries. A leading role was assigned, too, to the state in fostering technological development, with a proposed Ministry of Technology as the main instrument of state intervention.

Wilson's approach was also, however, technocratic and merito-cratic. In tune with what appeared then to be the prevailing national mood, he projected the vision of a modern classless society as the remedy for Britain's economic and social stagnation. In this way he made a clear appeal to the rising social groups – scientists, techni-cians, managers and skilled workers – whose advance was held to be blocked by a privileged, complacent and amateurish Establishment. Moreover, Britain's poor economic performance was the result, Wilson argued, not just of underinvestment but also of a situation in which 'the technician and expert in British industries are kept at a lower status than that of the well-born and well-connected amateurs in the company boardrooms', where 'the high command' was too often 'managed either dynastically or on the basis of a family, school or social network'.[90] In place of such anachronisms, Wilson therefore urged the need for the removal of class barriers in industry and society, for the development of the skills and talents of the new social groups, and for the enlargement of the individual's opportunities through the expansion of education and training.

The practical expression of these innovative themes became evident after the 1964 General Election in a number of policy initiatives and institutional developments. Economic planning was fostered through the creation of a Department of Economic Affairs, directed from October 1964 by George Brown. A new Ministry of Technology, too, headed by Frank Cousins, was set up to promote the new science-based industries. A National Plan, amounting to a strategic framework for achieving sustained economic growth, was drawn up by the DEA (Department of Economic Affairs) and presented to Parliament in 1965. An Industrial Reorganisation Corporation was also established, designed to direct state investment into corporate enterprises, to gain greater governmental control over the private sector, and to change the structure of private industry.

In addition, the planning of the scientific revolution in practice entailed proposals for the sponsorship of science through the Ministry of Science, the promotion of research and development in civil industry, the application of scientific techniques in industry, and the establishment, through the Ministry of Technology, of new state-owned industries based on government-sponsored research.

However, Labour's specific public ownership measures, outlined in its 1964 election manifesto, entitled *The New Britain*, were confined to the renationalization of steel, eventually achieved in 1967,[91] and the public ownership of water supplies. The 1966 election manifesto, *Time for Decision*, added proposals for the public ownership of ports, for the creation of a National Freight Authority, eventually established in 1968, and for public participation in the aircraft industry through the acquisition of holdings in the two largest airframe firms.

The 1966 proposal concerning the ports was taken up by the left-wing Minister of Transport, Barbara Castle, but was eventually rejected by her successor Richard Marsh. The 1970 General Election intervened before his alternative scheme could be implemented. In the case of the aircraft industry, the Labour Government rejected plans for public ownership when the long-standing policy of trying to merge the industry's two largest firms, BAC and Hawker Siddeley, proved abortive.

This apparent dilution of Labour's traditional commitment to the incremental nationalization of industry later drew criticisms from the Labour left that, under Wilson, Labour was abandoning socialism and embracing instead the benevolent management of capitalism.[92] Such criticisms gained greater force from the distinctive political climate of the time, which was marked by a drift to the left in the trade unions, including the Transport Workers and Engineers in particular, mounting industrial militancy and unrest, and a growing rift between the Labour Government and the Party's main policy-making organs – its Annual Conference and National Executive.

Nevertheless, Wilson's strategic approach, at least up to 1966, did appeal to the Labour left in important ways. With the use of traditional socialist rhetoric and symbolism, he denounced the old economic and social order in Britain as a backwater of privilege, complacency, snobbery and amateurish incompetence. Somehow, too, he managed to equate the qualities of managerial expertise and professionalism required in the New Britain with the enduring socialist values of social equality and collective responsibility in a manner that appeared convincing to traditional socialists, a feat which had eluded Crosland and Gaitskell. Moreover, with his attacks on the old order Wilson even conveyed to many on the left the impression that he sought to replace capitalism with a socialist alternative, based on central planning and public ownership, rather than with merely a modified and civilized form of market economy. For the strategy of modernization which he championed implied that Labour would secure major structural changes in the British economy.

Wilson strengthened this appeal to the left by attempting to justify the continuing relevance of democratic socialism as the vehicle for the planning and public control of the major new industrial and technological forces which the scientific revolution had unleashed. That involved rehabilitating the traditional socialist ideas of public ownership and central economic planning in the cause of the modernization of the British economy. Since 1963 he had prepared the ground for such an undertaking by seeking to restate British socialism in terms of the broadly defined concept of the scientific and technological revolution.

However imprecise the concept might have been, Wilson's constant promotion of it during this period helped to link socialism with contemporary themes of modernization, economic efficiency and expansion rather than with traditional socialist concerns with the nature, structure and distribution of economic power. His celebrated 1963 Scarborough speech – in which he had established the linkage between planning, science and socialism and thereby equated democratic socialism with the public control, and hence centralized planning, of economic and scientific resources – made explicit the ideological significance of these connections in its concluding section which stressed that 'In all our plans for the future we are re-defining and we are re-stating our socialism in terms of the scientific revolution'.[93] As for the substantive content of Wilson's brand of socialism, it did appear, with its modest programme of public ownership measures, to substitute planning and new forms of state intervention for the traditional socialist strategy of gradual collectivization of the economy through the extension of public ownership to specific industries or companies. As a result, this shift of emphasis did cause concern on the Labour left after 1966 and even more conspicuously by the end of that decade.

Nevertheless, as Peter Shore pointed out thirty years later, Wilson's movement away from the left's orthodox 'shopping-list' approach to public ownership did not imply an abandonment of the traditional importance attached by Labour to the extension of public ownership. According to Shore's own interpretation of the developments of this period,

> The old argument about nationalisation and private enterprise was left behind when Wilson advanced the new role of public enterprise, to be pressed forward to apply science and technology to new industries and processes which the private sector had neglected. Far from saying that public ownership was outmoded and irrelevant, Wilson championed public enterprise as an essential tool for the modernisation of British industry.[94]

Shore argues that Wilson, between 1963 and 1966, thereby 'united his Party with a strong Left steer in policy without alienating the Right'.[95] For Wilson's 'technocratic collectivist' version of socialism, emphasizing the efficient and purposeful public control of economic and scientific resources, did appeal, too, to the revisionist right of the Party since it envisaged the continued existence of a mixed economy, while promoting modernization as the precondition of both economic growth and social progress.

Furthermore, in specific policy terms, both the 1964 and 1966 election programmes embraced the revisionist goals of indicative planning, sustained economic growth and high social expenditure. In accordance with revisionist opinion, too, later developments placed, as we have seen, strict limits on the extension of public ownership. The Labour Government's economic strategy seemed instead to project as its central purpose the modernization and greater efficiency of a mixed economy through active government intervention. The ideological significance of such a strategy was clearly revisionist since it contained, as Howell has noted, 'no suggestion of any fundamental change in the structure of the economy', but fostered instead 'the expectation of a constructive partnership between government and industry' which 'left any public ownership measures as aids to modernisation, not as invasions of existing power structures'.[96]

It was also the case that Wilson's analysis, developed after 1963, of Britain's economic and industrial problems drew not just upon the prescriptions offered in the left-leaning policy documents of 1960 and 1961 but also upon the themes explored by revisionist thinkers since the mid-1950s – including the need to enhance the competitiveness of British industry and to strengthen the country's manufacturing base through increased research and investment. Wilson's subsequent strategic approach, too, involving a desire to present Labour as a progressive national, and hence cross-class, party of government, harmonized with the broader aims of Gaitskell, Crosland and other leading revisionists.

That approach had been pursued so effectively by Wilson that by the time of the 1964 General Election it appeared, as Horner has observed, that 'Labour had secured a "modernizing" image which had displaced its traditional identification (and preoccupation) with public ownership'.[97] One of the principal tasks of revisionism thus seemed on the verge of accomplishment, a process that was further assisted by Wilson's pragmatic approach to national economic problems, by the limited proposals for extending public ownership contained in the 1964 manifesto and by that document's optimistic social policy commitments, which were of the kind that revisionists had long advocated – such as the reorganization of secondary education along comprehensive lines, the raising of the school-leaving age to 16, and wage-related retirement, sickness and unemployment benefits.

Wilson's own underlying commitment to Labour's modernization was also apparent in his sporadic attacks on traditionalist thinking, as, for instance, at the 1966 Party Conference where he stressed that

> It is not enough to reject the organised conservatism of the Tory Party. We cannot afford to perpetuate any form of dinosaur-type thinking in our own Party. . . . We cannot afford to fight the problems of the sixties with the attitudes of the Social Democratic Federation, nor, in looking for a solution to those problems, seek vainly to find the answer in Highgate cemetery.[98]

One effect of such iconoclasm was that during that same year one of Wilson's left-wing critics was complaining that

> What the present Labour leaders are basically about is . . . the more efficient and . . . the more humane functioning of British capitalism. What distinguishes them from their Tory and Liberal political colleagues and competitors is not their will to create a socialist society on the basis of the social ownership and control of economic power . . . but a greater propensity to invoke state intervention in economic and social life than these competitors are willing to accept.[99]

Such charges had, of course, been regularly made by the Labour left against Gaitskell's leadership between 1956 and 1963.

Yet in spite of all these clear revisionist influences, Wilson's leadership brought about a dilution of revisionism itself in two important respects. First, his espousal of the cause of modernization in the light of the scientific revolution involved a restoration of the role of public ownership not just in rhetorical terms but also in the forefront of Labour policy. Second, the years of government from 1964 to 1970 witnessed a retreat from the revisionists' growth-based strategy as economic growth and higher public expenditure were sacrificed by July 1966 to deflationary measures, including public spending cuts, a statutory wage freeze and indirect tax increases, in order to correct the inherited balance-of-payments deficit and defend the value of sterling.

Crosland, as the chief intellectual architect of revisionism, was understandably critical of that retreat into orthodoxy, yet he still hoped that the next Labour government would pursue a growth-based strategy more resolutely. Later, looking back at the erosion of his revisionist objectives, he considered, too, that from 1964 to 1970 'there was little sign of a coherent, overall egalitarian strategy' and that, in consequence, 'extreme class inequalities remain, poverty is far from eliminated'.[100]

Recent works by political historians have, with considerable justification, offered a more favourable reassessment of the record of the 1964–70 Wilson Governments than had previously been presented.[101] None the less, there seems general agreement that those Governments' economic and social policy failures in the 1960s did indeed stem from such strategic shortcomings. These included the inability of the Department of Economic Affairs to change the shape of economic policy by supplanting the Treasury as the main agent of policy formulation; the abandonment by July 1966 of the National Plan and with it the target of an annual growth rate of 4 per cent; and, in general, the Labour Governments' lack of capacity for countering the long-term adverse trends affecting the British economy.

IV

In the light, then, of the collapse of the Labour Governments' growth-based strategy, Crosland's revisionist project seemed by the late 1960s to have been undermined. Certainly the experience of those years called into question two of its underlying assumptions – namely that sustained economic growth could be achieved and that governments had the policy instruments to promote that end.

With this retreat in practice from revisionist aims there could therefore be no smooth transition in the 1960s from traditional state socialism to some version of European social democracy. Instead,

Wilson's carefully ambiguous style of leadership, which combined a sharp awareness of the mythic importance of public ownership with a commitment to pragmatic policy-making, extended Labour's ideological truce – on the question of the nature and purpose of both public ownership and democratic socialism – into the period beyond 1963.

Under Wilson's leadership 'the incompatibility between socialist aims and integrative practice', between, that is, the fundamentalist goal of replacing capitalism with a new socialist order and the practical need to adapt to the realities of a market economy, had thus, as Middlemas has argued, 'been deep-frozen by the accord of 1963'.[102] That tension was subsequently to be 'thawed out and revived'[103] as a consequence of the power struggle within the Party which developed in the late 1960s and early 1970s. Yet instead of confronting the implications of such conflict, Labour leaders in the 1960s and 1970s, first Wilson and then Callaghan, decided, as Marquand later observed, 'to allow sleeping ideological dogs to lie'.[104]

Such ambiguity and evasion did, however, serve an important political purpose, since Wilson's approach, presented more positively in the language of 'technocratic collectivism', 'played a vital role in the internal dynamics of the Labour Party by providing a basis for party unity before the elections of 1964 and 1966'.[105] Indeed, that advantage had been recognized at the time by Richard Crossman when in 1964 he described the theme of the scientific revolution as 'the new creative Socialist idea needed to reconcile the Revisionists of the Right with the Traditionalists of the Left. Harold Wilson succeeded where Hugh Gaitskell failed'.[106] Crosland, too, later acknowledged the political benefits of this idea for a party exhausted by ten years of internecine strife. While he himself was highly sceptical about the substance of Wilson's pronouncements on the scientific revolution theme, Crosland considered none the less that it had a 'deeply therapeutic effort' on the Party.[107] For, 'unlike Clause 4 and unilateralism', the new theme was 'unifying and non-controversial' and the Party itself 'was sick of ideological dispute'.[108]

The significance of this reconciling role which the 'scientific revolution' assumed during this period was re-emphasized, over twenty years later, by Wilson when he maintained that, over public ownership, 'Hugh wanted to fight, I wanted to set the Party on a new path'.[109] For that purpose, Wilson, who on his own admission was 'never an avid nationalizer', believed that the idea of the 'scientific revolution' provided 'something exciting: it got rid of all the old silly arguments over public ownership'.[110] One political commentator in 1963 could almost be justified, he suggested, in describing his celebrated Party Conference speech of that year as 'a 50-year leap forward – for Labour and for Britain'.[111]

The 'scientific revolution', promoted in Wilsonian terms, clearly did present a theme conducive to party unity in the early 1960s. Such a benefit was itself a product of the theme's mythic resonance, of the way in which it rekindled Labour's 'socialist faith'. By providing, that is, a basis for unity, along with certain other attractive features, the idea of a 'scientific revolution' performed some of the main functions of a political myth. This 'new creative Socialist idea' was, for instance, directed towards a Party membership that was afflicted by internal schisms and demoralized by successive election defeats. To that audience it offered a convincing account of economic developments which both explained and deplored the stagnation and imbalance of contemporary British society.

Furthermore, the 'scientific revolution' presented the vision of an invigorating future, one that served to mobilize the Party against the Conservative enemy, thereby instilling a firm sense of political purpose. Tony Benn had even anticipated the idea's mythic force by proposing that Wilson's series of speeches, begun in 1964 and taking forward the Scarborough message, should follow the theme of 'regeneration', with 'a spiritual flavour and a suggestion of youth (new generation) about it'.[112] In programmatic terms, such a vision furnished a clear justification for the extension of both public ownership and economic planning and for restoring a thirty-year-old link between those Party commitments.

But, above all, the Wilsonian theme supplied the means of unifying the Party, transcending its bitter doctrinal and factional disputes. Through its critique of private industry and its renewed emphasis on public ownership, it appealed to those who aspired to the traditional goal of an alternative, non-capitalist form of economic organization. Through its demands for expertise and improved efficiency, it harmonized, too, with the revisionist advocacy of a more vigorous and dynamic mixed economy.

Concerned, then, with holding the Labour Party together as a loose coalition of interests and ideas, Wilson's approach to ideological revision by means of the flexible concept of the scientific revolution was both indirect and highly ambiguous, designed to convert Labour into Britain's natural party of government without openly breaking with its traditional aims and symbols. His underlying pragmatism, which, as Ponting has noted, was 'a considerable asset in electoral terms in 1964, and also within the complex, faction-ridden internal politics of the Labour Party',[113] led him to shelve emotive and divisive issues and to project a new, less controversial set of ideas around which the Party could unite.

This did not mean, as has often been alleged,[114] that, with his pragmatic leanings, Wilson lacked any interest in either socialist ideology or political ideas in general. Indeed, as Pimlott has argued, 'The notion that Wilson had a "contempt for ideas" ... comes from people who really mean that they regard the ideas that he did have contemptuously'.[115] For, in reality, Wilson's 'view of the future had far more clarity and intellectual content', embracing most notably the idea of linkage between planning, technological development and economic growth, than that of Attlee, Callaghan, Foot or Kinnock when they first faced the electors as Party leader.[116]

Nevertheless, with regard to Labour's ideological debate and to questions of socialist doctrine, Wilson remained a pragmatic centrist and a reconciler, who, in Morgan's words 'made a virtue, among his dogmatic brethren, of averting his gaze from theology'.[117] From such an approach certain tangible benefits, in terms of both Party unity and broad electoral appeal, clearly flowed. Yet the political vision which underlay Wilson's centrist appeal, and which his own pragmatism had fashioned, was limited in its scope. In place of the traditional socialist goal of a transformed economy and society, it promised no more and no less than a modernized and restructured mixed economy. In the longer term, therefore, it was likely that fundamentalists would be disappointed by such a modest goal and deterred by the prospect of streamlining rather than superseding capitalism. Similarly, it was probable that revisionists would eventually be dismayed by the anti-capitalist rhetoric and the restored status of public ownership which accompanied the Party's new concern with reconciliation.

The most serious drawback, then, of the intra-Party compromise fostered by this idea of a 'scientific revolution' was that it suppressed fierce and deep-rooted policy and doctrinal disputes. As Bill Rodgers later recalled, the unifying theme 'involved bypassing the question of public ownership. You couldn't get everybody travelling on that bypass. They were used to going down the traditional routes'.[118] Or, as Middlemas also observed, with a different analogy but the same reservation in mind: 'What had really occurred ... resembled the dosing of a malarial patient with quinine: the symptoms disappeared, but the Party was not really strengthened, nor were its ideological fevers cured.'[119] It was hardly surprising that those internal strains, and the deeper doctrinal tensions underlying them, resurfaced, sharply and divisively, during the 1970s and early 1980s.

5 Revisionist social democracy in retreat, 1970–83

I

The period of opposition from 1970 to early 1974 witnessed a severe ideological reaction within the Labour Party against revisionist social democracy and the policies and strategy which it had engendered in the 1960s. This development occurred against the economic background of a deepening international recession, marked by rising unemployment and surging inflation, that arose in the wake of the oil price crisis of 1973–4. Such a climate eroded the optimism that had characterized revisionist thought concerning both the possibility of achieving sustained growth through state economic management and the effectiveness of social and fiscal policy measures in reducing inequalities and promoting social welfare.

The reaction against revisionist social-democratic ideas and policies was accompanied after 1970 by a marked shift to the left within the Party's policy-making institutions – the National Executive Committee and Annual Party Conference – and by a revival of the appeal of traditional socialist remedies, albeit presented in a contemporary form. These developments were evident in the left's increasing control over the NEC, which by 1973 had reached a point where, among that body's constituency and women's section representatives, only two members – Shirley Williams and Denis Healey – were associated with the revisionist right. The left's control thereby led to its increased representation on the NEC's various policy-making committees, notably its Home Policy Committee, its Industrial Policy subcommittee and its offshoot the Public Sector group.

More widely, the growing strength of the left was reflected in the swelling ranks of both constituency activists and trade unionists disenchanted with the economic, industrial and international policies of the Wilson Governments. This in turn led to a resurgence of left-wing campaigning activity within constituency parties and trade unions. Furthermore, the Party's leftward shift was reinforced by the forging of closer links between the Labour left and trade union interests as a result of their combined opposition to the Heath Government's industrial relations legislation as well as to its application for British membership of the European Community. Such ties helped to raise the strength of the left within the Party to probably its highest level since 1945.

This major change in the Party's balance of power and influence was evident in a series of Conference decisions taken between 1970 and 1973, committing Labour to substantial extensions of public ownership into such areas as banking, insurance and building societies, the construction industry, road haulage, shipbuilding and ship-repairing.

These commitments derived after 1970 from the Party's complex policy-making process, which centred on its Research Department and the NEC Home Policy Committee, with both trade unions and the extra-parliamentary party exercising increasing influence. The eighty or so committees and study groups involved in that process[1] were united in the belief that the Party should be redirected towards traditional socialist objectives, from which the Wilson Governments had allegedly strayed. Indeed, as Hatfield has observed, Labour's policy-makers in the early 1970s 'shared one common conviction . . . the belief that successive Labour Governments had failed, and would continue to fail, unless there was a fundamental change in the balance of the public and private sectors of the economy'.[2]

On the level of Party policy, therefore, this swing to the left entailed a reaffirmation of Labour's traditional commitment to public ownership, together with a re-emphasis on the need to devise and implement new methods of state economic planning. Specifically, on the NEC's Industrial Policy subcommittee and its Public Sector Group, Stuart Holland, with Judith Hart and Ian Mikardo as prominent supporters, advocated a set of proposals which in due course became the foundations of the so-called Alternative Economic Strategy, evolving throughout the 1970s and developed most clearly after 1979.

This new interventionism was theoretically conceived by Holland and others against an economic background of growing concentration of ownership in British manufacturing industry. As a result of a series of mergers and takeovers, 100 large firms in Britain by 1970 produced nearly 50 per cent of total net manufacturing output. (In 1950 the same number of large firms had produced only 20 per cent of such output.)

The left's strategic response to these developments, as well as to the economic stagnation that accompanied them, was both a rejection of revisionist social democracy, with its foundation built on Keynesian macroeconomics, and an advocacy of an alternative programme based on a quasi-Marxist analysis of monopoly capitalism and corporate power and offering traditional socialist prescriptions reformulated in contemporary terms.

During the period of opposition from 1970 to 1974 Labour's industrial policy therefore became, as Peter Shore has recalled, 'the touchstone of socialist intent'.[3] This became evident as Tony Benn assumed an increasingly powerful position within the policy-making process. As Shadow Minister for Industry, as chairman of the NEC's Home Policy committee from 1974 and of its Industrial Policy subcommittee between 1970 and 1974, and subsequently as Secretary of State for Industry from February 1974 until the summer of 1975, Benn certainly 'had a special claim to be considered as the architect and custodian of party policy'.[4]

Driven, it seemed, by the belief 'that capitalism had broken down irretrievably and must be replaced by a new and predominantly publicly-owned economy',[5] Benn became the dominant political influence on the shape of Labour's domestic policy-making during those years, when, as Philip Whitehead has observed, he appeared as, 'once the youthful technocrat of the first Wilson era, now a born-again socialist radicalized by his experience of workers in struggle'.[6]

The policy proposals which emanated from the Party committees that Benn chaired included, most notably, plans for the creation of a State Holding Company designed both to coordinate the state's existing holdings in British industry and to take into public ownership a number of leading manufacturing firms, turning them into the competitive pacesetters of their respective industries.

This interventionist institution, presented in the form of a National Enterprise Board (NEB) and drawing on Italian industrial experience, would thus serve as a vehicle for flexible competitive public enterprise. It would be reinforced by a proposed system of compulsory planning agreements, based on French and Belgian planning practice, between government and large private-sector companies with regard to their investment and exports.

Both these proposals, therefore, involved a more direct, interventionist form of economic management, by means of a substantial extension of both public ownership and central planning, than had been attempted by the governments of either Macmillan or Wilson in the 1960s, with their various experiments in indicative economic planning. Eventually the proposals became embodied in the NEC policy statement, *Labour's Programme 1973*, arguably Labour's most left-wing document since *For Socialism and Peace* in 1934.

Labour's Programme 1973 amounted to a clear repudiation of a revisionist social-democratic approach to economic strategy. It declared that the Labour governments in the 1960s had 'made it increasingly evident that even the most comprehensive measures of social and fiscal reform can only succeed in masking the unacceptable face of a capitalist economy and cannot achieve any fundamental changes in the power relationships which dominate our society'.[7] In place of such ineffective reformism the document stated that its overriding aim was 'to bring about a fundamental and irreversible shift in the balance of power and wealth in favour of working people and their families',[8] a choice of words originally proposed by Tony Benn and destined to become 'the battle cry of the left'[9] in the Party's subsequent debate.

Further underlining its ideological standpoint, the 1973 document reaffirmed Labour's credentials as a 'democratic Socialist party' determined to 'put the principles of democracy and Socialism above considerations of privilege and market economics'.[10] Moreover, it projected Labour's visionary aim as 'no less than a new social order', which was attainable through the pursuit of the Party's 'basic Socialist goals', notably the extension of public ownership and central economic planning. For only measures of that kind could end 'the arbitrary exercise of economic power', in Tawney's phrase, that was characteristic of the capitalist system, and thereby transfer social control 'from a small elite to the mass of the people'.[11]

The policy instruments designed to give practical effect to these traditional socialist aims consisted, first, of the proposed National Enterprise Board as the main vehicle for extending both public ownership and economic planning. Its tasks would involve job creation in areas of high unemployment, and promotion of investment, exports and technological development. Its envisaged structure would consist not just of existing state shareholdings but also, most controversially, of a substantial number, twenty-five in all, of major profitable manufacturing companies from the private sector. For only, it was argued, through a substantial expansion of public ownership in profitable industries could such objectives as higher investment, increased exports and full employment be achieved. In addition, the remaining large private-sector companies would be

required to sign planning agreements with a future Labour government in order to set targets for investment, prices and exports within
private manufacturing industry. Each of these radical innovations
would in turn be incorporated in a new Industry Act which would
confer on a future Labour government greater powers of selective
intervention with regard to policies affecting investment, prices and
profits in the corporate sector.

These highly interventionist policy proposals, which were endorsed
by the 1973 Party Conference, clearly constituted a decisive break
with revisionist social-democratic strategy, with its underlying
Keynesian method of indirect, macroeconomic intervention. Indeed,
in terms of both policy and ideology the 1973 Programme represented a shift to the left that was unprecedented in the post-1945
period. The transformative rather than reformist implications of
its underlying aims were underlined by Benn at the 1973 Party
Conference when he declared: 'We are saying at this conference that
the crisis that we inherit when we come to power will be the occasion
for fundamental change and not the excuse for postponing it'.[12]
This economic transformation which Benn advocated rested on an
unequivocal support for extensive public ownership that had been
absent from Party policy for twenty years. In that important sense,
therefore, the 1973 Programme, and the 1974 manifestos which it
influenced, were, as David Coates has argued, 'important victories'[13]
for the Labour left, which tied the Party leadership when it entered
office in 1974 to a set of policy commitments 'more radical in tone
and aspiration than any that the Party had endorsed since 1945'.[14]

Reactions to such commitments, both on the revisionist right of
the Party and within the Party leadership itself, were highly
unfavourable. Upon publication of *Labour's Programme 1973*, which
Michael Foot later described as 'the finest Socialist Programme
I have seen in my lifetime',[15] Harold Wilson soon made clear his
opposition to plans to acquire twenty-five major manufacturing firms,
a major part of the NEB's proposed operations. While he favoured
the creation of a National Enterprise Board as a means of promoting
new enterprises and assisting ailing private-sector firms, he believed
that the twenty-five firms proposal would be both electorally unpopular and politically damaging for Labour.[16] He consequently
warned the NEC, at the Clause V joint NEC/Parliamentary Committee
meeting about the next election manifesto, that the Shadow Cabinet
would veto any such proposal.

In taking this stance, Wilson was supported by both Crosland and
Jenkins. Crosland had opposed the takeover plan since November

1972, regarding such extensive intervention as highly bureaucratic and electorally disastrous in its likely effects.[17] In general, the social-democratic right viewed the proposal, along with the idea of compulsory planning agreements, as symptomatic of the left's hostile attitude towards the private sector and of their consequent lack of support for the mixed economy.

The fact that Wilson did ensure that such a controversial proposal made no appearance in Labour's 1974 election manifestos gave comfort to social democrats. Nevertheless, the Party was still committed to an overtly left-wing economic programme since the February 1974 election manifesto, *Let Us Work Together*, proposed a major extension of public ownership into such fields as ship-building and ship-repairing, aircraft production, the ports, and land required for development. It also promised to acquire public holdings in profitable sections or firms of vital industries such as pharmaceuticals, road haulage and machine tools. It preserved, too, the envisaged status of the National Enterprise Board as a major interventionist instrument. Moreover, it underpinned all these proposals with the ultimate Bennite aim of achieving 'a fundamental and irreversible shift' in the balance of power and wealth within British society.

The left's alternative economic programme, albeit with one key proposal removed, was translated, therefore, into official Party policy documents during this period. One effect of these developments was to galvanize the Party's centre and right into forming, after the October 1974 General Election, the Manifesto Group, a purely parliamentary grouping which aimed to unify anti-left opinion within the PLP. Its name, initially suggested by James Wellbeloved, was itself misleading or ambiguous in view of the opposition of most social-democratic MPs to the highly interventionist proposals contained in the February 1974 manifesto. But, as Wellbeloved explained: 'when we call ourselves the Manifesto Group, we don't mean that we like the manifesto. What we mean is that the manifesto is as far as we're prepared to bloody well go!'[18] But in spite of this organized response by the Labour right, the left's economic programme was strengthened soon afterwards by a systematic attempt by one of its main architects, Stuart Holland, to provide it with a coherent theoretical justification. This appeared in his book *The Socialist Challenge*, published in 1975, which also constituted a major critique of the revisionist position on economic policy and strategy.

In 'The Socialist Challenge' Holland developed an economic analysis which focused upon the dominant power within British industry of a small number of very large, often multinational companies. These constituted what he referred to as a mesoeconomic sector of the economy which accounted for the bulk of industrial production, exports and employment. Furthermore, the economic power and political influence of these giant firms, Holland argued, had eroded the capacity of national governments for controlling them indirectly by means of Keynesian economic techniques. Macroeconomic intervention through the use of government fiscal and monetary policies had thus, in his view, proved an increasingly ineffective method of regulating these new concentrations of private economic power.

In the light of these developments, Holland maintained that 'It is on the key question of state power and government control that the Crosland analysis has been proved wrong, and with it the "revisionist" thesis of which he has remained the foremost advocate in post-war Britain'.[19] Indeed, the economic policy failures of the previous Labour Governments, including, for instance, the abortive National Plan, were largely due, in Holland's judgement, to the limitations of the Keynesian economic basis of social-democratic theory, as expounded most influentially by Crosland.

The growth of the mesoeconomic sector of big-league companies had also, Holland argued, undermined another important aspect of Crosland's analysis – his thesis of the divorce between ownership and control within private industry, for 'the rise of managerial capitalism has not diluted the power of capitalism as a mode of production, but has increased the power of managers in the dominant meso-economic sector'.[20]

In view of these shortcomings of what he referred to as 'Keynesian social democracy', as refined and updated by Crosland, Holland wanted to shift the focus of socialist economic thinking away from demand management towards a more traditional concern with controlling the processes of supply in a capitalist economy increasingly dominated by powerful multinational companies. For that purpose he therefore advocated more direct state intervention at the mesoeconomic level with the aid of traditional socialist policy instruments – namely, a large-scale extension of public ownership and central economic planning. Specifically, such intervention would occur through the formation of competitive public enterprises, a strong National Enterprise Board and planning agreements with major firms – proposals which had all appeared in *Labour's Programme 1973*.

Only by such directly interventionist methods, Holland insisted, could the unaccountable private economic power of multinational companies be controlled by a future Labour government. Only through such measures, too, could central goals of economic policy, such as higher levels of investment and exports and a more stable regional balance of resources and employment, be effectively attained in the wake of the failures of both the private sector and Keynesian economic management.

II

Holland's analysis did not go unchallenged by revisionist social democrats within the Party. Crosland, for example, in his essay 'Socialism Now', published in 1974, directly addressed the question of 'whether the revisionist thesis of the 1950s and early 1960s . . . now needs to be drastically revised' in the light of experience and, particularly, in the face of 'a revival of semi-Marxist thought in Britain',[21] which held that 'a major transformation of power-relationships has taken place in the British economy, due partly to the growing concentration of industry and partly to the growth of the multi-nationals'.[22] This left-wing thesis further maintained, Crosland noted, that economic power had consequently moved away from the state and the trade unions 'towards a small oligarchy of private manufacturing firms',[23] which had been able to frustrate the previous Labour Governments' attempts to achieve either greater equality or improved economic performance through faster growth and higher investment and exports.

The major conclusion drawn, therefore, by proponents of this 'semi-Marxist' viewpoint was that, contrary to the revisionist thesis, ownership of the means of production was still a dominant influence on society and that, consequently, 'a massive increase in public ownership is required, not so much for reasons specific to any particular firm or industry, but generally to transfer this concentrated power and wealth from a small economic oligarchy to the people'.[24]

But while conceding that concentration in manufacturing industry had greatly increased in Britain since around 1950, Crosland did not accept the view that this development had led to a major increase in the power of private industry relative to that of the state, the trade unions or the community in general. The activities of private manufacturing firms were more and more circumscribed, he argued, first, by government legislation and policy – both macroeconomic and microeconomic; second, by increased foreign competition – as, for instance, in the motor, aero-engine and electrical equipment industries; and, third, by a shift of employment out of manufacturing into services. British manufacturing industry, he concluded, 'with falling or stagnant profits, severe competition from imports and a declining share of total employment, is faced by ever-increasing activity (in terms of both expenditure and direct regulation), a trade union movement capable of blowing even governments off-course and . . . a growing consumer and environmental lobby'.[25]

As for the multinational companies, those powerful organizations, while clearly posing certain economic dangers, had also, in Crosland's view, brought tangible benefits in terms of inward investment and hence increased net income. Moreover, the necessary regulation of their activities could still be achieved, he believed, through government legislation, taxation and other controls.

On the basis, therefore, of the available evidence, Crosland found it 'hard to discern a massive shift of power to the private corporation' or to detect 'a drastic transformation of power relationships' within the British economy.[26] Indeed, he saw 'no reason to alter the revisionist thesis that government can generally impose its will (provided it has one) on the private corporation'.[27]

Crosland also rejected the second part of Holland's influential thesis – his view that a substantial extension of public ownership was required in the light of this questionable shift in the balance of economic power. Any policy of transferring the largest private firms to public ownership in order to redistribute that power would give rise, Crosland warned, to the danger of creating a series of 'managerial bureaucracies' across the British economy.[28] In addition, current arguments for a large-scale extension of public ownership into manufacturing industry were not supported, he maintained, by postwar experience of nationalization in Britain. In terms, for example, of its effect on the distribution of wealth, nationalization had had 'no visible influence'[29] as a result, first, of the payment of fair compen-sation to former shareholders in the form of government stock and, second, of the nationalized industries' practice of borrowing from the private sector in order to finance their expansion.

Nevertheless, Crosland did endorse 'an active policy of competitive public enterprise; that is the establishment (either from scratch or by take-over) of state companies or joint ventures to compete with private enterprise'.[30] That idea, which he had first supported twenty-five years before, still seemed 'a fresher and more attractive approach' to public ownership than the traditional emphasis on 'monolithic industry nationalization'.[31] He conspicuously failed, however, to admit the possibility that Holland and his left-wing colleagues might merely be urging the adoption, albeit on a larger scale, of a policy proposal first advanced by revisionists such as Jay and Crosland in the 1950s.

True, however, to his revisionist views, Crosland made it clear that any extension of public ownership, whether through competitive public enterprise or into particular areas of the economy (which in his case would preferably include development land, private rented housing or parts of the construction and insurance industries), should occur on a limited scale and within the surrounding framework of a 'genuinely mixed economy'.[32] The disappointing economic developments in Britain over the last decade could not, in his view, be attributed to the British pattern of ownership, since countries with much faster rates of growth also, like Britain, had mixed economies. Furthermore, no evidence had been presented 'to show how or why, in Britain alone, a massive transfer of ownership is either necessary to achieving our goals or would in fact help to achieve them'.[33]

Public ownership, therefore, remained for Crosland a useful policy instrument and a means of achieving socialist goals, not an end in itself. It took its proper place within a 'genuinely mixed economy', which ought to be 'not necessarily ... an economy in which whole sectors are privately and whole sectors publicly owned' but one 'based on a variety of ownership forms and social controls designed to provide the best possible blend of social efficiency, growth and choice'.[34]

Adding, too, a sceptical note on the limitations of state collectivism, Crosland commented, in a manner that anticipated later developments of economic theory and policy in Britain:

We must not expect too much from either more intervention or more nationalization. Little was left by 1970 of the glowing 1964 themes of industrial restructuring and technological revolution. ... Governments do not always see the public interest so much more clearly than private firms.[35]

Moreover, in terms of political priorities, 'we must decide', Crosland concluded, 'that greater equality, and not spawning new pieces of State bureaucracy, is what fundamentally divides us from the Tories'.[36]

Crosland had thus provided a carefully argued defence of the revisionist position in the face of the left's 'semi-Marxist' critique. The object of that intellectual exercise, to which other revisionist social democrats, notably Marquand, also contributed,[37] was essentially a negative one of demonstrating that there was 'no need to abandon the revisionist analysis of socialism in favour of a refurbished Marxism'.[38] But there was a more positive aspect, too, of Crosland's counter-attack. This consisted of a restatement of his ethical, and in particular his egalitarian, view of socialism. In the light of the last ten years' experience there was, he maintained, 'no need for revisionists to revise our definition of socialism'.[39] For in their view socialism was still 'basically about equality', by which he meant 'more than a merito-cratic society of equal opportunities' and also 'more than a simple . . . redistribution of income'. Instead, revisionists pursued the goal of 'a wider social equality embracing also the distribution of property, the educational system, social class relationships, power and privilege in industry – indeed all that was enshrined in the age-old dream of a more "classless" society'.[40] That ideal of social equality involved, too, what Crosland described as 'an improvement in our social capital; such that the less well-off have access to housing, health and educa-tion of a standard comparable, at least in the basic decencies, to that which the better-off can buy for themselves out of their private means'.[41]

The pursuit of social equality, then, together with 'the relief of poverty, distress and social squalor',[42] which Crosland had consis-tently stressed as the fundamental and distinctive socialist ideals, ought to remain, he insisted, Labour's key objectives in the 1970s. In order to achieve them, however, sustained economic growth – of around 4 per cent per year – was also still a necessary means, which was consistent, he believed, with environmental concerns with reducing pollution and conserving energy resources provided that there was 'social control and intervention in markets'.[43]

In what were to be the last major theoretical statements in defence of his revisionist stance, Crosland argued that what Labour needed was 'a sharper delineation' of its 'fundamental objectives' and 'a greater clarity about egalitarian priorities', together with, in practical terms, 'a stronger determination to achieve them'.[44] What, however, was not required was 'some great shift of direction',[45] one that would involve any radical reformulation of the revisionist positions which he had staked out in the 1950s. Crosland, therefore, did not just reaffirm the egalitarian and welfarist ideals of revisionist social democracy. He also continued to adhere to its key underlying assumptions – namely, that rapid and sustained economic growth could be achieved (though he did concede that he had been too complacent on this subject in the past);[46] that governments had the capacity both to promote such growth and to curb private economic power; and that social-democratic ideals could be fulfilled within the context of a market-oriented mixed economy and through the interventions of the British state.

What seemed absent, then, from Crosland's theoretical statements during this period was any concerted attempt to adapt those optimistic assumptions to meet the harsher 1970s climate of economic stagnation and industrial conflict. This lack of either doctrinal or strategic innovation in the face of such problematic questions as, for instance, the link between growth and redistribution was evident not just in Crosland's writings but also on the revisionist right in general.

Such theoretical limitations sprang largely from a specific political source: the absorption of most revisionist social democrats in the issue and cause of British membership of the European Community,[47] which dominated British politics during the first half of the 1970s. For in the deep Party split on that divisive issue, which first appeared with the large-scale rebellion of pro-European MPs against the party whip in October 1971,[48] Labour's pro-EC minority was drawn mainly from the ranks of the revisionist right, with a few notable exceptions such as Crosland and Healey.

Labour's schism reflected, therefore, not only deeply held differences over the European issue but also the configuration of power within the Party during the early 1970s. In that political climate pro-European revisionists, who increasingly described themselves as 'social democrats' as a symbol of their affinity with Continental social democracy,[49] became publicly identified with the European issue. This conferred the advantage of projecting them as a clearly organized grouping under the acknowledged leadership of Roy Jenkins. Their association with the European cause also, however, had the disadvantage of diverting their intellectual and strategic energies from the ideological conflicts which by that time clearly underlay central areas of domestic policy.

The growing political isolation of revisionist social democrats in a Party which was then predominantly hostile towards the European Community was a direct consequence of these developments. Their condition was aggravated by their own loss of intellectual initiative, which a preoccupation with the European issue had done nothing to restore, to the Bennite left with its apparently coherent and widely supported economic strategy and programme.

Revisionist influence was further eroded, too, as the focus of power within the Party during this period shifted away from the parliamentary party towards the left-leaning Party Conference and National Executive. With their mainly parliamentary political base and their avowed European sympathies, social democrats thus became increasingly distant from the main centres of Party policy-making as the 1970s progressed.

III

With Labour's unexpected return to office in February 1974, the leftward shift within the Party since 1970 was clearly underlined by the manner in which Tony Benn and Eric Heffer, ministers at the Department of Industry, presented their industrial strategy, with its radical proposals, derived from *Labour's Programme 1973*, for a substantial extension of public ownership and control, for compulsory planning agreements and for a highly interventionist National Enterprise Board.

Gradually, however, those proposals were diluted as Benn's strategy was transmuted into, first, a government White Paper and, second, subsequent government legislation. Benn's original draft for that White Paper, later derided by Wilson as 'sloppy and half-baked ... polemical, even menacing in tone',[50] was largely rewritten by a Cabinet committee chaired by the Prime Minister. The White Paper that eventually emerged in the summer of 1974, entitled *The Regeneration of British Industry*, reflected this moderating influence. It contained no list of large manufacturing firms earmarked for public ownership and only a reduced list of industries for complete public ownership. In addition, the initial proposal for compulsory planning agreements between government and private industry was transformed into plans for agreements of a voluntary nature. Furthermore, Benn's conception of the National Enterprise Board as an instrument of direct intervention evolved instead into Wilson's favoured idea of a state holding company largely designed for assisting ailing private-sector firms.

Underlying these modifications, too, was a shift of ideological emphasis evident in the White Paper's opening paragraph, which declared the Government's commitment to a mixed economy that would combine 'efficient publicly owned industries, with a vigorous, alert, responsible and profitable private sector'.[51] This was clearly a far cry from the anti-capitalist rhetoric of *Labour's Programme 1973*, with its denunciation of 'the arbitrary exercise of economic power'. The changes which the White Paper signalled even led Benn to record, later in 1974, his belief that 'there is a systematic social democratic betrayal of socialist policy and the Cabinet has got nothing in common with the aspirations of the movement'.[52]

In spite of Benn's suspicions, the 1974 White Paper, although modified in content and tone, did contain a number of proposals for extending state intervention and ownership into British industry. These included plans for the nationalization of the docks, development land and the aircraft and shipbuilding industries, together with a commitment to establishing a national corporation for the exploration and extraction of North Sea oil. All these proposals were subsequently enacted.

None the less, 'the betrayal of socialist policy' which Benn feared seemed confirmed, in left-wing eyes, by events following the EC referendum in June 1975. For with Benn removed from his post as Secretary of State for Industry and demoted in Cabinet to Minister for Energy, Wilson began to assume general direction of industrial strategy. The left-wing tide ebbed further after 1975 as the various elements of the Alternative Economic Strategy, of which Benn considered himself the chief political architect, were gradually dismantled. Its cornerstone, the National Enterprise Board, limited in its funds and powers, was reduced largely to a vehicle for rescue operations aimed at ailing 'lame duck' industries and companies, which included British Leyland and Rolls-Royce. Moreover, planning agreements, even in their modified, voluntary form, were in practice confined to just one instance, established with the American car company Chrysler. They increasingly gave way to the more familiar system of tripartite indicative planning through the NEDC.

The cumulative effect of these developments led Stuart Holland, the principal intellectual progenitor of the 1973 *Programme*, to reflect gloomily towards the end of 1975 that 'the rethink in theory and policy which followed the 1970 election defeat transformed under the present Government into a half-hearted State capitalism, rather than a major challenge to capitalism itself'.[53]

This dilution of the left's economic strategy and programme was made easier politically as a result of the temporary rupture of the alliance between the Labour left and the left-wing leadership of the big trade unions, notably the Transport Workers and Engineers. After 1975 the Government's domestic policy increasingly revolved around the Social Contract, a device by which union cooperation in establishing a voluntary incomes policy was achieved in return for the implementation of industrial and social policies in tune with union demands. This process, while protecting the Government from left-wing pressures, at the same time generated conflict between the left-leaning NEC and left-wing union leaders such as Jack Jones and Hugh Scanlon, who were chiefly responsible for managing the practical operation of the incomes policy.

Economic factors, too, played an increasingly central role in encouraging the Labour Government's retreat after 1975 from the left-wing policies and programme developed in Opposition between 1970 and 1974. The deteriorating economic situation, with the level of unemployment rising above 1 million and the rate of inflation approaching 30 per cent in 1975, and with the pound, too, under intense pressure, induced a highly cautious mood among Government ministers, as well as an aversion to radical and untested Bennite prescriptions.

The cause of economic orthodoxy was further promoted by the deepening financial crisis of 1976, following which the retreat from socialist policies, both traditional and revisionist, became more explicit. For the International Monetary Fund's (IMF) loan package of that year, designed to defend the pound and restore international confidence, entailed, as its attached conditions, major cuts in public expenditure in order to reduce substantially the Public Sector Borrowing Requirement. Crosland, who had originally opposed the loan and its conditions, reluctantly joined the rest of the Cabinet in December 1976 in supporting the IMF package out of fear both for the currency and for Party unity if the advice of the Prime Minister and Chancellor were to be repudiated. Yet Crosland remained convinced, as Benn later recorded, that the loan and its conditions were 'wrong economically and socially destructive of what he had believed in all his life'.[54]

While the recession of 1975–6 had the effect of completing the Government's dismantlement of the left's economic strategy, it also served, paradoxically, to extend left-wing influence within the Party and to push the social-democratic right on to the defensive, both politically and ideologically. In the first place, the Government's conduct provoked a further policy shift to the left in the form of *Labour's Programme 1976*, a document which proposed the extension of public ownership into banking, insurance and leading companies in every key sector of industry. Reaffirming the Bennite transformative aim of achieving 'a fundamental and irreversible shift in the balance of wealth and power', the policy statement was overwhelmingly backed by the 1976 Party Conference. That support was itself based on the widespread belief on the left, reinforced by political developments since 1975, that only through radical policy and constitutional changes within the Party could Labour rediscover its socialist purpose. As Benn declared at the 1976 Conference, 'we are also paying a heavy political price for 20 years in which, as a party, we have played down our criticism of capitalism and soft-pedalled our advocacy of socialism'.[55]

In furtherance of this restored policy initiative, the left also retained and even increased its leverage through its continuing predominance on Labour's main policy-making bodies, the NEC and the Annual Conference. Indeed, when the Chancellor of the Exchequer, Denis Healey, was voted off the NEC in 1976, the left's majority presence on that body was strengthened, while on its powerful Home Policy Committee Tony Benn, its chairman since 1974, continued to exert a major influence.

In broader terms, too, the Labour Government's economic difficulties for many observers signified an underlying crisis affecting the ideological position which the left rejected: revisionist social democracy itself, with its Keynesian economic foundation. For the acute economic problems of the mid-1970s, comprising a lethal combination of rapid inflation, high unemployment and sterling depreciation, appeared to undermine the viability of social democracy, resting as it did on its Keynesian strategy for maintaining full employment and promoting economic growth.

The resulting loss of confidence in Keynesian demand management even led to what amounted to a formal repudiation of Keynesianism itself by the Labour leadership when at the 1976 Party Conference James Callaghan, Wilson's successor as Prime Minister, stated:

> We used to think that you could spend your way out of a recession and increase employment by cutting taxes and boosting government spending. I tell you in all candour that that option no longer exists, and in so far as it ever did exist, it only worked on each occasion since the war by injecting a bigger dose of inflation into the economy, followed by a higher level of unemployment as the next step.[56]

But along with that highly significant retreat came a loss of commitment to the social-democratic project for which Keynesianism had provided the economic cornerstone. For while the Callaghan Government seemed unable or unwilling after 1976 to stimulate economic recovery through Keynesian economic techniques, it appeared equally unprepared to adhere to the social-democratic strategy of promoting greater equality and welfare provision through high social expenditure.

These changes gave rise to a period of ideological fragmentation within the Party between 1976 and 1979. The steady erosion of confident revisionist assumptions – both about effective economic management and rapid economic growth and about an advance towards egalitarian and welfarist goals by those means – in the face of acute economic problems had produced, in Minkin's phrase, 'a broad crisis of revisionist social democracy'.[57] As Peter Jenkins later observed, 'when the I.M.F. foreclosed on Britain, it foreclosed on Croslandism'.[58] Certainly the economic recession that had deepened since 1973, leading to the IMF crisis of 1976, had precluded the possibility of delivering either sustained economic growth or high levels of public expenditure, without which neither the redistribution of wealth and resources nor the promotion of social welfare, Crosland's most cherished aims, could be achieved.

To those on the left, meanwhile, these developments appeared to discredit not just Crosland's social-democratic goals but also his underlying theoretical analysis. In Anthony Arblaster's view, for example, the disappointment of so many of Crosland's expectations – of full employment and sustained economic growth, in particular – sprang from 'the wrongness of his analysis'.[59] For the three major claims which he had made in the 1950s about the transformation of capitalism in Britain had all been invalidated, Arblaster argued, by economic developments over the past twenty-five years.

In the first place, as the experience of Labour Governments in the 1960s and 1970s had indicated, the power of private industry remained 'far greater than Crosland was ever willing to admit', while 'the power of the state to control capitalism' was 'correspondingly far less than he supposed'.[60] Second, the increased power of the trade unions, which Crosland had also stressed in his analysis, 'far from being an accepted feature of British political and industrial life', had since the late 1960s become 'the focus of acute strains and open conflicts between the unions and the state'.[61] Finally, Crosland's emphasis on internal structural changes within private industry, involving the increasing divorce of ownership and control, had both greatly exaggerated that trend and misrepresented the nature of the pursuit of profit in contemporary capitalism. In reality the profit motive was still 'a corporate institutional necessity which imposes itself willy-nilly on individual managers, no matter how humane and non-acquisitive they may (or may not) be'.[62]

The failure, therefore, of the revisionist hopes and expectations which Crosland and other revisionists had fostered in the 1950s was, Arblaster concluded, 'not simply an error in prediction, like an inaccurate weather forecast', but rather 'the logical product of a fundamentally wrong, and over-sanguine, account of the supposed transformation of British capitalism into a system more stable, more humane and enlightened, more rational and controlled'.[63]

By the autumn of 1977, this left-wing commentator was even asking whether Crosland, who had died in February of that year, was really

'Labour's last revisionist'. For while Croslandite revisionism, 'with all its faults', had at least offered 'a clear and distinctive conception of socialism (essentially in terms of equality), together with a clear and coherent strategy for achieving it', to which Crosland had remained 'explicitly committed', Labour Governments since 1964 had not been operating 'with any coherent strategy, or socialist aims of any kind, whether revisionist or radical'.[64] By 1977, Arblaster maintained, Labour in power had in fact abandoned the revisionist strategy of the pursuit of greater equality through economic growth and high public expenditure. In the light of that retreat, did Labour any longer represent 'even the most limited kind of social democratic gradualism?' Meanwhile, he suggested, Crosland's survivors, with 'no alternative strategy to offer', showed 'little sign of realising that the strategy which he consistently advocated has already failed'.[65]

Arblaster's critique concisely summarized the principal objections levelled at that time by left-wing opponents of Croslandite social democracy, focusing both on its analysis of the changed pattern of economic power in Britain and on the political strategy based on that analysis. While that left-wing critique was itself flawed at various points – notably in its assertions about the power of private enterprise in Britain during the 1970s and about the intellectual limitations of Crosland's followers – it did at least underline the predicament of revisionist social democracy during this period, which was evident at both intellectual and practical political levels. Theoretically, as we have seen, Crosland had confined his efforts mainly to a defence of his revisionist thesis in the face of left-wing criticism that focused on the implications of the growing concentration of private industry. His conspicuous inability after 1974, arising from the pressures of office, to go beyond that defence and to revise his own analysis so as to address the economic and industrial problems of the 1970s was aggravated by a growing distance from his revisionist colleagues, particularly Jenkins and his pro-European supporters.[66] That personal tension was symbolized by Crosland's increasing use of the term 'democratic socialist' to describe his own position and by his disdainful references to a 'social democrat' as 'somebody about to join the Tory Party'.[67]

Furthermore, the intellectual malaise of Croslandite social democracy deepened as a result of the diverting prominence of the European issue, the demise of Keynesian economics in the face of rising unemployment and cutbacks in public spending, and the subsequent discrediting, in the eyes of its critics, of the revisionist strategy built on that Keynesian foundation.

In the light of this theoretical stagnation, revisionist social democracy seemed by the mid-1970s to have lost much of its intellectual and political coherence and appeal. Its continuing decline within the Party became even more apparent, politically and intellectually, with the departure from the Government of Roy Jenkins, following his disappointing performance in the 1976 Party leadership contest, to become President of the European Commission, and with the deaths of Crosland in 1977 and John Mackintosh in 1978. The declining intellectual influence of the social-democratic position was starkly illustrated, too, by the demise of *Socialist Commentary*, once the leading revisionist journal, in December 1978. Its last editor, Peter Stephenson, concluded his final comments by expressing his concern that 'those who share the Manifesto Group position ... find it much easier to define themselves in terms of their difference from the simplifications of the left than putting forward their own inevitably complex positive policies of democratic socialism'.[68]

By that time, in the depth of the Winter of Discontent, the strains of office to which Labour Governments had been subjected between 1974 and 1979, induced by the economic stagnation, sterling crises and bitter industrial disputes of those years, appeared to have undermined the major assumptions of Croslandite social democracy – both about the attainability of rapid economic growth and about the capacity of the central state for promoting that growth and, with it, desired social policy objectives.

IV

By the late 1970s, some social-democratic politicians and thinkers, recognizing the significance of those developments, were beginning to reappraise and restate the principles of social democracy in the light of the experiences of Labour in office. In 1977 John Mackintosh, for example, contended that the shortcomings of revisionism lay in its lack of a coherent economic theory for a mixed economy which could stimulate growth within it. Instead of Labour's 'outmoded obsession' with public ownership, which ought really to be 'judged as a technique and must be rejected if it is less effective than other techniques',[69] he argued that the Party's 'first task' was 'to evolve criteria for running a successful mixed economy where both the public and the private sectors feel they are useful'.[70] Indeed, Labour, in his view, needed to mount 'a positive theoretical defence of such a system on grounds of freedom and of economic performance' instead of viewing it 'simply as a stage on the road back to full public ownership'.[71]

Mackintosh even developed this point by advancing in 1977 the case for a realignment of the left in British politics in order 'to produce a major left-of-centre party which would be tied neither to Marxist dogma nor to the trade unions'.[72] Free of such ideological and institutional ties, he believed, a realigned party of that kind would bring to an end Labour's long-standing doctrinal 'ambivalence over the value of a mixed economy'.[73] For the truth was that Labour had never fully decided 'whether a mixed economy is desirable in itself or is a stage on the road to a better, alternative system'.[74] Nor had the Party 'decided whether the private sector is to be encouraged as a major source of growth and as an essential way of maintaining competition and free choice or whether it is to be sat on, taxed, regulated, pushed and pulled till it drops dead'.[75]

From that standpoint, too, he rejected as 'quite misguided' the left-wing critique, developed by Holland, Arblaster and others, of Crosland's view of the power of the modern state in relation to private industry. In Mackintosh's view, 'the great weakness of Crosland's position was not that he underestimated the resilience of capitalism but that he overestimated it'.[76] He failed, that is, to foresee that the private sector might lose its internal dynamic and its capacity for expansion and investment in an unfavourable or even hostile economic and industrial climate.

Shortly before he died in 1978, Mackintosh also expressed his doubts about the effectiveness of the egalitarian programme – built around comprehensive education, redistributive taxation and high social expenditure – which Crosland's ideas had inspired and which Labour Governments had promoted. By the late 1970s it seemed clear to him 'that in some senses the programme was a failure'.[77] For while class divisions in Britain might have been slightly reduced, Crosland's 'ideal of a more egalitarian society' was 'not markedly nearer' to fulfilment.[78]

The principal reason for this failure lay in the programme's heavy reliance on Crosland's 'assumption, typical of the 1950s, that growth could and would continue unabated'.[79] Such growth, it had also been assumed, would in time be generated by a mixed economy with a vigorous and resilient private sector, something to which Labour had never been unequivocally committed. Crosland's programme had therefore proved 'too superficial' in so far as he had not realized 'the need for an underpinning of economic theory which justified and maintained a mixed economy'.[80] In addition, his egalitarian project had been overambitious since it had promoted a form of 'social engineering' – based mainly on social and fiscal policy measures

– which had proved beyond the means of Labour Governments since 1964. For the various aspects of British society which such measures had sought to alter, whether in education or industry or the distribution of wealth, appeared 'too entrenched to be open to quick political solutions'[81] offered by government policy or legislation.

Writing from the same ideological standpoint, David Marquand considered that his friend Mackintosh had thus raised 'many of the thorniest issues with which a revised and libertarian social democracy will have to deal'. He believed, too, that by the late 1970s Mackintosh was moving towards 'the full-scale reassessment of social-democratic political theory . . . which he was better qualified to produce than anyone else in British political or academic life'.[82]

In recognizing the need for that ideological revision, Marquand took a highly pessimistic view of the current prospects for social democrats within the Labour Party. When Mackintosh was first elected to Parliament in 1966, he recalled, 'revisionist social democracy appeared to be the wave of the future', with 'even the sluggish, unadventurous, rather anti-intellectual British Labour Party . . . taking the revisionist road, in fact, if not in form'.[83] Yet ten years later revisionist social democracy was, in his view, 'unmistakably on the defensive',[84] with the NEC and Party Conference under left-wing control since the early 1970s, and with social democrats losing 'battle after battle' in the mass Party outside Parliament.[85]

Under challenge, then, on its left from a revived fundamentalist socialism and under pressure on its right from the market-liberal doctrines of Thatcherite Conservatism, the Labour leadership had clung, Marquand argued, to an outdated, bureaucratic form of social democracy instead of revising its ideological assumptions and 'developing a new and more libertarian version' of them.[86] Labour Governments of the 1960s and 1970s had been more concerned with extending the frontiers of the central state and expanding corporate power than with decentralizing decision-making. The steel, shipbuilding and aircraft industries, for instance, had been nationalized, 'in the old, bureaucratic Morrisonian way';[87] a panoply of Boards, Commissions and Corporations had been set up; and the power of the trade union establishment had been enlarged. Yet no progress had been made in the direction of constitutional reform by removing secrecy in government or by increasing parliamentary scrutiny of the executive. Nor had there been any serious attempt to decentralize economic power by, for example, making nationalized industries more responsive to consumers or by encouraging workers' participation in the running of industry.

In trying to explain those shortcomings, Marquand identified as one of the main historical causes of the decline of social democracy the dominant influence of the Fabian element in its intellectual inheritance. For while the decentralist New Liberal influence had been largely neglected over the years, the pervasive Fabian impact on social democracy had in practice degenerated into a centralist, bureaucratic form of social engineering.[88]

While describing the fading political and ideological allure of social democracy, Marquand underlined, too, the defensive posture of social democrats within a Party that had become increasingly left-wing in its composition, proletarian in its ethos and image, and anti-intellectual in its instincts. Echoing views expressed five years earlier by the former Labour MP Dick Taverne,[89] he concluded gloomily that he did not believe 'that the job of revising welfare-state social democracy can be done within the formal framework of the Labour Party or that active Labour politicians can contribute much to it'.[90]

In that same 1979 essay Marquand stressed the need for working out the purposes of 'a new-model libertarian decentralist social democracy'.[91] In reality, however, he and other like-minded social democrats within the Party, notably Mackintosh and Evan Luard,[92] were more concerned with developing a critique of the centralist and corporatist tendencies inherent in the state socialism to which Labour then appeared committed. Little systematic attempt was made by them or others to revise Croslandite social democracy to meet the changed economic and political circumstances of the late 1970s.

The increasingly marginalized position of social democrats within the Party at this time was even more starkly exposed after Labour's election defeat in 1979, which heralded a phase of factional 'civil war' and, with it, a sharp and dangerous polarization of policy and ideological positions. This period of bitter conflict arose, in the first place, from what Minkin has described as 'an unprecedented internal schism over Party democracy . . . unlike anything known before in Labour Party history',[93] which convulsed the Labour Movement between 1979 and 1983. After 1979 the debate within the Party centred not just around policy issues but also around the redistribution of power within the Party, with the left advocating constitutional changes designed to ensure that the parliamentary party and leadership should be accountable to the Party Conference and hence to the rank and file. The pressures for such changes, which had been instigated in 1973 by the Campaign for Labour Party Democracy, were coordinated after 1980 by the left-wing umbrella grouping the Rank and File Mobilising Committee, with Benn as its leading standard-bearer. Its efforts culminated in the acceptance by the Party Conference in 1979 of the principle of mandatory reselection procedures for sitting MPs and in 1980 of plans for a new electoral college for electing the Party leader, eventually established in 1981.

The effectiveness of this left-wing campaign was also underpinned by a leftward lurch in Party policy. Indeed, these two developments were interconnected since the left's demands for constitutional changes did not rest merely on arguments for intra-Party democracy. They were also fuelled by a desire to reduce the independence of the parliamentary party and, specifically, to curtail its control over the implementation of Party policy. For the left's shift of emphasis after 1979 on to organizational and constitutional concerns had itself arisen from its disillusioned experience of the conduct of the 1974–9 Labour Governments, which had either diluted or discarded approved Party policies.

With the left, then, in the ascendancy as a result of the constitutional changes of 1979–81, increasingly influential in constituency parties, and maintaining a presence in the unions 'unknown in any previous period of Labour-in-Opposition',[94] it had also by 1980 secured major policy victories with Conference support for commitments to unilateral nuclear disarmament, unconditional withdrawal from the EC and an Alternative Economic Strategy involving a substantial extension of public ownership and control.

These policy commitments, enshrined in the 1980 NEC document *Peace, Jobs and Freedom*, carried a stage further proposals made by left-wing pressure groups within the Party, notably, the Labour Co-ordinating Committee, founded in 1978 and chaired by Benn's close colleague Michael Meacher. In particular, the Alternative Economic Strategy restated the major proposals of Labour's *Programmes* of 1973 and 1976, including planning agreements with individual companies, a more vigorous National Enterprise Board as a vehicle for state holdings in private industry, public ownership in certain key sectors and restrictions on imports.

This development and adoption of overtly left-wing policies after 1979 eventually produced the wide-ranging NEC policy statement *Labour's Programme 1982*, which argued in fundamentalist terms that 'our social and economic objectives can be achieved only through an expansion of common ownership substantial enough to give the community decisive power over the commanding heights of the economy'.[95] In practical terms that meant restoring to public ownership all privatized industries as well as extending public ownership into new fields such as electronics and pharmaceuticals.

Labour's Programme 1982 was in turn translated, almost in its entirety, into the Party's 1983 General Election manifesto, *A New Hope for Britain*, which therefore contained commitments to a national economic strategy built upon large-scale public ownership and control and direct state planning, to unilateral nuclear disarmament and to withdrawal from the European Community. The manifesto was in those respects 'a thoroughly Bennite document'[96] and marked the culmination of the left's ascendancy since 1979, as exemplified by the constitutional changes and policy victories which it had secured, as well as by Foot's election as Party leader in 1980.

In the struggle for power, therefore, within the Party which erupted after 1979 the left appeared by 1983 clearly to have gained the upper hand. This was evident even though Benn's own influence, while still considerable, was on the wane following his narrow defeat by Healey in the acrimonious deputy leadership contest of 1981, after which the left itself became increasingly fragmented.

The reasons for the left-wing backlash, more severe than after 1970, which had produced this shift of power lay, above all, in the widespread disillusionment with the record of Labour Governments between 1974 and 1979. Indeed, the left's most serious charge against the Parliamentary leadership, that it had 'betrayed socialism' during those years, was a recurrent theme underlying demands for both policy and constitutional changes after 1979. But the move to the left derived its force from other factors, too – notably, the increasing influence of a radical and youthful activist middle-class membership, well represented in left-wing pressure groups within the Party, and the continuing appeal of the left's alternative strategy and programme.

In the face of these forces of change the social-democratic right was driven on to the defensive in Labour's 'civil war' after 1979. Unable to revise their ideological stance in a rigorous manner, in spite of the endeavours of Mackintosh and Marquand, social democrats concentrated largely on resisting the left's constitutional proposals, whilst in effect conceding defeat on major policy issues such as Europe, defence and economic strategy.

From this beleaguered position, leading social-democratic MPs David Owen, Shirley Williams and Bill Rodgers – the so-called 'Gang of Three' – warned in August 1980 that a 'new democratic socialist party . . . of conscience and reform' might even become desirable if Labour were to abandon 'its democratic and internationalist principles'.[97] They and twenty-five other Labour MPs eventually joined Roy Jenkins, together with former Labour politicians and influential social-democratic thinkers such as Marquand, Luard and Taverne, in founding the Social Democratic Party (SDP) in March 1981.

The loyalist group of social-democratic MPs, meanwhile, whose most prominent members included Denis Healey, Roy Hattersley and John Smith, continued to fight a rearguard action under the organizational banner of the group Labour Solidarity. Their main concerns were to counter the influence of the Bennite left and to restore the damaged credibility of Labour's centre-right in the wake of the defections to the SDP.

By 1981, then, with Labour's social democrats fragmenting into these loyalist and secessionist factions in the most serious Party split for fifty years, the Party's retreat from the revisionist positions of the 1950s and 1960s had been clearly signalled. Two years later, with Labour suffering its worst election defeat, in terms of its share of the popular vote, since 1918, the wider, destructive effects of its factional 'civil war', which had produced that split, were underlined even more glaringly and painfully.

6 Revisionism reborn? 1983–92

I

In the wake of Labour's electoral debacle of 1983, Neil Kinnock rapidly succeeded Michael Foot as the Party's new leader, after securing a clear majority in its electoral college. Although he had established his political reputation as an articulate left-wing critic of the Wilson and Callaghan Governments between 1974 and 1979, Kinnock was by 1983 drawing broadly based support within the Party – from both its soft left and its centre. This was a vital factor underlying his election as leader.

His inheritance seemed at first to be a dismal one, consisting of 'a badly-divided and demoralised Party permeated with intense suspicion of the leadership, and a programme that had been decisively repudiated by the electorate'.[1] In such unfavourable circumstances, therefore, he was convinced, as he later recalled, that 'there would have to be profound changes in the policies and in the organisation of the Labour Party – not simply as ends in themselves but also as contributions to a change in the mentality of the Labour Party'.[2] Those changes were essential, he believed, if Labour was to broaden its electoral appeal and win political power again.

Among the policies which Kinnock thought should consequently be altered were those concerning the European Community, nuclear defence and the 'general policy on nationalisation'.[3] He did not, however, immediately make 'major forays into changing policies', holding back, as he has recalled, for two reasons. First, any attempt to institute major policy changes would have been doomed 'without long preparation and a variety of actions to push and persuade people and organisations into changed positions'.[4] For internal party constraints at first prevented any radical policy innovations during this period, though partial but signficiant policy shifts were to occur in relation both to the European Community and to economic and industrial strategy. Kinnock himself was later to regret not having secured more radical changes at an earlier stage of his leadership.[5] In retrospect, however, he considered that 'if you make the change at a speed that is not agreed or acceptable to the Labour movement, then you smash into the wall of the block vote or uproar in the constituencies'.[6] With regard, therefore, to the current state of Party opinion at that time, he was continually aware of 'what I've described as the tanker problem: if you turn a tanker around too fast, you break it in half'.[7]

A second reason for proceeding with caution after 1983 was the fact that there was no tradition or institutional means within the Party for the Shadow Cabinet or Parliamentary Labour Party to instigate such changes. In addition, the National Executive Committee in 1983 was a body 'with a slight majority against the Leadership on most issues which involved a significant alteration in the policy and constitutional position of the Party'.[8]

Those political realities therefore impressed on Kinnock the need to pursue policy and organizational changes 'by very thorough and calculated means' and to avoid any 'direct challenges to established policy'.[9] Part of that elaborate, long-term process of change would involve overcoming that element within the Party which had, in Kinnock's words, 'treated realism as treachery . . . and scorned any emphasis on the importance of winning elections as a contaminating bacillus called "electorism"'.[10] Specifically, that meant combating the influence of the Bennite hard left – a task made easier both by Benn's defeat in the 1981 deputy leadership contest and by the blame widely attached to the hard left for Labour's crushing 1983 Election defeat.

Kinnock's movement for internal Party reform was, however, largely subordinated for the next two years to other concerns as Labour lived 'in the ideological shadow of the miners' strike and the local government problems of Liverpool'.[11] It was hardly surprising, therefore, that his cautious reformist efforts during that period were not accompanied by any obvious desire to revise central aspects of Labour's socialist strategy.

Nevertheless, there were indications of a growing revisionism in at least one ideologically crucial area: his attitude towards a market-oriented mixed economy. This was evident in an interview with the historian Eric Hobsbawm a year after Kinnock had been elected Party leader. At first he appeared here to maintain the fundamentalist stance on the role of public ownership which he had taken throughout the 1970s, insisting that 'As far as the "commanding heights" are concerned, we are committed to the process of re-nationalisation and that must proceed'.[12] As far as he himself was concerned, that was both an 'ideological commitment' on his part, one that was 'basic to my view of democratic socialism', and at the same time 'the only means . . . to give coherence to the most efficient organisation of our resources'.[13]

He revealed, however, an important modification of that traditionalist attitude by maintaining that 'To pose stark alternatives of the public economy and the market economy is a supreme folly . . . the one of which Mrs Thatcher is most guilty'.[14] Instead, he took the pragmatic view that it was necessary 'to find the system of stimulation and encouragement, the climate of enterprise' most conductive to meeting Labour's domestic and international obligations. That would involve 'deliberate encouragement for the small businesses and for co-operatives'.[15]

It was significant that Kinnock should make these ideologically contentious remarks in an interview with Eric Hobsbawm. For his thinking on Labour's strategy had already been reinforced by Hobsbawm's controversial lecture, *The Forward March of Labour Halted* and subsequent article, *Labour's Lost Millions*.[16] In those writings Hobsbawm had provided an analysis of a thirty-year-long process of decline in the British Labour movement, focusing on socioeconomic and political developments such as the numerical decline of the manual working class and the long-term fall in Labour voting support and membership. He had examined, too, major changes within capitalism since 1945 – among them, technological advances, improved working-class living standards and the increased size of the public sector.

Kinnock made no attempt to reproduce or develop Hobsbawm's analysis in his own writings and speeches. Yet his similar process of rethinking was carried a stage further in 1985 – the year in which Kinnock mounted a direct attack on Militant at the Party Conference, and in which the miners' strike was at last defeated – with his Fabian lecture on *The Future of Socialism*.[17] Here again he started from a traditional socialist premise. 'Britain', he declared, 'obviously remains a capitalist country with a society that is competitive without being meritocratic', and in which 'the combined inefficiencies and injusticies of the system still cause "moral revolt" to be a main chord in the tone of British socialism'.[18] As a remedy for those ills he championed the 'third way' of democratic socialism, a philosophy 'separate and distinct from the stale vanguardism of the ultra-left and from the atavistic and timid premise of social democracy'.[19]

But the 'harsh electoral reality', he stressed, was that Labour needed to broaden its appeal and hence its electoral base. The party could not rely 'merely on a combination of the dispossessed, the "traditional" and increasingly figmentary working class and minority groups for the winning of power'.[20] If Labour was to form a government, it had 'to relate to and draw support from the modern working classes whose upward social mobility, increased expectations and extended horizons are largely the result of opportunities afforded them by our movement in the past'.[21]

Labour's adjustment to those social changes would require, Kinnock argued, 'a shift in attitudes and presentation, not a change in principles'.[22] The party needed to re-emphasize the ethical character of its socialist heritage, to 're-assert democratic socialism as an effective body of values for modern needs rather than the ghost from the past'.[23] For it was those values – of fellowship, community and individual freedom – which underlay Labour's great achievements of collective provision, such as the creation of the National Health Service, the building of public-sector housing and the development of comprehensive education.

Moreover, an awareness of social and cultural trends in the mid-1980s, not least of 'upward social mobility' and 'increased expectations', led Kinnock to insist that 'there is no essential contradiction between collective provision and individual freedom'.[24] Indeed, historically collective provision had 'not been the enemy of individual freedom', but rather 'the agent of individual emancipation' and 'for that reason' would occupy 'a central position in the forging of the future of socialism'.[25] For 'individual freedom' was 'the objective, past, present and future of democratic socialism'[26]

Kinnock did not, however, develop this ethical approach to socialism into overtly revisionist conclusions. For, unlike Crosland or Gaitskell in the 1950s, he did not at this stage openly argue that socialist values could be effectively promoted within the framework of a market-oriented mixed economy. Instead, he still dissociated himself from that revisionist position by insisting on the unique ideological importance of 'that economic and social analysis which democratic socialism brings to the structural economic and social problems of capitalism'.[27] He thus did not appear to believe, unlike Crosland or Gaitskell, that socialist ideals and values could be separated from the supporting framework of a socialist economic analysis or from the programmatic implications of such an analysis.

For Kinnock, therefore, democratic socialism differed radically from the social-democratic position which Labour revisionists had to a large extent established within the Party. For he maintained that

> The essence of social democracy is that it is not concerned with the structure of property ownership, or the transfer of economic power; it is defined in terms not of social change, but social relief, not of eradicating inequality, but relieving its most gross manifestations.[28]

Social democracy was thus concerned, he argued, with mitigating social conditions 'without confronting the system which creates distress in the first place'.[29] Such complacency might, he conceded, have been credible during the 1950s. For the period of the post-war consensus – characterized by near-full employment, increased production and rising consumer spending – seemed to legitimize the revisionist assumption that economic growth would provide the means of reducing economic and social inequalities and promoting social welfare. But 'when that climate changed and the political consensus appeared to move to the right, so too', claimed Kinnock, 'did the social democrats', who then 'gave up on equality which they had previously espoused as the main credential of their "radicalism"'.[30]

It was clear, then, that Kinnock's readiness to explore ways in which Labour might widen its appeal by changing its attitudes did not yet extend to a desire to re-examine the traditional socialist analysis that underlay the democratic socialist values which he so ardently espoused.

He did, however, distance himself clearly from the centralist and bureaucratic tendencies inherent in Fabian state socialism. 'We do not believe', he stressed, 'in the centralisation of power in the hands of unaccountable bureaucracies'.[31] In support of that belief he cited the authority of such leading figures in the British socialist pantheon as Robert Owen and William Morris, in whose writings one would 'search in vain for the autocratic or state dominated vision of socialism'.[32] Instead of the model of a centralized, bureaucratic state, Kinnock commended to democratic socialists 'the state as community – the state as an enabling power – the idea of collective and purposive action'.[33]

This idea of an enabling state was itself inseparable from the ideal of positive freedom, of the self-development and wider opportunity of the individual. For the democratic state which Kinnock favoured was one that involved, as he told the 1985 Party Conference, ' . . . the collective contribution of the community for the purpose of individual liberty throughout the community'.[34] This was a significant emphasis because, in spite of his repudiation of social democracy and its revisionist precursors, those interrelated ideas – positive freedom and an enabling state – which could themselves be traced back to the social liberalism of both T. H. Green and the Edwardian New Liberals, formed the intellectual basis of the movement away from traditional socialist positions that Kinnock was to complete after 1987.

By 1986 that movement was anticipated with the publication of the Party policy statement *Social Ownership*. Defending its proposals at the 1986 Party Conference, Kinnock underlined both Labour's opposition to old-style Morrisonian nationalization and its support for diverse, wider forms of social ownership, ranging from 'small co-operatives to municipal enterprises and right through to the major utility corporations like British Telecom'.[35]

The document's publication had in fact coincided with the first stage of the Conservative Government's privatization of the public utilities, beginning with British Telecom and proceeding to British Gas. *Social Ownership* reaffirmed Labour's existing commitment to renationalize those industries, whilst declaring, too, that the next Labour government would 'embark upon an ambitious programme to move towards wider social ownership'.[36] To that end it revived, in particular, the idea of a state holding company in its new guise of British Enterprise, designed to acquire shares or to establish new companies in nationally important industries such as aerospace, steel and information technology.

This emphasis on more flexible forms of social ownership in preference to outright nationalization was supplemented by the increasingly pragmatic approach to Labour's economic and industrial strategy which Kinnock revealed in his book *Making Our Way*, published in 1986. Here, as part of an overall strategy of extending 'public involvement in the British economy', he advocated 'a plural public sector' embracing not only 'social ownership of national assets . . . of sectors of activity where there are natural or technical monopolies',[37] but also a growing number of regional, metropolitan and local enterprise boards and cooperative enterprises.[38]

The ideological justification for these varied forms of social ownership was that they would serve as necessary means of securing public and democratic control of the economy so as to promote the enduring ethical ends of democratic socialism: namely, 'the freedom and dignity of the individual' and 'the construction of a society which is compassionate and fair'.[39]

Making Our Way also signalled an important shift in Kinnock's thinking towards qualified support for a managed, reformed capitalism. Noting that the institutions and prócedures established since 1945 for 'managing the market' had laid the foundations of '25 years of remarkable prosperity' throughout the West, he regretted that those procedures had been neither developed nor adapted.[40] Yet democratic socalism could, he believed, carry the benefits of 'managing the market' a stage further. He thus advocated, in contrast to his previous, more fundamentalist pronouncements,[41] what had been a characteristic approach of Keynesian social democracy, that is, 'social control of the market' in order to 'maintain the efficient operation of that highly complex, interdependent system, the modern economy'.[42]

Moreover, Kinnock was now prepared to acknowledge openly the benefits of a market economy, pointing out that 'the market is potentially a powerful force for good. It can be a remarkable coordinating mechanism. [It] can stimulate innovation and productive efficiency, and provide an economic environment in which individuals can experiment'.[43] Labour's eventual acceptance in 1986 of this more flexible and market-oriented 'social ownership' strategy in place of further nationalization and renationalization commitments was later cited by Kinnock as evidence in support of the 'calculated approach' to the process of changing Party policy which he had adopted in 1984.[44] More broadly, he considered that during his 'first innings' as party leader – from 1983 to 1987 – 'some progress had been made in securing new policies and, increasingly, some changes were taking place in the "mindset" of the party', a process made easier by his having at last obtained by 1986 'a steady majority' for his 'view on crucial issues' on the party's central policy-forming body, the National Executive Committee.[45]

However, the ideological significance of those changes in policy and attitude was not yet clear by 1987. That much was apparent in Labour's General Election manifesto, *Britain Will Win*. The document either jettisoned or scaled down the left-wing proposals of 1983 – the Alternative Economic Strategy, the commitment to withdraw from the European Community, the pledges to extend public ownership, renationalize privatized assets and massively increase public expenditure. In their place, it proposed such measures as an Industrial Investment Bank; the 'social ownership', rather than renationalization, of major utilities; and new state-sponsored industries.

But the compromises and ambiguity inherent in the 1987 manifesto reflected the fact that between 1983 and 1987 Labour's policy changes had been tentative and piecemeal. In 1987, therefore, it was still uncertain to what extent those limited changes signified a corresponding ideological shift from traditional state socialism to some variant of European social democracy.

II

An ideological change of that kind soon, however, became apparent after Labour's 1987 Election defeat when Kinnock set a two-year deadline for a wide-ranging Policy Review. The results of that process were evident, first, in the interim *Statement of Democratic Socialist Aims and Values* (largely written by Deputy Leader Roy Hattersley with editoral assistance from Kinnock and published in 1988) and, eventually in the final Policy Review documents, passed at the 1989 Party Conference and synthesized in the policy statement, *Meet the Challenge, Make the Change.*

The Policy Review was, above all, a response to Labour's conspicuous electoral failure since 1979 and formed a central part of the attempt to widen the Party's appeal by abandoning electorally unpopular policies such as nationalization, high taxation and nuclear unilateralism.

The Review was therefore also prompted by the electoral success of Thatcherism and by its impact on British politics, evident both in its reshaping of the political agenda and in the institutional and political changes that it had brought about. More broadly, the Review was a policy response to the social and economic changes – many of them promoted by the Thatcher Governments – that had occurred in Britain in the 1980s: the decline of manufacturing industry, the shrinking size of the industrial working class, changes in occupational structure, the increase in the private sector and the spread of home ownership.

Furthermore, in terms of the Party's internal debate, the Policy Review can be seen, as Martin Smith has observed, as a reaction to Labour's 'ideological failings',[46] to both the decline of Keynesian social democracy and the failure of the left-wing state socialism that had dominated Party policy-making from 1970 to 1983. The latter's defects had appeared to be starkly illustrated at home by the electoral defeat of 1983 and abroad by Mitterand's abortive socialist experiment of 1981–3 in France.

Shaped by these factors, therefore, Labour's Policy Review was an attempt to 'develop policies that did not repeat the mistakes of the 1970s and which would be more popular than those of the 1980s'.[47]

The degree to which it would thereby challenge traditional Labour thinking was revealed by Kinnock's comments at the 1987 Party Conference. The Review, he warned, would offend those who seemed 'to have "do not disturb" notices hung on their minds', those who described 'the very activity of examination . . . as a "betrayal of fundamental principles"'.[48] Yet the reality, in his view, was that 'after losing three general elections any serious political party that did not undertake the assessment, the review, the examination . . . would be betraying its principles and its policies and its people'.[49]

But the Policy Review, he stressed, was wholly consistent with Labour's socialist purposes. It would seek 'to develop the means to further the ends of democratic socialism . . . the commitments to community, democracy and justice. And to real individual liberty'.[50] To that reaffirmation of socialist principle, however, he added a cautious and balanced, yet ideologically significant, reference to the strengths and weaknesses of the market economy. Labour's form of socialism, he stated, recognized

> that whilst the market is an adequate system for deciding the price and availability of many goods and services, the market has not been, and will never be, an adequate mechanism for deciding upon the supply or the quality of health care and education and so much that is fundamental to a decent life.[51]

Kinnock also sought to justify the Policy Review in terms of the realistic nature of democratic socialism. Its values, he insisted, were 'living purposes', not 'declarations, icons or holy relics'; they were there 'to be put into practice, not into storage'.[52] It was therefore essential to relate those values and purposes 'to the realities of our condition – and not to where we would like to be, or to some imagined environment that has yet to be created'.[53] Such realities included the social and economic changes that had taken place in the 1980s – the increase in home ownership, wider share-ownership, the shift in the pattern of work from mass-production manufacturing to high-tech custom production, and so on. They were 'the realities of a changing economy, a changing society, and . . . a changing electorate, too'.[54]

There was a striking resembalance between Kinnock's emphasis here – on the need for Labour to adapt to social change and to stress the living ethical purposes of its socialism rather than take a fixed view of some finite socialist goal – and the revisionist arguments advanced by Crosland thirty-one years earlier in *The Future of Socialism*. In support of his position Kinnock chose instead to quote

Bevan, his socialist mentor, who had warned of the danger of socialists becoming 'symbol worshippers', of their being imprisoned by 'old words' and categories used to describe social realities that had long since changed.[55]

The ideological basis for the re-examination of Labour's policies that Kinnock urged was provided by the 1988 *Statement of Democratic Socialist Aims and Values*. In tune with his fundamental ideals, the document stressed that the party's overriding aim, and indeed 'the true purpose of democratic socialism', was the 'creation of a genuinely free society . . . in which the fundamental objective of goverment is the protection and extension of individual liberty'.[56] But it also clearly confirmed the support for a market economy cautiously announced by Kinnock the previous year. 'In the case', it declared, 'of most . . . goods and services, the operation of the market, where properly regulated, is a generally satisfactory means of determining provision and consumption'.[57]

In his own book *Choose Freedom*, Roy Hattersley, the *Statement*'s main author, had already developed these ideological positions at greater length. 'Socialism', he had declared, 'exists to provide – for the largest number of people – the ability to exercise effective liberty'.[58] Tracing the historical roots of this viewpoint back through Tawney, Hobhouse and T. H. Green to the radical utilitarianism of John Stuart Mill,[59] Hattersley argued, in line with that tradition, both that liberty and equality were indissolubly linked and that the enabling, democratic state could be employed in pursuit of those twin ideals. Democratic socialism was thus, in his view, 'about an extension of freedom brought about by a more equal distribution of resources'.[60] It was a political ideology that also required 'the use of collective power to increase individual rights and to extend individual freedom'.[61] Its ultimate aim, therefore, was 'the real – as distinct from the theoretical – emancipation of previously powerless citizens'.[62]

With regard to the economic framework within which such socialist ends might be attained, Hattersley maintained that 'outside the area of natural monopoly, public utility and social service, markets are essential to any definition of socialism which includes the encourage-ment of diversity and individual liberty and the economic autonomy (public or private) that goes with those essential conditions'.[63]

In spite of its reiteration of firm support for a market economy, Hattersley's subsequent *Statement of Democratic Socialist Aims and Values* also clearly rejected Thatcherite views by underlining the limitations of the notion of an economically-based freedom of choice. 'Economic power and liberty', it maintained, 'are inextricably linked'.[64] Moreover, 'real freedom' for the individual could only be extended and sustained by 'co-operative action' and 'collective provision'.[65] The statement challenged market-liberal principles further by contending that a socialist government should intervene selectively in the market 'as a matter of conscious policy and for defined purposes' in order to 'monitor and regulate the market', thereby preventing 'market abuse and the unfair exploitation of market dominance'.[66]

Hattersley's statement, however revisionist in its open espousal of the market, made little political impact at the time. It was debated and approved without much controversy on the first morning of the 1988 Party Conference, 'disposed of before coffee time', as Hattersley later recalled, thereby allowing the Party 'to turn to the aspects of policy which we most enjoyed – not formulation but presentation'.[67]

When Kinnock came to defend once more the developing Policy Review at that 1988 Conference, he confronted the gravest doctrinal charge directed at it from the left: that Labour was now embracing the market and seeking to 'run capitalism better than the Tories'. In his most explicit endorsement to date of the market economy, he told Conference:

> the day may come when this conference, this movement, is faced with a choice of socialist economies. . . . But until that day comes, . . . the fact is that the kind of economy that we will be faced with when we win the election will be a market economy. That is what we have to deal with and we will have to make it work better than the Tories do.[68]

That realistic view was certainly reflected in the document that marked the completion of the Policy Review process. Published in 1989, *Meet the Challenge, Make the Change* both reaffirmed the fundamental socialist values stated a year earlier and set out the revised policies and strategy that a future Labour government would pursue. In his introduction to the document Kinnock confirmed that it 'starts from Labour's basic values – our commitment to individual freedom, to a more just and democratic society'.[69] The promotion of those values would require the deployment of 'a democratic and enabling state, at the disposal of the community'.[70]

The document also underlined Labour's abandonment of public ownership as a major instrument of Labour policy and socialist strategy. Indeed, Gamble has described the Policy Review as 'the most explicit rejection of the policy of expanding public ownership which the Party has ever made'.[71] For while it did not actually propose to repeal Clause IV of the Party Constitution, the Review, 'like Crosland', made it clear 'that the question of ownership has become irrelevant to the problems of managing the economy'.[72]

In justifying this major change, Kinnock pointed to the increasingly blurred dividing lines between the private and public sectors. 'In the past', he observed, 'much of the debate between Labour and Conservative parties centred on the boundaries' between them. But in present circumstances 'in many areas of economic activity … modern technology, modern markets, modern investment systems have dissolved the rigid boundaries'.[73] Moreover, in modern economies 'the success of the private sector depends in large part on public investment and involvement'.[74] The policy implications of such realities were a movement away from proposals either for renationalizing privatized companies or for major new extensions of public ownership and a consequent shift of emphasis to public regulation or control.

These important changes were underpinned in *Meet the Challenge, Make the Change* by a positive, if qualified, endorsement of the market economy. As Peter Kellner commented at the time: 'On the use of market mechanisms, the report comes within an inch of celebrating their use'.[75] The document recognized, for instance, that 'the market has a vital role to play', but added that 'it will not – left to itself – produce adequate investment in education and training, in science and technology, in new products and capacity'.[76] In similar vein, it described 'the free market' as 'possessing great strengths which must be utilised', yet considered it 'incapable of building unaided a strong and modern economy'.[77]

Moreover, the document clearly idenified what those strengths were, maintaining that

> in very many areas of the economy the market and competition are essential in meeting the demands of the consumer, promoting efficiency and stimulating innovation, and often the best means of securing all the myriad, incremental changes which are needed to take the economy forward.[78]

Kinnock, too, in his introduction endorsed this view, stating that 'private business can be the most efficient way of producing and distributing many goods and services – provided that government regulates commercial behaviour in the interests of the consumer, and restricts monopoly practices in the interests of competition'.[79] The 'economic role of modern government' was therefore 'to help the market system work properly where it can, will and should – and to replace or strengthen it where it can't, won't or shouldn't'.[80]

In spite of these qualifications and the consequent emphasis on the regulatory role of government, all this amounted to an acknowledgement of the merits of the market economy to a degree unprecedented in the historical development of Labour policy. As Kellner has noted, by 1989 'a subtle but vital shift in Labour's ideology had been completed. Instead of being a party which found the market guilty until proved innocent, it was now a party that regarded the market as innocent until found guilty'.[81] Crewe has even argued that what Labour was now proposing was 'not market socialism in which the state and planning agencies provide the main economic lever and markets are supplementary, but a social market economy in which the market is the motor of the economy and the state supplies the oil and does the tuning up'.[82]

Theoretical justification for this ideological shift had been provided not just by Hattersley but also by other Labour politicians and thinkers, such as Giles Radice and Bryan Gould. In his book *Labour's Path to Power: the New Revisionism*, Radice argued that, in order to demonstrate its credentials as 'a fully fledged revisionist party, capable of learning from the past, analysing the changing trends',[83] Labour ought 'to . . . have the honesty to come to terms with the market and admit that in many areas the competitive model, provided it is adequately regulated, works well in the allocation of goods and services'.[84] The Party should therefore, he believed, 'accept the role of markets in the economy not as an unfortunate necessity to be endured for a limited period but on principle'.[85]

Moreover, Bryan Gould, in his book *A Future for Socialism*, not only acknowledged and enumerated the advantages of the market economy[86] but also maintained that its acceptance by the Labour Party had ceased to be a meaningful issue of doctrinal controversy. For, as he pointed out, there was 'virtually no society in today's world that does not make some use of markets', since all modern large-scale economies make some use of the price mechanism, 'the essence of markets', as the means of allocating goods and services.[87] Debating the issue of whether socialists should accept or reject the market concept was therefore 'a ludicrous piece of self-delusion'.[88] The real question, he stressed, should be 'not whether or not the market, but where, how, and for what purposes?'.[89]

Defended in these unapologetic terms, the Policy Review's endorsement of the market economy did indeed represent, for all Gould's insouciance, a major, historic ideological shift as far as the

Party's official, public stance was concerned, even if it did not amount to a radical departure from the actual performance of previous Labour governments. None the less, the market-friendly Review did not simply offer a Thatcherite programme, since the 1989 document declined to embrace market-liberal principles. As we have seen, the narrow conception of economic freedom and the idea of an unregulated market economy were both firmly rejected. As Kinnock argued in his introduction, 'the market, left to itself, does not invest adequately in the education and training, the science, technology and research and development which a modern economy needs'.[90]

In place of those market-liberal principles, Labour and its leader stressed, therefore, the role of an interventionist, enabling state and hence the need for collective action and provision. The state, it was argued, should seek to intervene selectively in the market in order to remedy its imperfections as well as to reinforce its strengths. That meant active support for policy measures such as investment in training, infrastructure, research and development, and science and technology; for environmental regulation; and for public regulation of utilities and natural monopolies.

This agreed policy position concealed, however, a significant intra-Party debate in the early stages of the Policy Review. This was conducted between, on the one hand, an interventionist, neo-Keynesian school of thought led by Gould and, on the other, a more market-oriented approach favoured by Kinnock and his Shadow Chancellor John Smith.[91] Gould and his supporters advocated strategic intervention to regulate market activity in a concerted, long-term manner, whereas Kinnock and Smith proposed more selective, *ad hoc* intervention for specific purposes.

A balance between these rival viewpoints had been struck in *Meet the Challenge, Make the Change*. By the later stages of the Policy Review, however, the less interventionist approach, designed, above all, to promote market efficiency, had clearly prevailed, particularly after Gould had been replaced as industry spokesman in October 1989 by Gordon Brown. The role of the state in economic management was thereafter envisaged as an enabling one, performing tasks which the market was either unwilling or unable to accomplish. Moreover, the rationale underlying such intervention was to be partnership and cooperation between government and private industry, as later policy documents made clear.[92]

III

With its advocacy of this market-oriented, yet selectively interventionist, approach, did the culmination of the Policy Review
represent, then, for Labour a return to revisionist social democracy?
That certainly is the judgement of many commentators. Kellner,
for example, on the completion of the Review process, declared: 'If
it were not for the charged emotions that labels convey, Mr Kinnock
could now proudly proclaim Labour's conversion to social democracy'.[93] For 'a fundamental feature' of the Policy Review was 'its
wholesale abandonment of what we used to call socialism, when the
word was synonymous with state ownership of industry'.[94] Similarly,
Crewe, describing the Policy Review as 'the least socialist policy
statement ever to be published by the party', maintained that 'the
complaint of left-wingers that their party has jettisoned socialism for
social democracy is perfectly fair'.[95]

The outcome of this ideological transformation was, in Marquand's
view, that by 1989 a situation had been reached in which 'The Labour
Party was unmistakably another European social democratic party,
committed, like its continental sister parties, to further European
integration, continued membership of the Atlantic alliance and a
market-oriented mixed economy'.[96] 'Judged by results', therefore,
'Kinnock was now a better – or, at any rate, a more successful –
revisionist than Gaitskell had ever been'.[97]

This asssessment of the Policy Review's ideological significance
is supported by both general and specific considerations. First and
generally, Labour's Review, like the 1950s revisionism of Crosland
and Gaitskell, sought to reformulate socialist principles and to revise
Labour policies in the light of changed economic, social and political
conditions.

Second and specifically, there are clear similarities between
Crosland's revisionism and the main positions advanced in the Policy
Review. Both displayed an attitude towards public ownership that
was pragmatic, instrumental and to a large extent sceptical. Both
advocated, too, selective state intervention within a market-oriented
mixed economy for the purpose either of remedying the market's
deficiencies or of ensuring fairer or more efficient outcomes. Furthermore, both shared an underlying commitment to sustained economic
growth as the necessary basis for reducing social inequalities and
promoting social welfare.

There were, however, also some significant differences between the
revisionism of Crosland and Gaitskell and that of the Policy Review
and hence of Kinnock, its main instigator. First, the new rethinking

emerged without a Keynesian economic foundation. The Policy Review focused, after all, mainly on the strategy of 'supply-side socialism' – on the need for the state to intervene selectively on the supply side of the economy. It recognized, in the face of economic realities, both domestic and global, the limits to demand management and the need, too, for constraints on public expenditure and borrowing. In ideological terms, therefore, this stance could be regarded as promoting 'a post-Keynesian revisionism . . . for a different era which has learnt the lessons of the 1970s'.[98] Viewed in a harsher light, it could even be seen as heralding 'the abandonment of Keynesian social democracy in favour of pre-Keynesian orthodoxy'.[99]

That economic cautiousness evident in the Policy Review underlines a second difference of approach, for the radical egalitarianism which formed the main positive impulse behind Crosland's revisionism, and which largely depended on high public expenditure and sharply redistributive taxation, was diluted under Kinnock's leadership to suit the very different economic and political circumstances of the 1980s and 1990s. In this respect, it can be said that Labour's new outlook was 'a modernised, circumspect revisionism'.[100] In place of a commitment to full employment and to a growth-based redistribution of wealth and resources, it offered more modest, if arguably more realizable, objectives and aspirations and, as a consequence, lower expectations.

It has been argued, too, that Policy Review's constrained and measured approach stemmed from a third difference: its lack of a coherent theoretical basis. For, unlike the revisionism of Crosland, it was not rooted in a systematic analysis of social and economic developments over the last twenty years, even though its main proposals sprang from a recognition of those changes. The worst estimate of Kinnock's form of revisionism may therefore be, as Marquand has suggested, that it 'has been opinion-survey-driven' and 'not doctrine-driven'. Its strategic aim had thus been more 'to tailor a programme for a set of constituencies' than to provide 'a governing philosophy capable of guiding decision-makers through the unforeseeable contingencies of power'.[101]

Kinnock himself later acknowledged the force of this point, conceding that: 'A justifiable criticism could be that we were not sufficiently audacious and that there was no central philosophical theme to the exercise'.[102] He himself 'would have preferred greater boldness' and would have welcomed 'a neat and magnetic central theme for the work'.[103] Any public declaration on his part, however, that such a theme ought really to amount to nothing less than, in his own phrase, a radical 'Enterprise of Renewal' for the Party 'would have sent a repetitive electric shock through the Movement and allowed everyone to build their barricades of resistance'.[104] The Policy Review was designed, therefore, to offer 'a slice-by-slice approach'.[105] Kinnock was aware, too, of the awkward fact that 'as late as 1991 there was always a significant risk that any progressive lunge that was too big or too quick could have fractured the developing consensus and retarded the whole operation'.[106] Besides, the lack of a central philosophical theme could also be explained in terms of the primary importance which he constantly attached to the prize of electoral victory.[107]

IV

There is no question that under Neil Kinnock's leadership major changes were accomplished not just in the organizational structure of the Labour Party but also in its policy and doctrine. As part of his wider efforts to modernize the party and make it electable once more, from the mid-1980s he gradually and effectively guided it towards an essentially social-democratic programme that was pro-European, in support of collective security within the Atlantic Alliance and, most significant doctrinally, in favour of a market-oriented mixed economy.

Kinnock's achievement in ideological terms was to ensure for Labour a gradual transition from traditional state socialism to a variant of European social democracy – a task made easier both by the discrediting of state socialism in the 1980s and by the pressures of electoral politics as they affected his demoralized party. The ideological casualties of this process were, however, considerable. They included not just the traditional socialist nostrums of public ownership and central economic planning, but also major tenets of earlier Keynesian and Croslandite social democracy.

In spite of its disruptive implications for established socialist views, both traditional and revisionist, the ideological revision that Kinnock brought about was made easier, too, by his own immersion in the ethos of the Labour Party – in its characteristic values, traditions and practices, and in its distinctive culture and language.[108] It was that political asset, the fact that he was, in Peter Jenkins's words, 'at home in every twist and turn of the sub-culture of the Labour Movement',[109] which strengthened his hand in his struggle with the Bennite left after 1983 and in his attempts to change policies and attitudes in the Party as a whole after 1987.

But Kinnock's deep involvement in the insular world of the Labour movement may also have been an important reason why his re-fashioned form of democratic socialism failed to transmit itself with either conviction or appeal beyond Labour's core constituency to the wider society beyond. For perhaps, as Jeffreys has suggested, 'he was himself too much a product of 1970s-style Labourism to be able to escape its legacy without being accused of lacking consistency' and, partly because of that, 'was never quite able to make the leap between inspiring the party faithful and convincing the wider electorate'.[110]

Evidence of such uncertainty surrounding Kinnock's restyled and refurbished Party was amply provided by the result of the 1992 General Election. Against the background of a deep recession, and after entering the campaign with a sustained poll lead, Labour could still achieve a vote share of only 34.4 per cent (barely 3.6 per cent more than in 1987). The Conservatives under John Major were un-expectedly returned with a comfortable majority of twenty-one seats. Labour's decisive change of course after 1987, in terms of both policy and ideology, though demonstrably in line with current trends of public opinion, had yet to receive widespread popular recognition in the desired form of electoral success.

7 The triumph of revisionism?

Modernization under Smith and Blair

I

When John Smith succeeded Neil Kinnock as Party leader in July 1992, three months after Labour's fourth successive General Election defeat, it seemed clear that Kinnock's commitment to the modernization of the Party's policies and organization would be maintained. Smith's leadership indicated, too, that the process of ideological revision that had accompanied his predecessor's achievements would continue. The only doubts, expressed initially and subsequently, surrounding Smith's inheritance concerned the pace at which modernization would proceed and the manner in which ideological change would be promoted.

The main reason for such reservations lay in Smith's style of leadership. For in his approach to the divisions within the Party – between left and right and, since the late 1980s, between modernizers and traditionalists – he was above all a unifier. Indeed, many have concurred with Hugo Young's valedictory judgement that, in the Party's history, 'there has not been a less divisive leader, and none had fewer enemies', and that 'by comparison with Kinnock, Foot, Callaghan and Wilson, this leader's tragically shortened years were a time of tranquillity when the party members were finally prepared to let him get on with the job'.[1] Following Smith's sudden death in May 1994, Tony Benn, for example, recalled that the former leader had 'played a notable part in healing the personal breaches that had opened up during the Eighties' and had thus 'laid fresh foundations for the good will and co-operation between left and right that existed under Clem Attlee and Harold Wilson'.[2]

There were clearly substantial political benefits that flowed from this conciliatory approach to Labour's factional strife. By seeking to mediate in the debate between modernizers and traditionalists, Smith underlined the importance of the Party's painfully gained unity. The practical effect of his balanced attitude was that, without promoting the modernizers' cause as overtly as his predecessor had done, he nevertheless managed to extend the process of organizational change by establishing in October 1993 the principle of 'one member, one vote' for the selection of parliamentary candidates, thereby curbing the political power of the trade unions within the Party.

However, Smith's unifying approach, fostered by his deep roots in Scottish Labourism, also entailed a slackening in the pace of modernization that Kinnock had set since 1987. For, as some commentators have suggested, Smith's political style and background were such that 'he asked the party few awkward questions',[3] and that, 'nurtured in the collective culture of Scottish socialism, he failed to appreciate fully the urgency of reforming the party from top to bottom'.[4] Yet his persuasive political skills and Scottish socialist moorings were at the same time valuable assets during the difficult and protracted campaign to secure acceptance of the 'one member, one vote' principle in 1993.

With regard to the Party's ideological stance, Smith's inclination was to further Labour's gradual transition from traditional state socialism to a variant of European social democracy, a process that had been taking place since the Policy Review of the late 1980s. That ideological revision was entirely in harmony with Smith's own standpoint, which had remained consistently social-democratic. As a Labour MP since 1970 and as a minister in the Labour Governments of 1974–9, he had been a supporter of a mixed economy and an advocate of social improvement within its framework.

Moreover, Smith's social-democratic stance was rooted in a firm ethical, and specifically Christian, socialist base, as he made clear in his R. H. Tawney Memorial Lecture in March 1993.[5] For him the distinctive features of this ethical socialism were a belief in community and in the interdependence of individual freedom and collective action. As his socialist mentors, Tawney and William Temple, had both recognized, individual freedom was 'only meaningful and achievable within society' and, since 'human beings are naturally and incurably social, . . . freedom is best expressed in fellowship'.[6]

The moral basis, therefore, of this Christian socialism, bequeathed by Tawney, Temple and others, consisted of the overriding belief, which Smith reaffirmed 'with confidence and conviction', 'that the individual was best fulfilled in the context of a strong community, bound together in friendship'.[7] In 1994 Smith planned to publish a revised and secularized version of his lecture which would form a personal statement of democratic socialist values. His intention was then to offer his credo as a supplement to, rather than replacement of, Clause IV of the Party Constitution.[8] This move would help, he believed, to lower any residual tensions over Clause IV by demonstrating that it had in effect been superseded by his new statement, his own version of the 'New Testament' that Gaitskell had offered back in 1960.

This initiative on Clause IV, which was consistent with the gradualist and conciliatory style of Smith's leadership, contrasted with the more confrontational approach to that issue recommended during this period by two other leading Labour politicians. In March 1993 Jack Straw, Shadow Environment Secretary, had called, in his pamphlet *Policy and Ideology*, for a complete revision of Clause IV. Arguing that there was 'a disconnection between Labour's stated ideology and its approach to policy', he proposed that, 'there should be a recasting of the Party's objects in order to ensure that they relate directly to the circumstances, the challenges and the realities of life in the 20th and early 21st century'.[9] Such a move was necessary, Straw maintained, because Labour's ideology, its vision of society, as embodied in Clause IV, Part Four, had 'failed to keep pace not only with prosaic changes to Labour policy, but with more fundamental changes in Britain and in the world as a whole'.[10]

The only argument against what Straw called the 'refreshment of Clause IV' was an essentially negative one, based on the assumption 'that its reform would be too difficult to effect, too divisive, and that it is more sensible simply to let this redundant piece of ideological phraseology "wither on the vine"'.[11] Yet there were, in his view, 'overwhelming, substantive objections to the Nelson's eye approach to Clause IV'. These related, first, to the fact that Clause IV, Part Four, was 'a central plank of the Party's constitution', highlighted on Party membership cards, and, second, to the existence of 'the *cordon doctrinaire* which has been thrown up around Part 4',[12] stifling ideological debate. For Part Four had become 'a shibboleth of socialist belief' which had assumed 'some mystical significance'.[13] It was hard even to discuss for that reason and 'because there is fear of the charge of betrayal if any move is made against it'.[14]

Recalling that the publication of Sidney Webb's original statement had itself been 'an act of modernisation by the Labour Party, designed specifically to appeal to middle-class voters', including the 65,000 government officials employed by 1918 in the Ministry of Munitions,[15] Straw argued that the 'recasting of Clause IV' was needed in the 1990s if Labour was 'to refresh our appeal to the electorate as the governing party which takes Britain into the 21st century'.[16] But unlike Sidney Webb and his colleagues, Labour's current generation of modernizers ought, in Straw's judgement, to include in the revised Clause IV only 'a statement of ends', leaving statements of means to the Party's 'continuous process of policy formulation'.[17]

Straw's proposal, however, received no immediate support from the Party leadership. On the contrary, while wishing to supersede Clause IV with his own statement of values, Smith regarded Straw's initiative with displeasure in view of its timing. For the propagation of Straw's views on Clause IV coincided with the Party leader's struggle to secure the backing of trade union leaders for the principle of 'one member, one vote' in 1993.[18]

Nevertheless, Smith's predecessor, Neil Kinnock, later echoed Straw's views when in February 1994 he, too, advocated the re-writing of Clause IV. Recognizing the original clause's mythic force and appeal, Kinnock pointed out that Labour's 'tablet of stone' had achieved 'the status of political holy writ'.[19] It had become 'a hallowed part of Labour's political culture', regarded by many as 'the ideological definition of the Party's character' or even as 'its evidence of socialist identity'.[20] Yet although Kinnock conceded that public ownership and nationalization had once been 'central to my idea of socialism', by 1994 he was prepared to admit that he no longer believed 'that Clause IV is an adequate definition of modern democratic socialism'.[21]

In spite of these two contributions to the case for directly changing Clause IV,[22] Smith continued to adhere to his more indirect approach to this potentially divisive issue, making preparations, shortly before he died, for the drafting of his supplementary statement of values, which would in due course be discussed by the Party and, he hoped, eventually adopted by the 1995 Party Conference.[23] More broadly, he pursued his 'long game' strategy, shelving further organizational reforms and placing his emphasis on Party unity and on the preparation and development of Party policy.

Although that strategy appeared at times to Labour modernizers such as Tony Blair and Gordon Brown to be over-cautious,[24] John Smith's twenty-two-month period of Party leadership, cruelly cut short by his death in May 1994, ended with his popularity in the country at its peak, with the Labour Party at last broadly united and with the cause of its modernization cautiously sustained.

II

Tony Blair's election to the Labour leadership in July 1994, after securing 57 per cent of the votes of Party members, soon led to an acceleration of the pace of modernization within the Party. He himself, along with his friend Gordon Brown, had been among the most prominent of Labour's modernizers since the late 1980s, supporting Kinnock's policy changes and organizational reforms and, more recently, Smith's successful stand on 'one member, one vote' in 1993.

Modernization for Blair, as he later explained, was 'about returning Labour to its traditional role as a majority mainstream party advancing the interests of the broad majority of people', a role which, in his view, the Party had abandoned after 1979, when 'the activists steamrollered the leadership and put about the myth that we lost because we were not sufficiently traditionalist socialist'.[25]

Blair had earlier argued, in his post-mortem on Labour's election defeat in 1992, that 'The lesson in my view is clear . . . to continue and intensify the process of change. This must happen at the level of both ideas and organisation'.[26] In speeches and articles written during the early 1990s he therefore attempted to explore the main areas of ideological revision which he considered desirable for the Party. In a significant contribution, for example, to the journal *Marxism Today* in 1991, he argued that the challenge for socialists was 'to re-establish the agenda for public action without the old failings of collectivism'.[27] That meant recognizing the statist character of collectivism. For in the past, 'democratic socialists equated the public interest with public ownership', and 'had no developed analysis of the limitations of public ownership through the State as a means of helping the individual'.[28] But in practice it had become evident that the state could become 'a vested interest in itself, every bit as capable of oppressing individuals as wealth and capital'.[29]

In place of the inadequacies of state socialism, Blair wished to embrace the fundamental ideas of early ethical socialism – including its emphasis on 'the need of society to act together to achieve what the individual cannot do alone' and its advocacy of 'the use of the power of society to protect and advance the individual'[30] – and then to apply such ideas to the conditions of modern British society. Taken together, those socialist principles implied 'the notion of a clearly identified community, embodying the public interest or public good, standing up on behalf of individuals, against the vested interests that hold them back'.[31]

This reaffirmation of the enduring values of ethical socialism for Blair carried important policy and ideological implications. In the area of economic policy it underlay his view that:

the battle over theoretical forms of economic organisation is dead, or at least relegated to means, not ends. We need to develop instead a new economics of the public interest, which recognises that a thriving competitive market is essential for individual choice.[32]

Within that 'new framework of the public interest', he argued, it would be possible to appreciate the need not just for the existence of the market but also for government action designed to facilitate its efficient operation, while subjecting it to social needs. The practical effect of such a balanced approach would be that 'instead of government's relationship with industry being part of an ideological fight for territory between public and private sector, it becomes a partnership for the achievement of specific objectives in the public interest'.[33]

For Blair, then, modern socialism consisted not in a particular form of economic organization based on public ownership but rather in a collection of values such as community and mutuality which were strengthened by the 'over-reaching concept of the public interest'[34] invoked in support of the individual. The primary task of the 'new agenda' was to translate that concept into practical methods of public action aimed at enhancing the individual's freedom and interests.

The main features of the ideological revision which Blair was advocating as the 'governing philosophy of today's Labour Party'[35] were thus becoming reasonably clear. They appeared to comprise an espousal of the idea of an inclusive community promoting the public interest, a rejection of the elevated status previously ascribed to public ownership, and an unequivocal defence of the merits of a competitive market economy, once regarded by socialists as incompatible with their communitarian ideals.

These themes were developed further in a Fabian pamphlet published in July 1994, in which Blair maintained that the ethical socialism which he favoured had become 'since the collapse of Communism . . . the only serious view of the Left's future that can remain'.[36] Revived since 1983, in the wake of the fading appeal of the Marxist, quasi-scientific view of socialism so influential in the 1970s, the ethical socialist strand of thought rested, first, on the assumption 'that individuals are socially interdependent human beings [who] . . . owe a duty to one another and to a broader society' and, second, on the belief that, 'it is only through recognising that interdependence and by society as a whole acting upon it – the collective power of all used for the individual good of each – that the individual's interest can be advanced'.[37]

This ethical conception of socialism, which he underlined with the hyphenated use of the word 'social-ism',[38] was not something that Blair had recently come to embrace during Labour's ideological disputes. As a student at Oxford University in the early 1970s he had been strongly influenced by the communitarian ideas of the Scottish philosopher John MacMurray, who, in books such as *Persons in Relation* (1961) and *The Self as Agent* (1957), had combined ethical and Christian socialist views with a critique of liberal individualism.[39]

In the context of the revision of Labour's ideology, a theoretical approach of this kind had the advantage, Blair believed, not just of springing from deep historical roots but also of avoiding the limitations of a genus of socialist ideology based either upon sectional or class interests or upon 'particular economic prescriptions'.[40] For as society or the economy changed, so the disciples of such a time-bound ideology were 'left trying to fit the world to the ideology, not the ideology to the world'.[41] By contrast, ethical socialism, by defining itself as a set of values rather than in terms of economic formulae, was able, Blair maintained, to

> liberate itself, learning from history rather than being chained to it. It then no longer confuses means such as wholesale nationalisation with ends: a fairer society and more productive economy. It can move beyond the battle between public and private sector and see the two as working in partnership. It can open itself up to greater pluralism of ideas and thought.[42]

Such ideological benefits, in Blair's view, clearly included, therefore, both a rejection of an ownership-based definition of socialism and an acceptance of the broader socialist goal of 'a strong, united society which gives each citizen the chance to develop their potential to the full'.[43] Labour's identification of that goal, with 'the ideological compass reconstructed on true lines', would enable its socialist journey to be 'undertaken with vigour and confidence'.[44]

There were, however, at least two major problems that appeared to flow from Blair's ethical approach to socialism. In the first place, its sustained emphasis on the principle of community tended to obscure the abstract nature of that commitment. For that very reason this traditional socialist aspiration had not featured prominently in Labour revisionist thought during the 1950s. In *The Future of*

Socialism Crosland had placed much less emphasis on what he called 'the ideal of fraternity and co-operation' than on the ideals of social welfare and equality.[45] He was aware of the difficulty of developing practical policies, and specific social and economic arrangements, for pursuing the cooperative ideal, particularly in the face of the individualistic attitudes and the motive of personal gain fostered by a competitive market economy. While he recognized the possibility that the ideal might be beneficially applied in the field of industrial relations, he considered that a general conversion to altruistic motives throughout society might require 'either a change in the basic "social character" or the creation of a largely novel institutional framework'.[46]

Crosland could not envisage how such major changes might be brought about; nor was he sure 'that even if they were practicable, they might not lead to serious losses in other directions, such as privacy, individuality, personal independence, equality of opportunity, or the standard of living'.[47] He therefore admitted that he 'did not feel able, in what is intended to be a reasonably definite and practical statement of socialist aims' to include 'the ideal of fraternity and co-operation' as part of the contemporary socialist goal.[48] Gaitskell, too, took a similar view. Whilst valuing the ideal in the field of social and industrial relationships, he believed that it had lost much of its relevance in modern economic conditions.[49]

A second difficulty raised by Blair's ethical approach was of a more traditional ideological kind and likely to be emphasized by the Labour left. For by separating his socialist ideals from any particular form of economic organization and by supporting, too, 'a thriving competitive market', Blair was in effect wrenching those ideals, as Crosland had also done, away from the surrounding framework of a traditional socialist economic analysis. The ethical socialist tradition of Tawney and others which he invoked had, by contrast, stressed the interdependence of ethical and economic concerns.[50]

In this respect, at least, Blair was in harmony with earlier revisionist thinking. But by maintaining that socialist values were compatible with a market economy, he also thereby made himself vulnerable to a familiar traditional socialist charge – that there was a basic contradiction between the ideals of community, solidarity, mutual obligation and social responsibility, on the one hand, and the acquisitive and materialistic values of the market, on the other. Indeed, ethical socialism in the past had consistently maintained that 'the natural impulse of the market and economic individualism was to eat away at the bonds of community and mutual responsibility'.[51]

In spite of these problems posed by Blair's communitarian views, for advocates of a market economy and traditional socialists alike, it soon became clear that he was not concerned with developing his position purely on a level of abstraction. Instead, it was increasingly presented by him as the theoretical basis of a major part of his modernizing project: his iconoclastic proposal, advanced at the end of his first Conference speech as Party leader in October 1994, to rewrite Clause IV of the Party Constitution.

Blair had already, in the summer of 1994, confided in his close associates Gordon Brown and Peter Mandelson concerning his desire to rewrite Clause IV.[52] Both he and Mandelson were influenced by the Party's private poll findings, which indicated that 'there is still too great a fear of the unknown as far as the Labour Party is concerned',[53] since voters remained unconvinced that the Party had really changed its character.

Shortly afterwards Blair proceeded to discuss his plans to rewrite Clause IV with the Party's deputy leader, John Prescott, who was also the acknowledged but unofficial leader of Labour's traditionalist wing. Although initially doubtful about the strategic and tactical prudence of Blair's proposal, Prescott consented to it on condition that trade union leaders could be assured that there would be no more modernizing party reforms before the next General Election.[54]

When, on 4 October 1994, Blair finally came to advance his controversial proposal, it was in a brief passage towards the end of his first platform speech as leader at the Party Conference in Blackpool. He told his audience that Labour required 'a modern constitution that says what we are in terms the public cannot misunderstand and the Tories cannot misrepresent'.[55] Without directly mentioning Clause IV, he therefore promised that he and Prescott would shortly present 'a clear, up-to-date statement of the objects and objectives of our Party'.[56]

Blair invited a wide debate on that statement, with 'the whole Party involved'.[57] If, following the debate, his new Clause IV were to be accepted, then, he declared, 'let it become the objects of our Party for the next election and take its place in our constitution for the next century'.[58] Justifying his initiative, Blair reminded his audience:

> Parties that do not change die, and this party is a living movement not an historical monument. If the world changes and we don't, then we become of no use to the world. Our principles cease being principles and ossify into dogma.[59]

Blair thus became the first Labour leader since Gaitskell in 1959 openly to challenge the status of Clause IV as the formal expression of the Party's socialist purpose. Like Gaitskell, he considered that revising Clause IV was necessary not only in the light of important economic and social changes in Britain but also in order to dispel misunderstanding or misrepresentation. Like Gaitskell, too, the new Labour leader regarded the reform of Labour's constitution as an important symbol of the Party's modernization.

Media reaction, even in the Tory Press, to Blair's 'unexpected theatrical *coup*'[60] was highly favourable. *The Times*, for example, described Blair's speech as 'truly audacious' since he had 'faced his party with home truths, and redefined the party's very philosophy'.[61] Hugo Young in *The Guardian* considered, too, that the 'emblematic purpose' of Blair's decision to rewrite Clause IV was 'to speak to the country about Labour's honesty, not just to Labour about the party's identity'.[62]

Residual opposition, however, to Blair's adventurous move was underlined two days after his keynote speech when Conference narrowly carried a motion in favour of the original Clause IV. Following this, a Defend Clause Four campaign was launched in November 1994. Aimed at mobilizing support among trade unionists, Party activists and MEPs, the pressure group was headed by Arthur Scargill as its honorary president and supported by MPs from the hard-left Campaign Group.

Nevertheless, Blair's modernizing project gathered momentum in December 1994 when the Party's National Executive agreed a timetable for a special Party Conference to vote on the proposed constitutional change in April 1995. In January 1995 the NEC decided to urge constituency parties to ballot their members on the proposal, and Blair himself began a nationwide tour in order to argue his case for change face to face with party members.

He had presented that case in forthright terms earlier in January whilst addressing Labour MEPs in Brussels, a majority of whom had declared their support for the existing Clause IV. Blair told the MEPs:

> The Labour Party is not a preservation society. Those who seriously believe we cannot improve on words written for the world of 1918 when we are now in 1995 are not learning from our past but merely living in it.[63]

A party that preached change to others, he added, should be 'prepared to embrace change for itself'; and rewriting Clause IV was 'an essential, vital part of our crusade for change'.[64]

At the end of January 1995, Blair set out his case in more detail in a speech to his own Sedgefield constituency party. Describing the revision of Clause IV as 'the most important change we have made since the Constitution was adopted almost 80 years ago', he defended his undertaking as 'a process not of destruction but re-birth', which would 'allow our Party to replace an icon fashioned by human hands for one age with the spirit that motivates us and lasts for all ages'.[65] For Blair that timeless spirit, invoked by him in almost mythic terms, was one of 'social solidarity', derived from the belief that 'we are . . . members of a society or community of people who owe duties to one another and who, by acting together, can use the power of all for the good of each'.[66]

In Blair's judgement, the recasting of the original Clause IV, which had itself been 'a compromise designed to achieve unity through ambiguity',[67] was necessary because it was open to objection on three grounds. In the first place, Clause IV committed Labour to 'common ownership with no boundaries', and hence to 'common ownership of industry, retail and finance',[68] rather than to a mixed economy. Such a commitment made no sense on grounds of either socialist principle or economic reality. Second, Clause IV's provision of 'a statement of objectives which no government could or would implement' had 'helped to divide the party from its leaders'[69]. For no Labour election manifesto had ever contained a pledge to carry out Clause IV in practice. Furthermore, as Blair later observed, 'the gap between our stated aims and policies in government fed the constant charge of betrayal – the view that our problem was that the leadership was too timid to tread the real path to true socialism'.[70] Third, public ownership, as enshrined in Clause IV, was, Blair maintained, 'only ever a means to an end. It was not and is not a "value"' or a principle, but only 'the means, in certain circumstances, of achieving our principles'.[71] Clause IV, therefore, did not 'on its own, properly reflect our values or our total view of the economy'.[72]

Free of such limitations, the new Clause IV ought, in contrast, to 'define our purpose as a political party', embodying certain distinctive socialist values. These included, in particular, social justice, 'the foundation stone', expressing 'our belief in a fair society'; freedom, conceived in a broader sense than mere freedom from restraint, and involving 'not just . . . theoretical choice and power but the practical ability to exercise it'; equality, not in the sense of uniform equality of outcome, but pursued rather as the goals both of equality of respect and status and of a fairer distribution of rewards and opportunities; democracy, which embraced 'the real devolution of power to people' and 'the rejection of a centralised and unaccountable state'; and, finally, solidarity, 'which, expresses properly the bonds of humanity that tie people together ... the responsibilities and duties we owe to one another'.[73]

These were the enduring values which ought, in Blair's view, to underlie and inspire Labour's new statement of objects. But what of the economic means of realizing those values? As originally set out in Sidney Webb's Clause IV, the Party's specified means – the common ownership of the means of production – appeared, especially in the light of the collapse of Communism, to constitute 'not merely an anachronism but a statement of our economic beliefs that carries no conviction inside our Party whilst exposing us to maximum misrepresentation outside it'.[74] For the words of the existing Clause IV, however diversely they might in the past have been interpreted, 'amount on any basis to a command economy'.[75]

This rejection of the idea of wholesale public ownership did not, Blair stressed, invalidate the case for public ownership in specific instances. There was a need for 'both dynamic markets and strong public services'. There was also 'a role for different types of ownership – private, public, co-operative and combinations of these'. But the issue of ownership itself ought 'not [to] be a matter of ideology but of the best practical means to serve the public interest'.[76]

Shortly before this extended defence of Blair's project, Hugo Young underlined its wider symbolic importance. Seeking to explain the lingering opposition in many quarters to revising Clause IV, Young observed:

> This is a faithless age. . . . This is not a time when secular faith is replacing religious belief, but when faith of any kind is a condition uncongenial to educated people. That is the context in which Labour, a party of faith, is trying to re-make itself. It is the agnosticism against which Clause Four, an article of faith, fights to survive.[77]

In this faithless, secular era, therefore, it was the task of the Labour leader to replace the original Clause IV, 'the last text for lost souls unable to face the agnosticism of the modern world', with 'a looser-textured project than anything written in a time of faith, when socialist politics were a crusade still capable of attracting mass loyalty'.[78] In rewriting Clause IV, Blair thus had to 'find words which inspire modest confidence that he will make a better world; offer pragmatic promises that answer no extravagant dreams; construct a programme that has its roots in up-to-the-minute realism'.[79]

In attempting to fashion that more limited project, Blair would still have to overcome the intransigence of the defenders of Labour's traditional article of faith, who remained mesmerized by its mythic appeal. As another commentator, Andrew Marr, observed, Blair, who was 'not a traditional socialist nor a natural Labour man', would have to resist the conservatism of those in the Party who 'have not changed at all and are about as relevant to the Blair project as pre-Copernican scholars are to astrophysics, mentally inhabiting a world that is gone, one in which there is no strong global economy, no international mobility of labour or capital, in which strong states can deploy powerful and predictable levers, including the ownership of big corporations, for social ends'.[80]

None the less, by the beginning of 1995 the circumstances facing Blair seemed far more favourable, for at least three reasons, than those that had confronted Gaitskell over thirty-five years before. In the first place, unlike Gaitskell in 1959, Blair had carefully prepared the ground in advance. He had consulted, and gained the support of, prominent colleagues such as Prescott, Brown and Mandelson. He had made a point, too, of declaring that an open debate on the issue would take place among Labour's mass membership and that a new statement of aims, composed by himself and Prescott, would in due course be submitted both to the Party's National Executive and to a Special Party Conference.

Second, Blair's proposal was unlikely to face such fierce opposition from the trade unions as had been directed at Gaitskell in 1959–60. The new leader was, after all, dealing with a trade union movement which, as a result of Labour's organizational reforms since 1987, such as the reduction in 1993 of the unions' block vote to 70 per cent of total Conference votes, did not exercise the same decisive political leverage within the Party as in Gaitskell's day. Blair nevertheless needed to tread with some care in this area since many of Labour's affiliated unions still had objectives similar to those of Clause IV written into their own constitutions and rule books. Third, Blair was fortunate, too, in not having the daunting prospect of confronting that formidable alliance of fundamentalists of the Labour left and pragmatists and sentimentalists of the Party's centre which had been deployed against Gaitskell in 1959–60.

Against this background, and in accordance with the timetable agreed in December 1994, the new text of Clause IV was eventually published in March 1995 and approved by the National Executive on 13 March. The main emphasis of the final draft, of which Blair was principal author, but which had been shaped by the contributions of

Prescott and other senior colleagues, was upon the values of community, social justice and democracy rather than upon economic goals. Its Part One thus set out Labour's overriding belief in the principle of community, declaring that:

> The Labour Party is a democratic socialist party. It believes that by the strength of our common endeavour we achieve more than we achieve alone, so as to create for each of us the means to realise our true potential and for all of us a community in which power, wealth and opportunity are in the hands of the many not the few, where the rights we enjoy reflect the duties we owe, and where we live together, freely, in a spirit of solidarity, tolerance and respect.[81]

Part Two of the new Clause IV contained what remained for the left the most heretical aspect of Blair's undertaking: a redefinition of Labour's economic aims that embraced the notions of, first, a competitive market economy operating in the public interest and, second, a partnership between private and public ownership. For Labour, it stated, was now committed to the goal of

> A dynamic economy, serving the public interest, in which the enterprise of the market and the rigour of competition are joined with the forces of partnership and co-operation, to produce the wealth the nation needs and the opportunity for all to work and prosper, with a thriving private sector and high quality public services, where those undertakings essential to the common good are either owned by the public or accountable to them'.[82]

Part Two also referred to Labour's commitment to strive both for 'a just society, which judges its strength by the condition of the weak as much as the strong' and for 'an open democracy, in which the government is held to account by the people; decisions are taken as far as practicable by the communities they affect; and where human rights are guaranteed'.[83]

In justifying and explaining these commitments, Blair underlined their ethical socialist inspiration, stating that:

> The central belief of the Labour Party is in social cohesion. . . . The basic principle is solidarity, that people can achieve much more by acting together than by acting alone. I think that all this is best represented by the idea of community, in which each person has the rights and duties which go with community.[84]

Defending, too, the new statement's ideologically contentious references to 'the enterprise of the market' and 'the rigour of competition', Blair had already told the Scottish Labour Party conference a few days earlier that 'We know we live in an economy where there is, will be and should be a thriving private sector, where competitive markets exist alongside public ownership in an economy that works in the public interest'.[85] Such pronouncements clearly did not acknowledge any latent tensions between Blair's ideal of community, forged by 'common endeavour', and his celebration of the virtues of the market economy. His left-wing critics, however, were quick to underline such tensions[86] and to recall, too, that Sidney Webb, the main author of the original Clause IV, had drawn a stark contrast between the destructive 'competitive struggle for the means of life' inherent in economic individualism – which he repudiated – and the productive process of 'conscious and deliberate cooperation' that was favoured in Labour's newly embraced socialist ideology.[87]

Press reaction, however, to Blair's statement favourably emphasized the significance of this major ideological revision. *The Independent* described the new text as 'the boldest attempt undertaken by the post-war Labour Party to embrace a dynamic market economy',[88] while *The Times* considered that the National Executive's endorsement of the new Clause IV marked 'a defining moment in history', signifying that Labour had become 'a modern, progressive, left-of-centre party facing up to a new century with clarity and confidence'.[89] For the new statement involved 'the abandonment of the ancient pledge on common ownership ... and its replacement by the strongest ever support for the mixed economy'. If accepted by the Party's Special Conference in April, it would represent an ideological shift, 'a sharp move away from old-style socialism towards the language of social democracy'.[90]

In similar vein, *The Guardian* regarded the newly approved Clause as 'in every meaningful sense a defining document' which 'marks a fundamental change in the expressed general purposes of this country's leading party of reform'. For it had now been made crystal clear 'that Labour is no longer a party with a socialist project based on economic ownership but one with a socialist project based on community values'.[91]

The Independent acknowledged these points, but struck a more sceptical note. In rewriting Clause IV, Blair had 'broken with a great swathe of Labour history', yet his new statement, which contained 'potentially resonant thoughts, if expressed in the ungainly language of the composite motion', really summed up 'how the Labour Party, together with other modern social democratic parties, has been obliged to change'.[92] For his text reflected Labour's loss of past ideological certainty, confirming the present reality that

> The modern socialist, instead, accepts and acquiesces in a capitalist world which the traditionalist socialist would unequivocally have declared to be hostile. There is no ambition to transform the fundamental contours of that society. The days of social engineering and grand plans are gone. Globalisation, technical change and the bankruptcy of the old doctrine leave no alternative. All is now contingency laced with values and ethics.[93]

Boosted by this widespread press recognition of both its ideological significance and its underlying realism, Blair's revisionist project shortly reached the final stage of what had been in effect a six-month campaign. For at the Special Party Conference on 29 April 1995, held at the Methodist Central Hall, Westminster, where, ironically, the original Clause IV had been adopted in February 1918, the Party leader finally secured the approval, by a 65 per cent vote, of his new statement of aims and values. His support included 90 per cent of the constituency vote and 54.6 per cent of the union vote, in spite of the opposition of two of the biggest trade unions, the Transport and General Workers' Union (TGWU) and Unison. The vote thus provided overwhelming support for Blair's strategy and stance, though some sceptical observers suggested that it constituted not so much a clear endorsement of his cause of modernization and ideological revision as 'a plebiscite – a vote of confidence in the Leader'.[94]

Shortly before this outcome had been reached, a much respected veteran of the Labour left, Barbara Castle, whilst pledging loyalty to the leader, had made clear her underlying reservations on the issue at stake, warning that 'It is always dangerous for a political movement to repudiate its past. . . . Methodology must change as the world changes, but that is secondary to preserving the philosophy which inspires our aims'.[95] At about the same time, Roy Hattersley, Labour's former deputy leader, and the most prominent remaining advocate of Croslandite social democracy, had viewed Labour's ideological shift in a more sanguine manner, predicting that 'in political folklore, April 29, 1995, will become the day when Labour turned itself into a social democratic party',[96] for Labour's Special Clause IV Conference would be 'a symbol of an evolution, which, although gradual and sometimes imperceptible, has been inevitable since 1979'.[97] It would represent the climax of economic and social changes, occurring in British society over many years, to which Labour had been forced to adapt.

But this crucial moment in Labour's history, marking symbolically the ideological transition from traditional socialism to social democracy, also witnessed the formal burial of the Party's socialist myth, of the visionary idea of an economic and social transformation, of a future Socialist Commonwealth built on the foundation of the public ownership of the means of production, the idea that had been embodied and crystallized in the original Clause IV.

The apparent triumph of social democracy, with its modest aspiration to improve and reform rather than to transform the nature of existing society, in turn depended, then, upon the Party's willingness to turn away at last from the mythic allure of both public ownership and the goal of a socialist Jerusalem, the shining city on a distant hill, which that economic mechanism had once promised to bring nearer.

Blair himself had stressed the need for this symbolic break with the past, for this abandonment of the status of Clause IV as an 'icon' or a 'totem'.[98] In confronting his Party with that task, he had demonstrated a lack of sentimentality and an 'unconcern about the inner workings of Labour's heart'[99] which no Labour leader since Gaitskell had dared to display. But, unlike Gaitskell, he had also exercised tactical and strategic skills throughout the undertaking and had encountered generally favourable political circumstances.

For Blair his ultimately successful rewriting of Clause IV had amounted, in his own words, to 'the ideological re-foundation of the party' in certain enduring values or ideals rather than in economic dogma. The revisionist project which had come to fruition could thus be presented to his Party as an act of modernization, reappraising Labour's ideology in the light of economic and social changes and in the face of persistent electoral defeat.

Moreover, this process of ideological change could also be interpreted by Blair as a recapturing of Labour's ethical socialist tradition, drawing upon values derived from that heritage, including, in particular, community and mutual responsibility, as well as the more familiar social-democratic ideals of social justice and equality of opportunity. Blair hoped that such a collection of values, separated from outdated economic prescriptions, would serve both to distinguish Labour clearly from the economic individualism of free-market Conservatism and to provide the Party with a firm sense of common identity and purpose.

Such hopes, however, left certain problematic questions unanswered. Would, for instance, communitarian values provide an inspiring and distinctive core vision for Labour now that they had been divorced from the moral and economic critique of capitalism that earlier ethical socialist thinkers such as Tawney had once advanced? Untested, too, by events was Blair's belief that an ethical approach to socialism based on the principle of community could form the basis of a coherent governing philosophy capable of guiding a future Labour Government in new and unfamiliar policy directions. At the end, therefore, of the boldly executed first stage of Blair's modernizing project, it remained uncertain whether a set of such abstract principles could provide a firm ideological anchorage now that Labour had been cut adrift from its traditional socialist moorings.

8 Conclusion

Viewed against its historical background, Tony Blair's successful bid in 1995 to rewrite Clause IV of the Labour Party Constitution may with justification be regarded as the culmination of a revisionist project within the Party – concerned both with demoting public ownership and with endorsing the market economy – that was initiated in the 1950s. In a wider sense, too, Blair's achievement may be seen from that perspective as the symbolic fulfilment of the desire of Labour revisionists and their successors clearly to establish the Party's identity in the mainstream of European social democracy.

This book has examined the development of that revisionist undertaking. It has explored the character of the emerging revisionist position, and considered it as a response to the widespread perception that public ownership was inseparable from Labour's vision of a future Socialist Commonwealth, of a transformed economy and society. For revisionism challenged, above all, the established status of public ownership as the Party's leading, inspirational idea, which provided, in Crossman's words, 'the central tenet of Labour's creed',[1] and hence the main strand in its loosely-knit ideological fabric.

Moreover, it has been argued here that the concept of political myth, viewed both as an emotive account of a party's past and as an inspiring vision of its future, helps to explain, first, the potency and enduring appeal of the idea of public ownership throughout the Labour movement since 1918 and, second, the sustained vehemence of the reaction to revisionist attempts to relegate that idea to a lower status in Labour policy and ideology, illustrated most dramatically by the indignant response to Gaitskell's abortive attempt to revise Clause IV in 1959–60.

In the past, Labour's socialist myth – of a new social order founded on the public ownership of the means of production – had helped to imbue the Party's members and supporters with a spirit of collective identity and common endeavour and purpose. With its account of earlier struggles, it had dramatically underlined the Party's declared socialist character, reinforcing its supporters' conviction that their cause went beyond the piecemeal reforms of social liberalism. With its inspiring vision of a transformed world, it had expressed, too, their deeply held aspirations. It had offered them the goal of conquering the commanding heights of the economy, the necessary stage on the road to the Socialist Commonwealth.

Embodied in Clause IV, this socialist myth had endured as an 'article of faith' and a source of inspiration for generations of British socialists. It had functioned, too, as a social binding force, helping to unite a loose and fragmented political organization. Through the formal expression of Clause IV, it had presented itself as a 'rallying-point',[2] which drew together Labour's diverse factions and interests, overriding their tactical and doctrinal differences. A common belief in the central importance of public ownership, and of nationalization in particular, had contributed vitally to that process, forming, in Crosland's words, 'a familiar mental sheet-anchor'[3] that gave the Party some kind of stability and ideological coherence. Hostile reactions to the revisionist attempt in the 1950s to break the ideological link between socialism and public ownership, thereby, in a sense, demythologizing the latter, were continually evident, as we have seen, in two major arenas of Party debate frequently explored in this study – namely, the Party Conference and the British socialist Press. Those who, for a variety of reasons – doctrinal, sentimental or tactical – continued to cherish the beguiling vision of an alternative, socialist society eagerly used those platforms to deplore the revisionists' devaluation of the significance, both symbolic and ideological, of public ownership. Revisionism itself they regarded as a dangerous challenge to their conception of Labour as a party with a distinctively socialist character and purpose.

Such fears and suspicions were aroused, in particular, by the revisionists' approval of the mixed economy, by their insistence on the clear distinction between socialist ends and means, and by their pragmatic emphasis on public ownership as a means and not an end. For conceptual subtleties of the latter kind were regarded on the left as a mere pretext for relegating public ownership to a secondary role in Labour policy. More broadly, the revisionist threat to the Party's socialist character was located in the blurred distinction that many drew between revisionism and radical Liberalism. There was a widespread unease that Labour revisionists, by understating the importance of such a central socialist idea as public ownership, had become little more than, in Strachey's words, 'rootless, drifting social reformers'.[4]

During the late 1950s, then, revisionist ideas and policies were widely perceived as sharpening differences within the Party over both its fundamental purpose and its underlying character. In the period following Labour's heavy election defeat in 1959 these disturbing effects were intensified by Gaitskell's controversial proposal to amend Clause IV of the Party Constitution. His plans represented the culmination of the revisionist attempt to demythologize public ownership. The indignant response which they evoked provided, too, the clearest expression of earlier anxieties induced by that rationalistic undertaking. For Gaitskell's behaviour was widely mistrusted and denounced because it signified an indifference to the symbolic importance and appeal both of public ownership and of Clause IV as the formal expression of Labour's socialist myth.

This study has traced and examined the various stages of this deepening process of ideological conflict which culminated in the confrontation over Clause IV in 1959–60. It has explored, too, the manner in which the potentially divisive implications of that conflict were contained by a deliberate and subtle compromise within the Party after 1960 which obscured and even suppressed, under the unifying cover of the idea of the scientific revolution, fundamental questions about the nature and purpose of democratic socialism – including, in particular, its attitude towards a market-oriented mixed economy.

To what extent, therefore, did Labour revisionism in the 1950s and early 1960s really succeed in the first part of its challenge to Party orthodoxy – in its attempt, that is, to promote a more secondary role for public ownership in Labour policy and ideology, and consequently to endorse unequivocally the mixed economy? By the time of Gaitskell's unexpected death in January 1963, had the revisionist position on public ownership thereby become entrenched within the Party? In broader terms, had revisionism triumphed or was it being gradually superseded as a major ideological influence?

On this question a substantial body of opinion has inclined towards the view of revisionist ascendancy in the early 1960s.[5] Haseler, for example, has depicted a 'modern, revisionist Labour Party'[6] emerging from a decade of internal discord. In similar vein, Morgan has maintained that within the Party during this period: 'We were all revisionists now, it seemed'.[7] Not all commentators, however, have favoured this interpretation. Minkin, for example, has argued that the pre-eminence of revisionist ideas, particularly with regard to public ownership, was anything but firmly rooted. It was achieved, in fact, only 'at elite level within the Party – amongst the parliamentarians and amongst trade union leaders'.[8] Furthermore, he has asserted that, so far from there being a 'revisionist victory',

> There was no fundamental transformation of opinion within the Party towards the revisionist position on public ownership. The change of policy on public ownership was achieved by a remarkable and complex mixture of factors which included deliberate ambiguity, a significant pattern of mandate distortion and the manipulation and bias of the Conference procedures.[9]

Minkin's argument facilitates an understanding of the Party's official acceptance of such a controversial document as *Industry and Society* in 1957. More broadly, his analysis makes it easier to comprehend the powerful resurgence of support for traditional socialist commitments to public ownership at Party Conferences after 1970. For the basis of such support 'amongst Party and union activists had changed little in the previous fifteen years'.[10]

Such scepticism about the long-term influence of revisionism is supported by a number of observations. First, it should be noted that, while from 1956 to 1959 revisionist attitudes – particularly towards public ownership and economic strategy – were translated into major policy statements, they none the less provoked widespread unease throughout the Party and, on the left, outright hostility. Second, Gaitskell's attempt to amend Clause IV – an exercise that could be regarded as carrying through the practical implications of revisionist thought – succeeded in arousing only deep suspicion and bitter opposition. Finally, the price of restoring Party unity in the aftermath of that conflict required both a retreat from revisionist positions and a restoration of public ownership to a position close to its traditionally central place within Labour policy and strategy.

The Party's post-1960 settlement was, however, provisional as well as unsatisfactory since it blurred fundamental differences of opinion and principle by, above all, maintaining Labour's ambiguity over the extent of its commitment to public ownership as well as its doctrinal ambivalence over the mixed economy and private industry. It was hardly surprising, therefore, that vital questions about Labour's long-term direction, and the deeper ideological tensions underlying them, resurfaced, sharply and divisively, during the 1970s and early 1980s. One of the disturbing aspects of the revisionist project of the 1950s was that it anticipated these later conflicts. The issues which it raised foreshadowed what John Mackintosh identified as the dilemma facing the Party in the 1970s – the choice of 'socialism or social democracy'.[11] Contrasting attitudes towards the role and significance of public ownership, and towards the mixed economy, were at the very heart of that choice.

After 1970, as we have seen, the increasing strength of the left within the Party ensured the revival of a fundamentalist socialist response, based on the advocacy of widespread public ownership and state economic planning, to Labour's ideological dilemma. The Labour left's temporary ascendancy came to an end, however, in the wake of the electoral débâcle of 1983, after which Kinnock's leadership fostered a gradual restoration of social-democratic, or at any rate more centrist, policy positions and attitudes.

The subsequent ideological revision after 1987 eventually led to the completion of the first part of the revisionist undertaking – the breaking of the historic link in Labour policy and ideology between democratic socialism and public ownership. The implications of that departure from past orthodoxy also became evident in the form of the Party's public and unequivocal endorsement of the market economy.

Shaw has argued that this belated ideological conversion was really much 'exaggerated'[12] by political commentators since an acceptance of the market had not only been made explicit in revisionist thought during the 1950s but was also implicit in the policy-making of Labour Governments after 1945. Yet he also concedes that the 'fulsome approval for the market' expressed in the Policy Review document of 1989, *Meet the Challenge, Make the Change*, was 'unique in a major policy statement'.[13]

What was, indeed, unprecedented in the history of the Labour Party was the extent of its unambiguous acknowledgement of the merits of a market economy. For since the 1950s support for a market-oriented mixed economy had continued to constitute what one perceptive commentator, Peter Jenkins, called Labour's 'official heresy' – clearly reflected both in Party policy documents and in the conduct of the Labour governments of the 1960s and 1970s, yet widely viewed with suspicion and even hostility by the Party's rank and file members.

To the social-democratic heirs of 1950s revisionism this public legitimation of such an important 'heresy' had seemed long overdue. Back in the late 1970s John Mackintosh had thus deplored Labour's long-standing doctrinal 'ambivalence over the value of a mixed economy'.[14] The Party, he regretted, had never fully decided 'whether a mixed economy is desirable in itself or is a stage on the road to a better, alternative system'.[15]

A decade or more later Giles Radice had also drawn attention to that same 'ambivalence over the role of the market and private enterprise',[16] for 'in contrast to most other European Socialist parties', he noted, Labour had 'never officially come to terms with private ownership, the mixed economy and the role of the market, though in practice, of course, it has for many years accepted their existence'.[17] Moreover, the Party's reticence on this central issue had helped to instil the widespread public fear, however misplaced, that Labour's ultimate goal was the construction, on the basis of large-scale state ownership and control, of an 'authoritarian and arthritic command economy'.[18]

By 1989, then, this major ideological shortcoming seemed to have been remedied. Furthermore, by April 1995 Labour's acceptance of the market economy had been officially legitimized by the rewriting of Clause IV in terms which both celebrated 'the enterprise of the market' and 'the rigour of competition' and removed any trace of commitment, however imprecise or symbolic, to wholesale public ownership.

But what of the second part of the original revisionist undertaking – its restatement of democratic socialist values and ideals? Did the ideological viewpoint that Labour now expressed represent in any meaningful sense an updated form of revisionist or Croslandite social democracy? Some commentators have certainly taken this view,[19] whilst others have rejected it, pointing to new Labour's 'abandonment of Keynesian social democracy'.[20]

Elaborating the latter interpretation, Shaw depicts Labour's ideological revision since 1987 as a process involving 'the dilution or renunciation of Keynesian social democratic tenets'[21] rather than a 'long-delayed conversion to European-style social democracy'.[22] For, in his view, Labour has departed from the Keynesian social-democratic tradition, first, and most obviously, by abandoning the belief that macroeconomic intervention can be vigorously employed to promote economic growth and full employment. Second, the Party has also moved away, for both international economic and domestic electoral reasons, from a strategy for pursuing egalitarian and welfarist goals that was built in the 1950s and 1960s upon high levels of public expenditure and sharply redistributive taxation.

For these reasons, Shaw argues, Labour's 'new ruling doctrine is in fact "post-revisionist"'[23]. Bereft of its original Keynesian foundation, this stunted new orthodoxy may well have lost, he suggests, its dynamic and even its *raison d'être*. For Labour's current form of 'post-revisionist social democracy'[24] has done little more than renegotiate the historic compromise of European social democracy – between capitalism and the democratic state – on 'terms much more favourable to capitalism'[25] than in the past.

Some part of this interpretation clearly seems to carry force. But in defence of Labour's ideological adaptation, it may be argued not only that its damaging ambiguity, or ambivalence, over the market economy has at last been removed, but also that the Party has come to embrace a more realistic view of the limits imposed on national governments both by global economic forces and by the pressures of electoral politics. In the difficult process of changing policies and doctrine, Labour has thus, according to this view, betrayed neither its idealism nor its heritage, but rather has undergone 'a withdrawal from fantasy and self-deception'.[26] For Labour's rethinking rests on a recognition of the fact that the economic and technological revolution that has occurred since the Party last held power in the late 1970s has 'buried its statist thinking'.[27] In the face of these developments, Labour therefore 'no longer falsely promises to change the world', believing instead that 'Western societies are broadly moving along the right track'.[28]

This informed pragmatism inherent in Labour's 'post-revisionist social democracy' may, therefore, offset the effects of the dilution of its former, underlying Keynesian assumptions. It is arguable, however, that the very notion of such an ideological position, of one that remains distinctively and recognizably social-democratic whilst abandoning both its Keynesian and its Croslandite foundations, is self-contradictory. 'The political fact of the age', Gray has thus written, 'is the passing of social democracy' in the face not only of the globalization of economic activity but also of the domestic policy and institutional changes in Britain since 1979.[29]

'The use', in particular, 'of tax and welfare systems for egalitarian redistribution – a central strategy of social democratic governments in Britain and much of Europe – is now', he points out, 'precluded by voter resistance and the global mobility of capital'.[30] As a consequence, 'the emerging social-democratic consensus in Britain', though in itself 'a considerable advance on the formulaic debates of the New Right and the Old Left, . . . nevertheless,' Gray maintains, 'embodies assumptions and modes of thought that belong to an historical context that has vanished beyond recovery'.[31]

It may well be, therefore, as Gray argues,[32] that the task of developing a successor to Thatcherism as a viable political project in Britain rests not on a vain attempt to refurbish an obsolete social-democratic ideology, but rather on the formulation of a social or communitarian liberalism that seeks to reconcile the individual's thirst for autonomy and freedom of choice with the benefits and responsibilities of community.

In the face of this view of the exhaustion of social democracy it should be remembered, of course, that as a political ideology it has prospered in the past through its flexibility and pragmatism. Labour's accommodation to, and eventual public endorsement of, the market economy provides a good example of those attributes. Yet the task of revitalizing social democracy, or, in the preferred phrase of probably most Labour politicians, democratic socialism, remains an uncertain prospect. The attempt, for instance, under Blair's leadership to reconnect Labour with its ethical socialist roots by reviving and re-emphasizing the principle of community runs into the serious practical problem of translating that ideal into concrete programmatic commitments.

Labour has accomplished the first part of the revisionist task to which Crosland, Gaitskell and others were committed in the 1950s and early 1960s – to remove the Party's doctrinal ambiguity over the market economy and to discard the obsolete link between democratic socialism and public ownership. Yet, arising from the second part of their undertaking – the reformulation of socialist aims and values – problems of ideological identity and coherence have clearly re-appeared for Labour in the 1990s. For what does the Party stand for, what are its guiding principles and governing ideals, now that the idea of public ownership has been relegated in importance, with the old Clause IV rewritten, and now, too, that its egalitarian commitment, forged in an earlier, more optimistic era to supersede fundamentalist socialism, has been diluted in terms of both policy and ideology?

In abandoning traditional shibboleths and in reappraising earlier revisionist assumptions, both Keynesian and Croslandite, Labour may well, as Blair has argued, have instigated a realistic 'process of change and reconstruction' in which all modern left-of-centre political parties have had to engage.[33] That process has therefore been 'not one simply of modernising old state socialism, but of modernising Sixties' democratic socialism or social democracy'.[34]

But while recognizing the benefits of a hard-won political realism in the face of major economic and technological changes and the prudence, too, of more cautious and modest reformist aspirations in an age of lost ideological certainties, thorny, unresolved questions of doctrine and strategy remain. What, for instance, are the long-term implications for Labour of its demotion of public ownership from its traditionally central place in Labour Party thought, policy and strategy? Can a party with such a strong sense of its own past easily downgrade a leading idea such as public ownership, one that for so long carried such a powerful emotional charge and which appears still to command the general support of a majority of grass-roots Party members?[35] For them, it seems, 'public ownership remains a touchstone issue' that raises 'a symbolic question about the nature of socialism rather than merely a public policy question about the role of the state in running British industry'.[36]

In the event, too, of a fifth consecutive election defeat for Labour, an unlikely prospect in 1995–6, but to be weighed none the less as a distinct possibility in the light of past failures, the probable revival and promotion of such traditional attachments throughout the Party would unquestionably pose problems for the leadership's modernizing ambitions.

Perhaps even more problematic is the question of the future appeal and practical application of Labour's, and Blair's, communitarian core vision. In the mid-1990s it appears uncertain whether such an abstract ideal will in the years ahead supersede the idea of public ownership as another major socialist 'touchstone', as both an inspirational idea for Party members and an ideological compass for future Labour governments, guiding them across the unfamiliar terrain of a global market economy.

Notes

1 LABOUR, PUBLIC OWNERSHIP AND SOCIALIST MYTH

1 Labour Party Annual Conference Report, 1957, pp. 139–40.
2 K. O. Morgan, 'The Rise and Fall of Public Ownership in Britain', in J. M. W. Bean (ed.), *The Political Culture of Modern Britain*, London, Hamish Hamilton, 1987, p. 279.
3 Ibid.
4 B. Crick, 'Britain's "Democratic Party"', *The Nation*, 10 December 1960.
5 See F. Bealey (ed.), *The Social and Political Thought of the British Labour Party*, London, Weidenfeld & Nicolson, 1970, p. 1.
6 Ibid., p. 11.
7 See R. Barker, 'Socialism and Progressivism in the Political Thought of Ramsay MacDonald', in A. J. Morris (ed.), *Edwardian Radicalism, 1900–1914*, London, Routledge & Kegan Paul, 1974, for a discussion of the influence of MacDonald's political ideas and of their relationship with social liberalism during the Edwardian period.
8 H. Pelling, *The Challenge of Socialism*, London, A. & C. Black, 1954, p. 291. See E. Eldon Barry, *Nationalisation in British Politics*, London, Cape, 1965, especially ch. 5, for an examination of the role of nationalization and public ownership in the British socialist tradition.
9 'Basis' of the Fabian Programme, 1887: see E. R. Pease, *The History of the Fabian Society*, London, Frank Cass, 1918; 3rd edn, 1963, Appendix II.
10 S. Webb, *Socialism: True and False* (Fabian Tract 51), London, Fabian Society, 1894.
11 Independent Labour Party Annual Conference Report, 1893.
12 See E. Hughes, *Keir Hardie*, London, Allen & Unwin, 1956, p. 37.
13 See S. H. Beer, *Modern British Politics* (first published 1965), London, Faber, 1982, pp. 123–5.
14 Ibid.
15 R. P. Arnot, *The Miners: Years of Struggle*, London, Allen & Unwin, 1953, p. 132; quoted in Beer, 1982, pp. 166–7.
16 Labour Party Annual Conference Report, January and February 1918, Appendix 1, Constitution of the Labour Party, Section 3(d) (later known as Clause IV, Part Four, of the Party Objects).

17 See, for instance, Bealey, 1970, p. 13; and R. Barker, *Education and Politics*, Oxford, Oxford University Press, 1972, pp. 6–7.
18 E. Wertheimer, *Portrait of the Labour Party*, London, Putnam, 1929, p. 50.
19 G. D. H. Cole, *A History of the Labour Party from 1914*, London, Routledge, 1948, p. 56.
20 Bealey, 1970, p. 89.
21 H. Pelling, *A Short History of the Labour Party*, London, Macmillan, 10th edn, 1993, pp. 43–4.
22 Beer, 1982, pp. 125, 140.
23 Ibid., p. 126.
24 R. Miliband, *Parliamentary Socialism*, London, Merlin Press, 1961, 2nd edn, 1972, p. 61.
25 *Labour and the New Social Order*, London, Labour Party, 1918.
26 Ibid.
27 Ibid.
28 R. McKibbin, *The Evolution of the Labour Party, 1910–1924*, Oxford, Oxford University Press, 1974, p. 91.
29 Ibid., p. 102.
30 B. Pimlott, 'The Labour Left', in C. Cook and I. Taylor (eds), *The Labour Party*, London, Longman, 1980, p. 166.
31 Ibid.
32 McKibbin, 1974, pp. 96–7.
33 Ibid.
34 Ibid.
35 Beer, 1982, p. 149. For a critique of Beer's interpretation, see R. Harrison, 'The War Emergency Workers' National Committee, 1914–1920', in A. Briggs and J. Saville (eds) *Essays in Labour History, 1886–1923*, London, Macmillan, 1971, pp. 257–9.
36 Beer, 1982, p. 145.
37 Cole, 1948, p. 60.
38 See B. Webb, *Diaries, 1912–1924*, (ed. M. Cole), London, Longman, 1952, p. 167; quoted in R. Kelf-Cohen, *Twenty Years of Nationalisation*, London, Macmillan, 1969, p. 20.
39 Ibid.
40 Quoted in Kelf-Cohen, 1969, p. 18.
41 On the importance of the influence of wartime economic conditions, see Eldon Barry, 1965, ch. 8.
42 See J. M. Winter, *Socialism and the Challenge of War*, London, Routledge & Kegan Paul, 1974, pp. 259–63, 274. See, too, Harrison, 1971, pp. 211–59.
43 Winter, 1974, pp. 273–4.
44 Ibid., p. 274.
45 Ibid.
46 See McKibbin, 1974; H. Perkin, *The Rise of the Professional Society*, London, Routledge, 1989.
47 R. H. Tawney, 'The Choice Before the Labour Party', *Political Quarterly*, July–September 1932; reprinted in R. H. Tawney, *The Attack and Other Papers* (first published 1953), Nottingham, Spokesman Books, 1981, p. 58.

48 H. M. Drucker, *Doctrine and Ethos in the Labour Party*, London, Allen
    & Unwin, 1979, pp. 1–2.
49 Ibid., pp. 9–17.
50 Ibid., p. 39.
51 Ibid., p. 25.
52 Ibid.
53 R. Barker, 'Political Myth: Ramsay MacDonald and the Labour Party',
    History, February 1976, p. 51n.
54 Ibid., pp. 48–9.
55 Ibid., p. 49.
56 Ibid., p. 46.
57 H. Tudor, *Political Myth*, London, Pall Mall, 1972, pp. 16, 137.
58 Ibid., p. 17.
59 R. Leach, *Genesis as Myth and other Essays*, London, Cape, 1969, p. 7.
60 H. Lasswell and A. Kaplan, *Power and Society*, New Haven,
    Connecticut, Yale University Press, 1946, p. 280.
61 E. Cassirer, *The Myth of the State*, London and New York, Oxford
    University Press, 1946, p. 280.
62 Ibid., p. 283.
63 Ibid., p. 282.
64 G. Sorel, *Reflections on Violence*, Riviere, 1908; trans. by T. E. Hulme
    and J. Roth, Glencoe, Illinois, Free Press, 1950, p. 59.
65 E. Durkheim, *The Elementary Forms of the Religious Life*, trans. by
    J. W. Swain, London, 1915, New York, Free Press, 1965, p. 420.
66 Cassirer, 1946, p. 47.
67 Sorel, 1950, p. 57.
68 J. R. Jennings, *Georges Sorel*, London, Macmillan, 1985, p. 122.
69 M. Duverger, *The Study of Politics*, trans. by R. Wagoner, London,
    Nelson, 1972, p. 99.
70 Tudor, 1972, p. 91.
71 Ibid., p. 16, chs 3 and 4.
72 Sorel, 1950, p. 48.
73 Tudor, 1972, p. 15.
74 Barker, 1976, p. 49.
75 Ibid.
76 Ibid., p. 51.
77 Drucker, 1979, p. 26.
78 See Tudor, 1972, pp. 110–14, for a discussion of the wider implications
    of this aspect (which he refers to as 'the demand for a morally coherent
    world') of eschatological myths.
79 *Labour and the New Social Order* (revised in accordance with resolu-
    tions of the Labour Party Conference, June 1918), London, Labour
    Party, 1918, pp. 3, 4.
80 Beer, 1982, p. 135.
81 Ibid.
82 See Beer, 1982, p. 128n; E. J. Hobsbawm, *Labouring Men*, London,
    Weidenfeld & Nicolson, 1964, ch. 18, p. 378.
83 Pimlott, in Cook and Taylor (ed.), 1980, p. 180.
84 See P. Cross, *Philip Snowden*, London, Barrie & Rockliff, 1966, pp. 38,
    53.

85 Pimlott, in Cook and Taylor (ed.), 1980, p. 181.
86 S. Desmond, *Labour: The Giant with the Feet of Clay*, London, Collins, 1921, p. 14.
87 Ibid., p. 197.
88 Drucker, 1979, p. 41.
89 R. Eccleshall et al., *Political Ideologies*, London, Hutchinson, 1984, p. 7.
90 Ibid., p. 8.
91 Duverger, 1972, p. 98.
92 Ibid., pp. 99–100.
93 G. Sorel, *Materials for a Theory of the Proletariat*, Riviere, 1919, p. 337; cited in G. Sorel, *From Georges Sorel* (ed. J. Stanley), New York, Oxford University Press, 1976, p. 45.
94 Beer, 1982, p. 135.
95 J. R. MacDonald, 'Foreword', *Labour and the Nation*, London, Labour Party, 1928.
96 Labour Party, 1928, p. 5.
97 *For Socialism and Peace*, London, Labour Party, 1934.
98 Ibid.
99 *Let Us Face the Future*, London, Labour Party, 1945.
100 Labour Party, 1928.
101 Ibid.
102 Labour Party, 1934.
103 *The Labour Party's Call to Power*, General Election manifesto, October 1935, London, Labour Party, 1935.
104 For Morrison's early views on nationalization, see H. Morrison, *Socialisation and Transport*, London, Constable, 1933.
105 See Labour Party Conference Report, 1933, pp. 204–9. See also Eldon Barry, 1965, pp. 302–3, on uses within the Labour Party of the terms 'nationalization' and 'socialization'.
106 *Labour's Call to Action*, General Election manifesto, October 1931, London, Labour Party, 1931.
107 Labour Party, 1934.
108 Morgan, in Bean (ed.), 1987, p. 280.
109 See Labour Party, 1945
110 See A. Rogow and P. Shore, *The Labour Government and British Industry 1945–51*, Oxford, Blackwell, 1955. For a summary of the principal measures, see R. Punnett, *British Government and Politics*, 6th edn, Aldershot, Dartmouth, 1994, ch. 12. See also Morgan, in Bean (ed.), 1987, p. 282.
111 See Punnett, 1994, pp 377–8.
112 Labour Party, 1945.
113 R. H. Tawney, 'The Choice Before the Labour Party', *The Attack and Other Papers*, p. 60.
114 Ibid., pp. 62, 64–5.
115 R. H. Tawney, *The Acquisitive Society*, London, Bell & Sons, 1921, p. 155; and 'We Mean Freedom', lecture delivered for the Fabian Society, 1944; reprinted in R. H. Tawney, 1981, p. 91.
116 'We Mean Freedom', in R. H. Tawney, 1981, pp. 92, 98.
117 C. A. R. Crosland, *The Future of Socialism*, London, Cape, 1956; rev. edn 1964, p. 328. (All future references to revised edition.)

118 I. Taylor, 'Ideology and Policy', in Cook and Taylor (ed.), 1980, pp 1, 26.
119 Ibid., p. 1.
120 See Beer, 1982, ch. VI.
121 Ibid., p. 126.
122 Ibid., p. 153.
123 Ibid., p. 154.
124 See, for example, Cole, 1948, p. 56; Pelling, 1993, p. 44.
125 Miliband, 1972, p. 62.
126 On Tawney's ideological influence, see Taylor, in Cook and Taylor (ed.),
     1980, p. 12; and G. Foote, *The Labour Party's Political Thought*,
     London, Croom Helm, 1985, p. 72.
127 D. Coates, *The Labour Party and the Struggle for Socialism*, Cambridge,
     Cambridge University Press, 1975, p. 41.
128 Ibid., p. 78.
129 Beer, 1982, p. 136.
130 Ibid., p. 237.
131 Ibid., p. 133.
132 Ibid., p. 135.
133 J. Tomlinson, *The Unequal Struggle? British Socialism and the Capitalist
     Enterprise*, London, Methuen, 1982, p. 63.
134 Ibid.
135 Ibid.

2 THE EMERGENCE AND REFINEMENT OF LABOUR REVISIONISM, 1951–9

1 L. Labedz (ed.), *Revisionism*, London, Allen & Unwin, 1962, p. 9.
2 W. H. Greenleaf, *The British Political Tradition, vol. 2: The Ideological
   Heritage*, London, Methuen, 1983, p. 475.
3 Ibid., p. 476.
4 L. Minkin, *The Labour Party Conference*, Manchester, Manchester UP,
   1980, p. 125.
5 Socialist Union was founded in 1951 and dissolved in 1959. Its leading
   members and writers included Allan Flanders, its chairman, and Rita
   Hinden, its secretary and editor of *Socialist Commentary* from 1955.
6 See P. Williams, *Hugh Gaitskell: A Political Biography*, London, Cape,
   1979, p. 320, n. 164.
7 See Minkin, 1980, p. 48; S. Haseler, *The Gaitskellites*, London,
   Macmillan, 1969, p. 8; Greenleaf, 1983, pp. 476–8; and, especially,
   Elizabeth Durbin, *New Jerusalems*, London, Routledge & Kegan Paul,
   1985, passim.
8 See Elizabeth Durbin, 1985.
9 For the major literary expressions of this rethinking, see H. Dalton,
   Practical Socialism for Britain, London, Routledge, 1935; D. Jay, *The
   Socialist Case*, London, Faber & Faber, 1937; and Evan Durbin, *The
   Politics of Democratic Socialism*, London, Routledge, 1940.
10 Jay, 1937, p. 195.
11 S. H. Beer, *Modern British Politics* (first published 1965), London,
    Faber, 1982, p. 237.

12 C. A. R. Crosland, *The Future of Socialism* (first published 1956), London, Cape; rev. edn 1964, p. 41. (All future references to revised edition.)
13 See, for instance, Beer, 1982, ch. VIII.
14 Labour Party Conference Report, 1952, p. 83.
15 See K. O. Morgan, 'The Rise and Fall of Public Ownership in Britain', in J. M. W. Bean (ed.), *The Political Culture of Modern Britain*, London, Hamish Hamilton, 1987, pp. 287–8.
16 See Labour Party Conference Report, 1948, p. 155.
17 For examples of the Morrisonian approach to the issue, see *Labour and the New Society*, London, Labour Party, 1951; *Facing the Facts*, London, Labour Party, 1952.
18 R. H. S. Crossman (ed.), *New Fabian Essays*, London, Turnstile Press, 1952, p. xi.
19 Crosland, 'The Transition from Capitalism', in Crossman, 1952, p. 37.
20 Crosland, 1964, p 1.
21 See Crosland, 1964, Part 1.
22 See A. Berle and G. Means, *The Modern Corporation and Private Property*, New York, Macmillan, 1932.
23 See J. Burnham, *The Managerial Revolution*, London, Putnam, 1942.
24 T. Smith, *The Politics of the Corporate Economy*, Oxford, Martin Robertson, 1979, p. 132.
25 For data concerning the extent of the divorce between industrial ownership and control in Britain, see T. Nicholls, *Ownership, Control and Ideology*, London, Allen & Unwin, 1969; and N. Abercrombie and A. Warde, *Contemporary British Society*, Oxford, Polity Press, 1988, pp. 17–27. For critical assessments of the validity of the 'managerialist' aspect of Crosland's analysis, see E. Burns, *Right-Wing Labour: Its Theory and Practice*, London, Lawrence & Wishart, 1961; S. Holland, *The Socialist Challenge*, London, Quartet Books, 1975, chs 1 and 2; and A. Arblaster, 'Anthony Crosland: Labour's Last Revisionist?', *Political Quarterly*, vol. 48, no. 4, October–December 1977.
26 See, for example, Socialist Union, *Twentieth Century Socialism*, London, Penguin, 1956, pp. 126–7.
27 See J. Strachey, *Contemporary Capitalism*, London, Gollancz, 1956. On the question of Strachey's distance from revisionist opinion, see H. Thomas, *John Strachey*, London, Eyre Methuen, 1973, pp. 276–7. For an extended discussion of Strachey's doctrinal position, see D. Bryan, 'The Development of Revisionist Thought Among British Labour Intellectuals and Politicians, 1931–1964', unpublished D.Phil. thesis, University of Oxford, 1984.
28 See *Industry and Society*, London, Labour Party, 1957, pp. 17, 18, 23. For an unfavourable view of the 'corporate elite' produced by the managerial revolution, see P. Shore (the author of the first draft of the economic analysis developed in *Industry and Society*), 'In the Room at the Top', in N. MacKenzie (ed.), *Conviction*, London, MacGibbon & Kee, 1958, pp. 23–54.
29 Crosland, 1964, pp. 19–20.
30 Ibid., p. 22.
31 Ibid.

32 J. Strachey, 'The New Revisionist', *New Statesman*, 6 October 1956.
33 Ibid.
34 Crosland, 1964, p. 43.
35 Ibid., p. 328.
36 See H. Gaitskell, *Socialism and Nationalisation* (Fabian Tract 300), London, Fabian Society, 1956.
37 For earlier expressions of the revisionist critique of the traditional egalitarian case for public ownership and nationalization, see Crosland, in Crossman (ed.), *New Fabian Essays*, 1952, p. 63; H. Gaitskell, 'Public Ownership and Equality', *Socialist Commentary*, June 1955; and R. Jenkins, 'Equality', in Crossman, 1952.
38 See Crosland, in Crossman, 1952, p. 63; R. Jenkins, *Pursuit of Progress*, London, Heinemann, 1953, p. 107; and Socialist Union, *Socialism: A New Statement of Principles*, London, Socialist Commentary Publications, 1952, p. 22.
39 See A. Bevan, *In Place of Fear* (first published 1952), London, Quartet Books, 1978, pp. 127–30; and R. H. S. Crossman, 'Towards a Philosophy of Socialism', in Crossman, 1952.
40 Crosland, 1964, p. 316
41 See C. A. R. Crosland, 'The Future of the Labour Party', *National and English Review*, July 1955.
42 See Socialist Union, 1956, pp. 123–4.
43 See, for example, Jenkins, 1953, p. 107.
44 See Crosland, 1964, p. 324.
45 This policy idea had first been developed with regard to land by Hugh Dalton in his work of 1920, *Inequality of Income in Modern Communities*. Douglas Jay had favoured the payment of death duties in kind in his book *The Socialist Case*, 1937, p. 277.
46 Personal correspondence from the Rt Hon. Douglas Jay, 11 January 1989. See also D. Jay, *Change and Fortune*, London, Hutchinson, 1980, p. 263.
47 Personal correspondence from the Rt Hon. Douglas Jay, 11 January 1989.
48 Jay, 1980, p. 264.
49 Ibid.
50 Ibid.
51 See Gaitskell, 1955, and 1956, p. 35.
52 Personal correspondence from the Rt Hon. Douglas Jay, 11 January 1989.
53 Labour Party Conference Report, 1957, p. 140.
54 Ibid.
55 Ibid., pp. 132–3.
56 B. Castle, *Tribune*, 13 September 1957.
57 See Crosland, 1964, chs 12, 13, 15 and 17.
58 See D. Jay, 1937, and his review of J. Strachey's *Contemporary Capitalism*, in *Forward*, 7 September 1956.
59 See Strachey's reply to Jay, *Forward*, 7 September 1956.
60 Crosland, 1964, p. 340.
61 See Socialist Union, 1956, p. 125.
62 Ibid., pp. 146, 147.
63 See, for example, H. Gaitskell, 'The Economic Aims of the Labour Party', *Political Quarterly*, January–March 1953.

64 For left-wing criticisms of the revisionist defence of the mixed economy, see G. D. H. Cole, 'Twentieth-century Socialism?', *New Statesman*, 7 July 1956; and W. Camp, 'Is This Really 20th Century Socialism?', *Tribune*, 29 June 1956.
65 Gaitskell, 1955.
66 Crosland, 1964, p. 44.
67 Ibid., p. 64.
68 Ibid., p. 69.
69 Ibid., p. 67.
70 Ibid.
71 See Chapter 7 below.
72 Crosland, 1964, p. 76.
73 Ibid., p. 77.
74 Ibid.
75 C. A. R. Crosland, 'Foreword' to the Japanese edition of *The Future of Socialism*, October 1960; Crosland Papers IV, 13/4.
76 See R. Hinden, 'The New Socialism', *Socialist Commentary*, November 1956.
77 Crosland, 1964, p. 66.
78 See P. Williams, 1979, p 69; Gaitskell, 1955.
79 R. Jenkins, in Crossman, 1952, p. 83.
80 R. H. Tawney, *The Radical Tradition* (ed. R. Hinden), London, Penguin, 1966, p. 176.
81 Gaitskell, address at R. H. Tawney's memorial service, 8 February 1962; quoted in Tawney, 1966, p. 221.
82 R. H. Tawney, 'The Choice Before the Labour Party', *Political Quarterly*, July–September 1932; reprinted in Tawney, 1981.
83 Tawney, 'We Mean Freedom', Fabian Society lecture, 1944; reprinted in Tawney, 1981.
84 Socialist Union, however, did not go this far. They retained a traditional socialist distaste for capitalist values and stressed the need for public control of private economic power. On this point, see Socialist Union, 1956.
85 Beer, 1982, p. 239.
86 Crosland, 1964, p. 64.
87 J. Strachey, 1956.
88 See, for example, the debate on *Industry and Society*, Labour Party Conference Report, 1957, pp. 131–55.
89 R. Miliband, *Parliamentary Socialism*, London, Merlin Press, 1972, p. 332.
90 Ibid.
91 See G. D. H. Cole, review of *Industry and Society*, *New Statesman*, 28 September 1957.
92 For differing accounts of this episode, see P. Williams, 1979, ch. 16; and M. Foot, *Aneurin Bevan, vol. 2: 1945–60*, London, Davis-Poynter, 1973, ch. 15.
93 See *For Socialism and Peace*, London, Labour Party, 1934; and F. Bealey (ed.), *The Social and Political Thought of the British Labour Party*, London, Weidenfeld & Nicolson, 1970, p. 27.
94 For a discussion of the lack of emphasis on economic planning in the 1950s, see T. Smith, 1979, ch. 6.

3 THE CLIMAX OF REVISIONISM: GAITSKELL AND THE CLAUSE IV DISPUTE

1 See, for instance, S. Haseler, *The Gaitskellites*: London, Macmillan, 1969, p. 15; M. Foot, *Aneurin Bevan, vol. 2: 1945–60*, London, Davies-Poynter, 1973, pp. 629–30; J Lee, *My Life with Nye*, London, Cape, 1980, p. 244.

2 The party was held at Gaitskell's house in Frognal Gardens, Hampstead, London, on Sunday, 11 October 1959. Among Gaitskell's guests were Herbert Bowden, Tony Crosland, Hugh Dalton, Patrick Gordon Walker, John Harris, Douglas Jay and Roy Jenkins. See P. Williams, *Hugh Gaitskell: A Political Biography*, London, Cape, 1979, pp. 538–9.

3 See Williams, 1979, pp. 539, 549.

4 M. Foot, 1973, p. 629.

5 D. Jay, *Change and Fortune*, London, Hutchinson, 1980, p. 272.

6 D. Jay, *Forward*, 16 October 1959.

7 Ibid.

8 M. Foot, 1973, p. 630.

9 Ibid.

10 P. Williams, 1979, p. 539.

11 Jay, 1980, p. 272.

12 Interview with the Rt Hon. Douglas Jay, Oxford, 16 January 1984.

13 Jay, 1980, p. 275.

14 Ibid.

15 Dalton to Gaitskell correspondence, November 1959, quoted in P. Williams, 1979, p. 543.

16 See, for instance, *Tribune* editorial, 23 October 1959; B. Levy, 'The Double Image', *New Statesman*, 31 October 1959; I Mikardo, 'Why Labour Can Attack', *Tribune*, 27 November 1959; *New Statesman* editorial, 28 November 1959.

17 See P. Williams, 1979, pp. 546, 916.

18 Gaitskell in private conversation with Alastair Hetherington, editor of the *Manchester Guardian*, reported in Hetherington's diary, 12 November 1959; quoted in P. Williams, 1979, p. 545.

19 Labour Party Constitution, Party Objects: Clause IV, Part Four. The words 'distribution and exchange' were added to Part Four in 1929.

20 Gaitskell in an address to the 1951 Society, Manchester; BBC North of England Home Service, 31 October 1955; quoted in P. Williams, 1979, pp. 546–7.

21 Jay, 1980, pp. 276–7.

22 See P. Williams, 1979, p. 550.

23 Ibid.

24 Interview with the Rt Hon. Douglas Jay, Oxford, 16 January 1984.

25 Jay, 1980, p. 277.

26 See P. Williams, 1979, p. 550; see also Crosland interviewed in *The Day Before Yesterday*, Thames Television, 29 September 1970: quoted in A. Thompson, *The Day Before Yesterday*, London, Sidgwick & Jackson, 1971, p. 205; S. Crosland, *Tony Crosland*, London, Cape, 1982, p. 93.

27 S. Watson, 'Winning the Trade Unions', in W. T. Rodgers (ed.), *Hugh Gaitskell, 1906–63*, London, Thames & Hudson, 1964, p. 112.
28 See P. Williams, 1979, p. 551.
29 J. Griffiths, *Pages from Memory*, London, Dent, 1969, p. 135.
30 Labour Party Conference Report, 1959, p. 107.
31 Ibid.
32 Ibid., p. 109.
33 Ibid., p. 108.
34 Ibid., p. 110.
35 Ibid.
36 Ibid.
37 Ibid.
38 Ibid., p. 111.
39 Ibid.
40 Ibid.
41 Ibid., p. 122.
42 Ibid., p. 111–12.
43 Ibid., p. 112.
44 Ibid.
45 Ibid.
46 Ibid.
47 Ibid., p. 113.
48 Ibid.
49 Ibid.
50 In her Chairman's Address, Labour Party Conference Report, 1959, pp. 83–6.
51 Labour Party Conference Report, 1959, p. 84.
52 Ibid., p. 85.
53 Ibid., pp. 121, 120. (Taverne had been the Labour candidate for Wandsworth, Putney, at the 1959 General Election.)
54 Ibid., p. 121.
55 Interview with Dick Taverne, QC, London, 29 August 1984.
56 Labour Party Conference Report, 1959, p. 120.
57 Ibid., p. 122.
58 See P. Williams, 1979, pp. 551, 556; M. Foot, 1973, pp. 638–9; D. Jay, 1980, p. 277.
59 See P. Williams, 1979, pp. 556–7.
60 Labour Party Conference Report, 1959, p. 153.
61 Ibid.
62 For further development of Jay's ideas on nationalization, see *Forward*, 20 November 1959; and D. Jay, 'Beyond State Monopoly', in *Where? 5 Views on Labour's Future* (Fabian Tract 320), London, Fabian Society, 1959 .
63 Jay, 1980, p. 277.
64 See M. Foot, 1973, p. 647; P. Williams, 1979, p. 557.
65 A. Bevan, 'How to Avoid Shipwreck', *Tribune*, 11 December 1959.
66 See G. Goodman, *The Awkward Warrior. Frank Cousins: His Life and Times*, London, Davis-Poynter, 1979, p. 247.
67 See F. Boyd, *The Guardian*, 26 February 1960; cited in P. Williams, 1979, p. 563.

168   *Remaking the Labour Party*

68 See P. Williams, 1979, p. 564.
69 See *Tribune* editorial, 19 February 1960.
70 See P. Williams, 1979, p. 566.
71 Ibid., p. 564.
72 Ibid., pp. 566, 616.
73 Personal correspondence from Philip Williams, 31 October 1984.
74 Labour Party Conference Report, 1959, p. 111.
75 Richard Crossman proposed the words 'amplifies' and 'clarifies'; C. W. Evans, the National Union of Railwaymen (NUR) delegate, proposed the word 'reaffirms'. See R. H. S. Crossman, *The Backbench Diaries of Richard Crossman* (ed. J. Morgan), London, Hamilton & Cape, 1981, p. 830 (entry for 22 March 1960).
76 *Labour's Aims*, London, Labour Party, 1960, section J.
77 P. Williams, 1979, p. 568.
78 Goodman, 1979, p. 248.
79 Crossman, 1981, p. 830.
80 Gaitskell letter to Rita Hinden, 7 July 1960, Socialist Union Papers 7.
81 The survey findings were republished in M. Abrams and R. Rose, *Must Labour Lose?*, London, Penguin, 1960.
82 See C. A. R. Crosland, *Can Labour Win?* (Fabian Tract 324), London, Fabian Society, 1960, p. 9.
83 C. A. R. Crosland, 'The Future of the Left', *Encounter*, March 1960.
84 Ibid. For hostile responses to Crosland's articles, see R. H. S. Crossman, 'The Spectre of Revisionism', *Encounter*, April 1960; B. Castle, 'Open Letter to Tony Crosland', *New Statesman*, 24 September 1960.
85 P. Gordon Walker, 'The Future of the Left', *Encounter*, July 1960.
86 For a detailed account of these developments, see Haseler, 1969, pp. 170–6.
87 See Goodman, 1979, p. 249.
88 *New Left Review* editorial, May–June 1960.
89 Labour Party NEC Minutes, 13 July 1960; quoted in D. Howell, *British Social Democracy*, London, Croom Helm, 1980, p. 224.
90 See P. Williams, 1979, p. 570.
91 For an account of the organizational development of CDS, see Haseler, 1969, ch. 10. On CDS in general, see B. Brivati, 'Campaign for Democratic Socialism', *Contemporary Record*, vol. 4, no. 1, 1990, pp. 11–12; Witness Seminar: 'The Campaign for Democratic Socialism, 1960–64', *Contemporary Record*, vol. 7, no. 2, 1993.
92 Interview with Dick Taverne, QC, London, 29 August 1984.
93 Interview with the Rt Hon. William Rodgers, London, 20 September 1984.
94 Haseler, 1969, p. 216.
95 See Haseler, 1969, p. 210. This point was confirmed in personal correspondence from Philip Williams, 31 October 1984.
96 See Campaign for Democratic Socialism, 'A Manifesto Addressed to the Labour Movement', 18 October 1960.
97 Labour Party Conference Report, 1960, p. 219.
98 Ibid.
99 Ibid.
100 Ibid.

101 L. Minkin and P. Seyd, 'The British Labour Party', in W. Paterson and A. Thomas (eds), *Social Democratic Parties in Western Europe*, London, Croom Helm, 1977, p. 124.
102 P. Williams, 1979, p. 571.
103 Ibid.
104 Personal correspondence from Philip Williams, 31 October 1984.
105 R. T. McKenzie, *British Political Parties*, 2nd edn, London, Heinemann, 1963, p. 607; D Wood, 'The Inheritance', in W. T. Rodgers (ed.), *Hugh Gaitskell, 1906–63*, London, Thames & Hudson, 1964, p. 156.
106 Interview with Lord Wilson of Rievaulx, Oxford, 12 May 1984.
107 R. Jenkins, 'Hugh Gaitskell: A Political Memoir', *Encounter*, February 1964.
108 P. Williams, 1979, p. 569.
109 Interview with the Rt Hon. William Rodgers, London, 20 September 1984.
110 See P. Williams, 1979, p. 547 on the reaction of Conservative Central Office.
111 See P. Williams, 1979, p. 560.
112 M. Foot, 'The Future of the Left', *Encounter*, July 1960.
113 E. Shinwell, *I've Lived Through It All*, London, Gollancz, 1973, p. 232.
114 Jenkins, 1964.
115 Wood, in Rodgers, 1964, p. 157.
116 Interview with Ian Mikardo, London, 12 July 1984.
117 Interview with Lord Wilson of Rievaulx, Oxford, 12 May 1984.
118 Interview with the Rt Hon. Douglas Jay, Oxford, 16 January 1984.
119 C. A. R. Crosland, *The New Socialism, Dissent* pamphlet, Melbourne, Australia, 1963: Crosland Papers, Appendix, 34.
120 P. Williams, 1979, p. 570.
121 Interview with Lord Wilson of Rievaulx, Oxford, 12 May 1984.
122 See P. Foot, *The Politics of Harold Wilson*, London, Pengiun, 1968, p. 127.
123 Interview with the Rt Hon. Douglas Jay, Oxford, 16 January 1964.
124 *Tribune*, 25 March 1960.
125 P. Williams, 1979, p. 549.
126 Ibid.
127 Ibid., p. 570.
128 Ibid.
129 R. H. S. Crossman, *Labour in the Affluent Society* (Fabian Tract 325), London, Fabian Society, 1960, p. 7.
130 *New Statesman*, 12 March 1960.
131 BBC radio interview with Harold Wilson, February 1964: published in *The Listener*, 29 October 1964.
132 H. Wilson, 'Memories of Hugh Gaitskell', *The Guardian*, 8 September 1983.
133 R. H. S. Crossman, 'The Spectre of Revisionism', *Encounter*, April 1960. For an anticipation of this point, see also Crossman's earlier article 'On Political Neuroses', *Encounter*, May 1954.
134 H. M. Drucker, *Doctrine and Ethos in the Labour Party*, London, Allen & Unwin, 1979, p. 38.
135 Ibid.

170 *Remaking the Labour Party*

136 *Tribune*, 8 January 1960.
137 Jenkins, 1964.
138 Interviews with Lord Jenkins of Hillhead, London, 27 October 1987; Lord Wilson of Rievaulx, Oxford, 12 May 1984.
139 P. Williams, 1979, p. 570.
140 P. Williams, 1979, p. 549.
141 F. S. Oliver, *The Endless Adventure*, London, Macmillan, 1930, pp. 45–6.
142 Oliver, 1930, pp. 46, 48.
143 H. Lasswell and A. Kaplan, *Power and Society*, New Haven, Connecticut, Yale University Press, 1946, p. 280 (see above, ch. 1).

4 REVISIONISM DILUTED, 1960–70

1 Interview with the Rt Hon. Peter Shore, MP, London, 2 August 1984.
2 *Labour in the Sixties*, London, Labour Party, 1960, p. 5.
3 Ibid.
4 Ibid., p. 6.
5 Ibid., p. 7.
6 Labour Party Conference Report, 1960, p. 137.
7 Ibid., p. 149.
8 Ibid.
9 Ibid., p. 151.
10 Ibid.
11 Ibid.
12 *Tribune* editorial, 7 October 1960.
13 'Can Labour Look Forward?', *New Statesman* editorial, 13 January 1961.
14 Ibid.
15 See also Wilson's elaboration of his case for public ownership and economic planning in his 'A Four Year Plan for Britain', *New Statesman*, 24 March 1961.
16 *Signposts for the Sixties*, London, Labour Party, 1961, p. 7.
17 Ibid.
18 Ibid., p. 9.
19 Ibid., p. 8.
20 Ibid., p. 10.
21 Ibid.
22 Ibid., p. 35.
23 Ibid., p. 16.
24 Ibid., pp. 16, 17.
25 D. Howell, *British Social Democracy*, London, Croom Helm, 1976; 2nd edn, 1980, p. 232.
26 D. Coates, *The Labour Party and the Struggle for Socialism*, Cambridge, Cambridge University Press, 1975, p. 93.
27 Interview with Ian Mikardo, London, 12 July 1984.
28 L. Minkin, *The Labour Party Conference*, Manchester, Manchester University Press, 1980, p. 287.
29 Ibid., p. 125.
30 C. A. R. Crosland, Memo for Campaign for Democratic Socialism, July 1961, Crosland Papers, II, 6/1.

31 W. Norman, *Signposts for the Sixties*, *New Left Review*, vol. 11, September–October 1961.
32 Ibid.
33 *New Statesman* editorial, 30 June 1961.
34 Ibid.
35 Labour Party Conference Report, 1961, p. 105.
36 Labour Party Conference Report, 1959, pp. 83–6.
37 P. Anderson, 'The Left in the Fifties', *New Left Review*, vol. 29, January–February 1965.
38 Interview with the Rt Hon. Peter Shore, MP, London, 2 August 1984.
39 Anderson, 1965.
40 Ibid.
41 See R. H. S. Crossman, '*Labour in the Affluent Society*' (Fabian Tract 325), London, Fabian Society, 1960.
42 Interview with the Rt Hon. Peter Shore, MP, London, 2 August 1984.
43 See, for instance, *For Socialism and Peace*, London, Labour Party, 1934. For a discussion of this point see F. Bealey (ed.), *The Social and Political Thought of the British Labour Party*, London, Weidenfeld & Nicolson, 1970, p. 27.
44 See Labour Party, 1961, pp. 16, 17. See also Wilson's reference to 'industrial mendicants' within the private sector, Labour Party Conference Report, 1961, p. 104.
45 Labour Party Conference Report, 1961, p. 106.
46 Labour Party, 1961, p. 7.
47 Labour Party Conference Report, 1961, p. 101.
48 'Our Outside Left', *Socialist Commentary* editorial, November 1961.
49 See, for instance, *Tribune* editorial, 13 October 1961; 'Missing Signposts', *New Left Review*, vol. 12, editorial, November–December 1961.
50 See Labour Party Conference Report, 1961, pp. 188–94.
51 Interview with the Rt Hon. Douglas Jay, Oxford, 27 July 1984.
52 Crosland, memo for CDS, July 1961, Crosland Papers, II, 6/1.
53 C. A. R. Crosland, *The Conservative Enemy*, London, Cape, 1962, p. 7.
54 See C. A. R. Crosland, 'The Transition from Capitalism', in R. H. S. Crossman (ed.), *New Fabian Essays*, London, Turnstile Press, 1952; C. A. R. Crosland, *The Future of Socialism*, London, Cape, 1964, pp. 16–17.
55 Crosland, 1962, p. 68.
56 See, for instance, 'The Insiders', *Universities and Left Review*, Winter 1958; M. Barratt-Brown, 'The Controllers', *Universities and Left Review*, vol. 4, 1959.
57 Interview with the Rt Hon. Douglas Jay, Oxford, 16 January 1984.
58 Ibid.
59 Crosland, 1962, p. 7.
60 See Crosland, 1964, pp. 43–4, 66–7.
61 See D. Jay, *Socialism in the New Society*. London, Longman, 1962, pp. 3–4, 44–5.
62 Jay, 1962, p. 45.
63 See Crosland, 1964, pp. 53, 328, 330–1; Gaitskell, *Socialism and Nationalisation*, London, Fabian Society, 1956.
64 Jay, 1962, p. 45.
65 Ibid.

66 Jay, 1962, p. 180. For a similar, earlier view, see Jay, *Forward*, 28 July 1956.

67 See Crosland, 1962, p. 41. Discussion of this point was contained in a chapter entitled 'The Role of Public Ownership' which had originally been published as what Crosland later referred to as a 'very revisionist article' in *Encounter*, May 1961. (See Crosland, memo for CDS, July 1961, Crosland Papers, II, 6/1.)

68 See Jay, 1962, p. 21.

69 See, for instance, Crosland, 1964, p. 330.

70 See Crosland, 1962, p. 41.

71 See Jay, 1862, pp. 278, 283, 285.

72 Crosland, 1962, p. 44; cf Crosland, 1964, p. 340.

73 See Jay, *Forward*, 16 October 1959; 20 November 1959; and 'Beyond State Monopoly', in *Where? 5 Views on Labour's Future*, London, Fabian Society, 1959.

74 Jay, 1962, p. 295.

75 Ibid., p. 301.

76 Ibid., p. 339.

77 See Crosland, 1962, p. 49; cf Crosland, 1964, pp. 140, 340.

78 For unfavourable views of Crosland's *The Conservative Enemy*, see B. Castle, 'The Radical Without Roots', *Tribune*, 23 November 1962, and G. Lichtheim, 'New Right', *New Statesman*, 30 November 1962. For a critique, too, of Jay's *Socialism in the New Society*, see R. Hinden, 'Socialism by Half', *Socialist Commentary*, March 1962.

79 Howell, 1980, p. 235.

80 See P. Williams, *Hugh Gaitskell: A Political Biography*, London, Cape, 1979, pp. 757–9; Minkin, 1980, pp. 288–9; S. Haseler, *The Gaitskellites*, London, Macmillan, 1969, p. 237.

81 Howell, 1980, p. 235. For a similar view see also Haseler, 1969, p. 253; A. Warde, *Consensus and Beyond*, Manchester, Manchester University Press, 1982, p. 65; K. Morgan, 'The Labour Party since 1945', in A. Seldon (ed.), *UK Political Parties Since 1945*, Hemel Hempstead, Philip Allan, 1990, p. 6.

82 M. Edelman, *Tribune*, 13 November 1959.

83 See Warde, 1982, pp. 94–118.

84 Ibid., p. 202

85 Ibid., p. 97.

86 See A. Howard, *Richard Crossman: The Pursuit of Power*, London, Pimlico, 1991, p. 250; R. H. S. Crossman, *The Backbench Diaries of Richard Crossman* (ed. J. Morgan), London, Hamilton & Cape, 1981, entry for 17 July 1963.

87 See D. Horner, 'The Road to Scarborough: Wilson, Labour and the Scientific Revolution', in R. Cooney, S. Fielding and N. Tiratsoo (eds), *The Wilson Governments 1964–1970*, London, Pinter, 1993. See also S. Fielding, 'White Heat and White Collars: The Evolution of Wilsonism', in Cooney et al. (eds), 1993, on the intellectual background of Wilson's 1963 Scarborough speech.

88 Labour Party Conference Report, 1963, p. 135.

89 See H. Wilson, *The New Britain*, London, Penguin, 1964; *Purpose in Politics: Selected Speeches*, London, Weidenfeld & Nicolson, 1964, pp. 14–28.

90 Wilson, *The Relevance of British Socialism*, London, Weidenfeld & Nicolson, 1964, pp. 22–3, 24.
91 See K. Ovenden, *The Politics of Steel*, London, Macmillan, 1978.
92 See R. Williams (ed.), *May Day Manifesto*, London, Penguin, 1968.
93 Labour Party Conference Report, 1963, pp. 139–40.
94 P. Shore, *Leading the Left*, London, Weidenfeld & Nicolson, 1993, p. 89.
95 Ibid., p. 91.
96 Howell, 1980, p. 252.
97 D. Horner, in Cooney et al. (eds), 1993, p. 67.
98 Labour Party Conference Report, 1966, p. 163.
99 R. Miliband, 'The Labour Government and Beyond', in *The Socialist Register 1966*, London, Merlin Press, 1966, pp. 12–13.
100 C. A. R. Crosland, *Socialism Now and Other Essays*, London, Cape, 1974, pp. 21, 26.
101 For a generally favourable reassessment of the record of the 1964–70 Wilson Governments, see, in particular, R. McKibbin, 'Homage to Wilson and Callaghan', *London Review of Books*, 24 October 1991; B. Pimlott, *Harold Wilson*, London, Harper Collins, 1992; and K. O. Morgan, *Labour People, Leaders and Lieutenants: Hardie to Kinnock*, Oxford, Oxford University Press, 1987, pp. 252–3. For an outline of various interpretations of the record of the 1964–70 Governments, see Introduction to Cooney et al. (eds), 1993, pp. 1–8.
102 K. Middlemass, *The Politics of Industrial Society*, London, Deutsch, 1979, p. 455.
103 Ibid.
104 D. Marquand, 'Inquest on a Movement', *Encounter*, July 1979.
105 Warde, 1982, p. 113.
106 R. H. S. Crossman, 'Scientists in Whitehall', *Encounter*, July 1964; reprinted in Crossman, *Planning for Freedom*, London, Hamilton, 1965, p. 135.
107 A. Crosland's Notebook, 1967–72: entry for Christmas 1968, Crosland Papers, IV, 16/7.
108 Ibid.
109 Interview with Lord Wilson of Rievaulx, Oxford, 12 May 1984.
110 Ibid.
111 Ibid.
112 A. Benn, *Out of the Wilderness: Diaries, 1963–67*, London, Hutchinson, 1987, entry for 23 January 1964, p. 90.
113 C. Ponting, *In Breach of Promise: Labour in Power, 1964–1970*, London, Hamish Hamilton, 1989, p. 403.
114 For expressions of this view, see, for instance, G Foote, *The Labour Party's Political Thought*, London, Croom Helm, 1985, p. 236; B. Crick, *Socialist Values and Time* (Fabian Tract 495), London, Fabian Society, 1984, p. 13.
115 B. Pimlott, *Harold Wilson*, Harper Collins, 1992, p. 273.
116 Ibid.
117 K. O. Morgan, in A. Seldon (ed.), *UK Political Parties Since 1945*, London, Philip Allan, 1990, p. 7.
118 Interview with the Rt Hon. Bill Rodgers, London, 20 September 1984.
119 Middlemass, 1979, p. 417.

5 REVISIONIST SOCIAL DEMOCRACY IN RETREAT, 1970–83

1 See M. Hatfield, *The House the Left Built: Inside Labour Policy-Making 1970–75*, London, Gollancz, 1978, p. 17.
2 Ibid., p. 18.
3 P. Shore, *Leading the Left*, London, Weidenfeld & Nicolson, 1993, p. 103.
4 Ibid., p. 105.
5 Ibid., p. 106.
6 P. Whitehead, 'The Labour Governments, 1974–79', in A. Seldon and P. Hennessy (eds), *Ruling Performance*, Oxford, Blackwell, 1987, p. 243.
7 *Labour's Programme 1973*, London, Labour Party, 1973, p. 30.
8 Ibid., p. 7.
9 Hatfield, 1978, p. 161. (Benn proposed the words at a meeting of the NEC Industrial Policy subcommittee.)
10 Labour Party, 1993, p. 7.
11 Ibid., p. 30.
12 Ibid., p. 187.
13 D. Coates, *Labour in Power?*, London, Longman, 1980, p. viii.
14 Ibid., p. 2.
15 *The Guardian*, 3 October 1973.
16 See Shore, 1993, p. 105.
17 See Hatfield, 1978, p. 149.
18 Quoted in R. Desai, *Intellectuals and Socialism: 'Social Democrats' and the Labour Party*, London, Lawrence & Wishart, 1994, p. 171.
19 S. Holland, *The Socialist Challenge*, London, Quartet, 1975, p. 26.
20 Ibid., p. 70.
21 C. A. R. Crosland, 'Socialism Now', in *Socialism Now and Other Essays*, London, Cape, 1974, p. 26.
22 Ibid., p. 27.
23 Ibid.
24 Ibid., p. 28.
25 Ibid., p. 30.
26 Ibid., p. 33.
27 Ibid.
28 Ibid.
29 Ibid.
30 Ibid.
31 Ibid., p. 39.
32 ibid.
33 Ibid., p. 43
34 Ibid., p. 39
35 Ibid.
36 Ibid., p. 44.
37 See D. Marquand, 'Clause Four Rides Again', *Times Literary Supplement*, 26 September 1975.
38 Crosland, 1974, p. 43.
39 Ibid., p. 15.
40 Ibid.

41 Crosland, 'A Social Democratic Britain', in Crosland, 1974, p. 71 (originally published as Fabian Tract 404, London, Fabian Society, January 1971).
42 Ibid.
43 Ibid.
44 Crosland, 'Socialism Now', in Crosland, 1974, p. 44.
45 Crosland, 'A Social Democratic Britain', in Crosland, 1974, p. 73.
46 Ibid.
47 For an extended discussion of this question, see Desai, 1994, ch. 6.
48 Sixty-nine Labour MPs voted against a three-line party whip in the parliamentary vote on the principle of British entry into the European Community in October 1971.
49 See, for instance, J. P. Mackintosh, 'Socialism or Social Democracy? The Choice for the Labour Party', *Political Quarterly*, vol. 43, no. 4, October–December 1972.
50 H. Wilson, *Final Term: The Labour Government 1974–76*, London, Weidenfeld & Nicolson, 1979, p. 33.
51 Cmnd 5710, HMSO, 1974, p. 2.
52 A. Benn, *Against the Tide: Diaries 1973–76*, London, Hutchinson, 1989, p. 263, entry for 13 November 1974.
53 *Tribune*, 14 November 1975, p. 5.
54 Benn, 1989, p. 674.
55 Labour Party Conference Report, 1976, p. 157.
56 Ibid., p. 188.
57 L. Minkin, *The Contentious Alliance*, Edinburgh, Edinburgh University Press, 1991, p. 208.
58 P. Jenkins, *Mrs Thatcher's Revolution*, London, Cape, 1987, p. 8.
59 A. Arblaster, 'Anthony Crosland: Labour's Last Revisionist?', *Political Quarterly*, vol. 48, no. 4, October–December 1977, p. 424.
60 Ibid., p. 425.
61 Ibid., p. 426.
62 Ibid., p. 427.
63 Ibid.
64 Ibid.
65 Ibid.
66 See Desai, 1994, pp. 137–8; S. Crosland, *Tony Crosland*, London, Cape, 1982, p. 229.
67 See P. Jenkins, *Guardian Weekly*, 27 February 1977.
68 *Socialist Commentary* editorial, December 1978.
69 J. P. Mackintosh, 'Is Labour Facing Catastrophe?', in *John P. Mackintosh on Parliament and Social Democracy* (ed. D. Marquand), London, Longman, 1982, pp. 176, 170 (originally published in *Encounter*, January 1977).
70 Ibid., p. 176.
71 Ibid.
72 J. P. Mackintosh, 'The Case for a Realignment of the Left', in Mackintosh, 1982, pp. 193–4 (originally published in *The Times*, 22 July 1977).
73 Ibid., p. 195.
74 Ibid.

75 Ibid.
76 J. Mackintosh, 'Has Social Democracy Failed in Britain?', in Mackintosh, 1982, p. 227 (originally published in *Political Quarterly*, vol. 49, no. 3, July–September 1978).
77 Ibid., p. 225.
78 Ibid.
79 Ibid., p. 230.
80 Ibid., p. 232.
81 Ibid., pp. 229–32.
82 D. Marquand, 'Introduction', in Mackintosh, 1982, pp. 19–20.
83 Ibid., p. 13.
84 Ibid.
85 Ibid., p. 14.
86 D. Marquand, 'Inquest on a Movement', *Encounter*, July 1979, p. 11.
87 Ibid.
88 Ibid., p. 9.
89 See D. Taverne, *The Future of the Left: Lincoln and After*, London, Cape, 1974.
90 Marquand, 1979, p. 18.
91 Ibid.
92 See E. Luard, *Socialism Without the State*, London, Macmillan, 1979.
93 Minkin, 1991, p. 126.
94 Ibid., p. 132.
95 *Labour's Programme 1982*, London, Labour Party, 1982.
96 J. Callaghan, *Socialism in Britain Since 1884*, Oxford, Blackwell, 1990, p. 45.
97 D. Owen, W. Rodgers and S. Williams, open letter to *The Guardian*, 1 August 1980.

6 REVISIONISM REBORN? 1983–92

1 E. Shaw, *The Labour Party Since 1979: Crisis and Transformation*, London, Routledge, 1994, p. 29.
2 N. Kinnock, 'Reforming the Labour Party', *Contemporary Record*, vol. 8, no. 3, Winter 1994, p. 536 (originally delivered as a lecture at the Institute of Historical Research, University of London, 8 December 1993).
3 Ibid., pp. 539–40.
4 Ibid., p. 536.
5 Interview with the Rt Hon. Neil Kinnock, London, 28 February 1994.
6 Ibid.
7 Ibid.
8 Kinnock, 1994, p. 536.
9 Ibid., p. 538.
10 Ibid., p. 540.
11 P. Jenkins, *Mrs Thatcher's Revolution: The End of the Socialist Era*, London, Cape, 1987, p. 224.
12 E. Hobsbawm, 'The Face of Labour's Future' (Eric Hobsbawm interviews Neil Kinnock), *Marxism Today*, October 1984, p. 11.

13 Ibid.
14 Ibid.
15 Ibid.
16 See E. Hobsbawm, 'The Forward March of Labour Halted', lecture delivered in 1978 and subsequently published in M. Jacques and F. Mulhearn (eds), *The Forward March of Labour Halted?*, London, New Left Books, 1981; and E. Hobsbawm, 'Labour's Lost Millions', *Marxism Today*, October 1984.
17 N. Kinnock, *The Future of Socialism* (Fabian Tract 509), London, Fabian Society, 1985.
18 Ibid., p. 1.
19 Ibid.
20 Ibid., p. 2.
21 Ibid.
22 Ibid.
23 Ibid., p. 3.
24 Ibid., p. 4.
25 Ibid., p. 5.
26 Ibid., p. 3.
27 Ibid., p. 8.
28 Ibid., p. 9.
29 Ibid.
30 Ibid.
31 Ibid., p. 6.
32 Ibid.
33 Ibid.
34 Labour Party Conference Report, 1985, p. 123.
35 Labour Party Conference Report, 1986, p. 49.
36 *Social Ownership*, London, Labour Party, 1986, p. 2.
37 N. Kinnock, *Making Our Way: Investing in Britain's Future*, Oxford, Blackwell, 1986, pp. 185, 186.
38 Ibid., pp. 186–7.
39 Ibid., p. 188.
40 Ibid., p. 189.
41 On Kinnock's earlier traditional socialist views, see T. Jones, 'Neil Kinnock's Socialist Journey: From Clause Four to the Policy Review', *Contemporary Record*, vol. 8, no. 3, Winter 1994, pp. 567–72.
42 Kinnock, 1986, p. 193.
43 Ibid., p. 42.
44 Kinnock, 1994, p. 542.
45 Ibid.
46 M. J. Smith, 'A Return to Revisionism? The Labour Party's Policy Review', in M. Smith and J. Spear (eds), *The Changing Labour Party*, London, Routledge, 1992, p. 17.
47 Ibid.
48 Labour Party Conference Report, 1986, p. 46.
49 Ibid.
50 Ibid.
51 Ibid.
52 Ibid.

53 Ibid.
54 Ibid.
55 Ibid.
56 *Statement of Democratic Socialist Aims and Values*, London, Labour Party, 1988, p. 3.
57 Ibid., p. 10.
58 R. Hattersley, *Choose Freedom: The Future for Democratic Socialism*, London, Penguin, 1987, p. xvi.
59 Ibid., p. xvii.
60 Ibid., p. 188.
61 Ibid., p. 129.
62 Ibid., p. 148.
63 Ibid., p. 170.
64 Labour Party, 1988, p. 4.
65 Ibid., p. 5.
66 Ibid., p. 10.
67 R. Hattersley, *Who Goes Home? Scenes from a Political Life*, London, Little, Brown & Co., 1995, p. 292. There had, however, been an earlier debate amongst members of the Shadow Cabinet over the extent of support for the market economy expressed in the statement of *Aims and Values*. See C. Hughes and P. Wintour, *Labour Rebuilt: The New Model Party*, London, Fourth Estate, 1990, pp. 69–71.
68 Labour Party Conference Report, 1988, p. 64.
69 *Meet the Challenge, Make the Change*, London, Labour Party, 1989, p. 5.
70 Ibid., p. 8.
71 A. Gamble 'The Labour Party and Economic Management', in Smith and Spear (eds), 1992, p. 65.
72 Ibid. (cf C. A. R. Crosland, *The Future of Socialism*, London, Cape, 1964, p. 41).
73 Labour Party, 1989, p. 6.
74 Ibid.
75 P. Kellner, 'Labour Learns to Love the Market', *The Independent*, 8 May 1989.
76 Labour Party, 1989, p. 9.
77 Ibid., p. 10.
78 Ibid.
79 Ibid., p. 6.
80 Ibid.
81 P. Kellner, 'Labour Adaptions Since 1979', *Contemporary Record*, vol. 3, no. 2, November 1989, p. 14.
82 I. Crewe, 'The Policy Agenda', *Contemporary Record*, vol. 3, no. 3, February 1990, p. 6.
83 G. Radice, *Labour's Path to Power: The New Revisionism*, London, Macmillan, 1989, p. 10.
84 Ibid., p. 14.
85 Ibid., p. 92.
86 B. Gould, *A Future for Socialism*, London, Cape, 1989, pp. 95–6.
87 Ibid., p. 94.
88 Ibid.
89 Ibid., p. 95.

90 Labour Party, 1989, p. 6.
91 On this particular debate, see E. Shaw, 1994, pp. 90–4. For an examination of the Policy Review as a whole, see Shaw, 1994, ch. 4; E. Shaw, *The Labour Party Since 1945*, Oxford, Blackwell, 1996, pp. 181–8; and M. J. Smith, in Smith and Spear, 1992.
92 See, for example, *Opportunity Britain*, London, Labour Party, 1991, p. 4.
93 Kellner, 8 May 1989.
94 Ibid.
95 Crewe, 1992, p. 5.
96 D. Marquand, *The Progressive Dilemma*, London, Heinemann, 1991, p. 201.
97 Ibid.
98 M. J. Smith, in Smith and Spear, 1992, p. 27.
99 Shaw, 1996, p. 201.
100 M. J. Smith, in Smith and Spear, 1992, p. 28.
101 Marquand, 1991, pp. 201–2.
102 Kinnock, 1994, p. 545.
103 Ibid.
104 Interview with The Rt Hon. Neil Kinnock, London, 28 February 1994.
105 Ibid.
106 Kinnock, 1994, p. 545.
107 Ibid.
108 On the significance of Labour's ethos within its ideology, see H. M. Drucker, *Doctrine and Ethos in the Labour Party*, London, Allen & Unwin, 1979. For an interesting discussion of Kinnock's empathy with Labour's ethos, see Marquand, 1991, ch. 17.
109 P. Jenkins, 1987, p. 221.
110 K Jefferys, *The Labour Party Since 1945*, London, Macmillan, 1993, p. 128.

7 THE TRIUMPH OF REVISIONISM? MODERNIZATION UNDER SMITH AND BLAIR

1 H. Young, 'Never Did a More Decent Man Rise to the Top of British Politics', *The Guardian*, 13 May 1994.
2 *The Observer*, 15 May 1994.
3 Young, 13 May 1994.
4 'Man of Honour in Cynical Times', *The Independent* editorial, 13 May 1994. For a discussion of Smith's approach to modernization of the Party, see G. Brown and J. Naughtie, *John Smith. Life and Soul of the Party*, Edinburgh, Mainstream, 1994, pp. 48–55.
5 Smith's lecture was subsequently published in J. Smith et al., *Reclaiming the Ground* (ed. C. Bryant), London, Spire, 1993, pp. 127–42.
6 J. Smith, 1993, pp. 130, 129.
7 Ibid., p. 138.
8 See J. Rentoul, *Tony Blair*, London, Little, Brown & Co., 1995, pp. 413–14. See also P. Webster, *The Times*, 20 September 1995.
9 J. Straw, *Policy and Ideology*, Blackburn, Blackburn Labour Party, March 1993, p. 2.

10 Ibid., p. 4.
11 Ibid., p. 10.
12 Ibid., p. 11.
13 Ibid., p. 12
14 Ibid.
15 J. Straw, 'Clause that Drew Blood', *The Guardian*, 24 February 1993; Straw, March 1993, pp. 21–3.
16 Ibid., p. 28.
17 Ibid.
18 See Rentoul, 1995, pp. 413–14. Straw himself, however, was unaware at the time, in spite of conversations with Smith shortly before the pamphlet's publication in 1993, of this particular reason for the leader's displeasure (personal correspondence from Jack Straw MP, 19 February 1996).
19 N. Kinnock, *Tomorrow's Socialism*, BBC 2 Television, 5 February 1994.
20 Ibid.
21 Ibid.
22 For further support at this time for the idea of revising Clause IV, see also G. Radice, *Southern Discomfort*, London, Fabian Society, 1992, p. 24; G. Radice and S. Pollard, *More Southern Discomfort*, London, Fabian Society, 1993, p. 16.
23 See Rentoul, 1995, p. 414.
24 Ibid., pp. 346–7
25 A. Blair, interview with P. Riddell and P. Webster, *The Times*, 18 September 1995.
26 *Fabian Review*, 9 May 1992.
27 A. Blair, 'Forging a New Agenda', *Marxism Today*, October 1991, p. 32.
28 Ibid.
29 Ibid.
30 Ibid.
31 Ibid.
32 Ibid., p. 33.
33 Ibid.
34 Ibid., p. 34
35 Ibid.
36 A. Blair, *Socialism* (Fabian Pamphlet 565), London, Fabian Society, 1994, p. 3.
37 Ibid., p. 4.
38 Ibid.
39 See J. Rentoul, 1995, pp. 41–4.
40 Blair, 1994, p. 4.
41 Ibid., pp. 4–5.
42 Ibid., p. 4.
43 Ibid., p. 7.
44 Ibid.
45 See C. A. R. Crosland, *The Future of Socialism*, London, Cape, 1964, pp. 67, 69–76.
46 Ibid., p. 73.
47 Ibid.
48 Ibid., p. 76.

49 H. Gaitskell, *Socialism and Nationalisation*, London, Fabian Society, 1956, pp. 5, 17–18; Labour Party Conference Report, 1959, p. 111.
50 See above, chs 1 and 2.
51 E. Shaw, *The Labour Party Since 1945*, Oxford, Blackwell, 1996, pp. 228–9.
52 See Rentoul, 1995, p. 412; J. Sopel, *Tony Blair: The Modernizer*, London, Michael Joseph, 1995, pp. 272–4.
53 Blair, in a note of a discussion with Mandelson, quoted in Sopel, 1995, p. 273.
54 See Rentoul, 1995, p. 416; Sopel, 1995, pp. 273–4.
55 Labour Party Conference Report, 1994.
56 Ibid.
57 Ibid.
58 Ibid.
59 Ibid.
60 P. Riddell, 'Theatrical Blow Struck in Battle to Banish the Old Dogma', *The Times*, 5 October 1994.
61 *The Times* editorial, 5 October 1994.
62 H. Young, 'Why Blair is Now More than Mr Nice Guy', *The Guardian*, 6 October 1994.
63 A. Blair, speech to Labour MEPs, Brussels, 10 January 1995; quoted in *The Times*, 11 January 1995.
64 Ibid.
65 A. Blair, 'Socialist Values in the Modern World', speech to Sedgefield Constituency Labour Party, 28 January 1995.
66 Ibid.
67 Ibid.
68 Ibid.
69 Ibid.
70 A. Blair, lecture at a commemoration organized by the Fabian Society to mark the fiftieth anniversary of the 1945 General Election, 5 July 1995.
71 A. Blair, 'Socialist Values in the Modern World', 1995
72 Ibid.
73 Ibid.
74 Ibid.
75 Ibid.
76 Ibid.
77 H. Young, 'The Crusade is Over for an Electorate of Deserters', *The Guardian*, 26 January 1995.
78 Ibid.
79 Ibid.
80 A. Marr, 'He's Not One of Them – and It Shows', *The Independent*, 11 January 1995.
81 Labour Party Constitution: *Labour's Aims and Values*, London, Labour Party, 1995.
82 Ibid.
83 Ibid.
84 A. Blair, quoted in *The Guardian*, 13 March 1995.
85 A. Blair, quoted in *The Daily Telegraph*, 13 March 1995.

86 See, for instance, K. Coates, *Common Ownership: Clause IV and the Labour Party*, Nottingham, Spokesman, 1995.
87 Sidney Webb, article for *The Observer*, 1917, explaining the thinking behind the constitutional proposals; quoted in Coates, 1995, p.10.
88 *The Independent*, 13 March 1995.
89 *The Times*, 14 March 1995.
90 Ibid.
91 'A Defining Break with Labour's Past', *The Guardian* editorial, 14 March 1995.
92 'A Clause for the Future', *The Independent* editorial, 14 March 1995.
93 Ibid.
94 Shaw, 1996, p. 200.
95 B. Castle, 'Going for a Quid Pro Quo', *Tribune*, 28 April 1995.
96 R. Hattersley, 'Tone of the Times', *The Guardian*, 27 April 1995.
97 Ibid.
98 See A. Blair, 'Socialist Values in the Modern World', 1995; Fabian Society lecture, 5 July 1995.
99 A. Marr, 1995.

8 CONCLUSION

1 R. H. S. Crossman, *Labour in the Affluent Society*, London, Fabian Society, 1960, p. 7.
2 See R. Harrison, 'The War Emergency Workers' National Committee, 1914–1920', in A. Briggs and J. Saville (eds), *Essays in Labour History, 1886–1923*, London, Macmillan, 1971, p. 259.
3 C. A. R. Crosland, 'The Future of the Left', *Encounter*, March 1960.
4 J. Strachey, 'The New Revisionist', *New Statesman*, 6 October 1956.
5 For expressions of this view, see D. Howell, *British Social Democracy*, London, Croom Helm, 1980, p. 235; S. Haseler, *The Gaitskellites*, London, Macmillan, 1969, p. 253; and A. Warde, *Consensus and Beyond*, Manchester, Manchester University Press, 1982, p. 62.
6 Haseler, 1969, p. 237.
7 K. O. Morgan, 'The Labour Party since 1945', in A Seldon (ed.), *UK Political Parties Since 1945*, Hemel Hempstead, Philip Allan, 1990, p. 6.
8 L. Minkin, *The Labour Party Conference*, Manchester, Manchester University Press, 1980, p. 240.
9 Ibid., p. 80.
10 Ibid., p. 326.
11 J. P. Mackintosh, 'Socialism or Social Democracy? The Choice for the Labour Party', *Political Quarterly*, vol. 43, no. 4, October–December 1972.
12 E. Shaw, *The Labour Party Since 1979*, London, Routledge, 1994, p. 206.
13 Ibid., p. 86.
14 J. P. Mackintosh, 'The Case for a Realignment of the Left', in *John P. Mackintosh on Parliament and Social Democracy*, (ed. D. Marquand), London, Longman, 1982, p. 195.
15 Ibid.
16 G. Radice, *Southern Discomfort*, London, Fabian Society, 1992, p. 24.

17 G. Radice, *Labour's Path to Power: The New Revisionism*, London, Macmillan, 1989, p. 10.
18 Radice, 1992, p. 18.
19 See, for example, M. J. Smith, 'Continuity and Change in Labour Party Policy', in M. J. Smith and J. Spear (eds), *The Changing Labour Party*, London, Routledge, 1992, p. 223; D Marquand, *The Progressive Dilemma*, London, Heinemann, 1991, p. 201.
20 E. Shaw, *The Labour Party Since 1945*, Oxford, Blackwell, 1996, p. 201.
21 Ibid., p. xi.
22 Ibid., p. 201.
23 E. Shaw, 1994, p. x.
24 Ibid., p. 103.
25 Ibid., p. 106.
26 A. Marr, 'Welcome Back From the Wilderness', *The Independent*, 19 December 1995.
27 Ibid.
28 Ibid.
29 J. Gray, 'Putting Britain together again', *The Guardian*, 29 January 1996.
30 Ibid.
31 J. Gray, *After Social Democracy*, London, Demos, 1996, pp. 7–8.
32 Ibid.
33 A. Blair, 'True Story of the Wilderness Years', *The Observer*, 17 December 1995.
34 Ibid.
35 See P. Seyd and P. Whiteley, 'Red in Tooth and Clause', *New Statesman and Society*, 9 December 1994, pp. 18–19, for survey evidence indicating that two-thirds of Labour Party members are still generally in favour of the public ownership of industry and, particularly, of the water, gas and electricity utilities. These findings were consistent with the authors' previous survey evidence published in P. Seyd and P. Whiteley, *Labour's Grass Roots: The Politics of Party Membership*, Oxford, Oxford University Press, 1992.
36 Seyd and Whiteley, 1994, p. 19.

BIBLIOGRAPHY

Abercrombie, N. and Warde, A., *Contemporary British Society*, Oxford, Polity Press, 1988.

Abrams, M. and Rose, R., *Must Labour Lose?*, London, Penguin, 1960.

Anderson, P., 'The Left in the Fifties', *New Left Review*, vol. 29, January–February 1965.

Arblaster, A., 'Anthony Crosland: Labour's Last Revisionist?', *Political Quarterly*, vol. 48, no. 4, October–December 1977.

Arnot, R. P., *The Miners: Years of Struggle*, London, Allen & Unwin, 1953.

Barker, R., *Education and Politics: A Study of the Labour Party*, Oxford, Oxford University Press, 1972.

——, 'Socialism and Progressivism in the Political Thought of Ramsay MacDonald', in A. J. Morris (ed.), *Edwardian Radicalism 1900–1914*, London, Routledge & Kegan Paul, 1974.

——, 'Political Myth: Ramsay MacDonald and the Labour Party', *History*, February 1976.

Barratt-Brown, M., 'The Controllers', *Universities and Left Review*, vol. 4, 1959.

Bealey, F., (ed.), *The Social and Political Thought of the British Labour Party*, London, Weidenfeld & Nicolson, 1970.

Beer, S. H., *Modern British Politics*, London, Faber, 1965; 2nd edn, 1982.

Benn, A., *Out of the Wilderness: Diaries 1963–67*, London, Hutchinson, 1987.

——, *Against the Tide: Diaries 1973–76*, London, Hutchinson, 1989.

Berle, A. and Means, G., *The Modern Corporation and Private Property*, New York, Macmillan, 1932.

Bevan, A., 'How to Avoid Shipwreck', *Tribune*, 11 December 1959.

——, *In Place of Fear*, London, Heinemann, 1952; new edn with intro. by N. Kinnock, London, Quartet, 1978.

Blair, A., 'Forging a New Agenda', *Marxism Today*, October 1991.

——, *Socialism*, London, Fabian Society, 1994.

——, 'True Story of the Wilderness Years', *The Observer*, 17 December 1995.

Bogdanor, V., 'The Labour Party in Opposition, 1951–64', in V. Bogdanor and R. Skidelsky (eds), *The Age of Affluence, 1951–1964*, London, Macmillan, 1970.

Brivati, B., 'Campaign for Democratic Socialism', *Contemporary Record*, vol. 4, no. 1, 1990.

Brown, G. and Naughtie, J., *John Smith. Life and Soul of the Party*, Edinburgh, Mainstream, 1994.

Bryan, D., 'The Development of Revisionist Thought Among British Labour Intellectuals and Politicians, 1931–64', unpublished D.Phil. thesis, University of Oxford, 1984.

Burnham, J., *The Managerial Revolution*, London, Putnam, 1942.

Burns, E., *Right-Wing Labour: Its Theory and Practice*, London, Lawrence & Wishart, 1961.

Callaghan, J., *Socialism in Britain Since 1884*, Oxford, Blackwell, 1990.

Camp, W., 'Is This Really 20th Century Socialism?', *Tribune*, 29 June 1956.

Cassirer, E., *The Myth of the State*, London and New York, Oxford University Press, 1946.

Castle, B., 'Open Letter to Tony Crosland', *New Statesman*, 24 September 1960.

——, 'The Radical Without Roots', *Tribune*, 23 November 1962.

——, 'Going for a Quid Pro Quo', *Tribune*, 28 April 1995.

Coates, D., *The Labour Party and the Struggle for Socialism*, Cambridge, Cambridge University Press, 1975.

——, *Labour in Power?*, London, Longman, 1980.

Coates, K., *Common Ownership: Clause IV and the Labour Party*, Nottingham, Spokesman, 1995.

Cole, G. D. H., *A History of the Labour Party from 1918*, London, Routledge, 1948.

——, 'Twentieth-century Socialism', *New Statesman*, 7 July 1956.

——, review of *Industry and Society*, New Statesman, 28 September 1957.

Cooney, R., Fielding, S. and Tiratsoo, N. (eds), *The Wilson Governments, 1964–1970*, London, Pinter, 1993.

Crewe, I., 'The Policy Agenda', *Contemporary Record*, vol. 3, no. 3, February 1990.

Crick, B., 'Britain's "Democratic Party"', *The Nation*, 10 December 1960.

——, *Socialist Values and Time*, London, Fabian Society, 1984.

Crosland, C. A. R., 'The Transition from Capitalism', in R. H. S. Crossman (ed.), *New Fabian Essays*, London, Turnstile Press, 1952.

——, 'The Future of the Labour Party', *National and English Review*, July 1955.

——, *The Future of Socialism*, London, Cape, 1956; rev. edn 1964.

——, *Can Labour Win?*, London, Fabian Society, 1960.

——, 'The Future of the Left', *Encounter*, March 1960.

——, *The Conservative Enemy*, London, Cape, 1962.

——, *Socialism Now and Other Essays*, London, Cape, 1974.

Crosland, S., *Tony Crosland*, London, Cape, 1982.

Cross, P., *Philip Snowden*, London, Barrie & Rockcliff, 1966.

Crossman, R. H. S. (ed.), *New Fabian Essays*, London, Turnstile Press, 1952.

——, 'Towards a Philosophy of Socialism', in R. H. S. Crossman (ed.), *New Fabian Essays*, 1952.

——, 'On Political Neuroses', *Ecounter*, May 1954.

——, *Labour in the Affluent Society*, London, Fabian Society, 1960.

——, 'The Spectre of Revisionism', *Encounter*, April 1960.

——, *Planning for Freedom*, London, Hamilton, 1965.

——, *The Backbench Diaries of Richard Crossman*, (ed. J. Morgan), London, Hamilton & Cape, 1981.

Dalton, H., *Practical Socialism for Britain*, London, Routledge, 1935.

Desai, R., *Intellectuals and Socialism: 'Social Democrats' and the Labour Party*, London, Lawrence & Wishart, 1994.

Desmond, S., *Labour: The Giant with the Feet of Clay*, London, Collins, 1921.

Drucker, H. M., *Doctrine and Ethos in the Labour Party*, London, Allen & Unwin, 1979.

Durbin, Elizabeth, *New Jersualems*, London, Routledge & Kegan Paul, 1985.

Durbin, Evan, *The Politics of Democratic Socialism*, London, Routledge, 1940.

Durkheim, E., *The Elementary Forms of the Religious Life*, trans. by J. W. Swain, London, 1915; New York, Free Press, 1965.

Duverger, M., *The Study of Politics*, trans. by R. Wagoner, London, Nelson, 1972.

Eccleshall, R., Geoghegan, V., Jay, R. and Wilford, R., *Political Ideologies*, London, Hutchinson, 1984.

Eldon Barry, E., *Nationalisation in British Politics*, London, Cape, 1965.

Elliott, G., *Labourism and the English Genius*, London, Verso, 1993.

Fielding, S., 'White Heat and White Collars: The Evolution of Wilsonism', in R. Cooney, S. Fielding and N. Tiratsoo (eds), *The Wilson Governments, 1964–1970*, London, Pinter, 1993.

Foot, M., *Aneurin Bevan, vol. 2: 1945–60*, London, Davis-Poynter, 1973.

——, 'The Future of the Left', *Encounter*, July 1960.

Foot, P., *The Politics of Harold Wilson*, London, Penguin, 1968.

Foote, G., *The Labour Party's Political Thought*, London, Croom Helm, 1985.

Gaitskell, H., 'The Economic Aims of the Labour Party', *Political Quarterly*, January–March 1953.

——, 'Public Ownership and Equality', *Socialist Commentary*, June 1955.

——, *Socialism and Nationalisation*, London, Fabian Society, 1956.

Gamble, A., 'The Labour Party and Economic Management', in M. J. Smith and J. Spear (eds), *The Changing Labour Party*, London, Routledge, 1992.

Goodman, G., *The Awkward Warrior. Frank Cousins: His Life and Times*, London, Davis-Poynter, 1979.

Gordon Walker, P. 'The Future of the Left', *Encounter*, July 1960.

Gould, B., *A Future for Socialism*, London, Cape, 1989.

Gray, J., *After Social Democracy*, London, Demos, 1996.

Greenleaf, W. H., *The British Political Tradition, vol. 2: The Ideological Heritage*, London, Methuen, 1983.

Griffiths, J., *Pages from Memory*, London, Dent, 1969.

Hamilton, M. B., *Democratic Socialism in Britain and Sweden*, London, Macmillan, 1989.

Harrison, R., 'The War Emergency Workers' National Committee, 1914–1920', in A. Briggs and J. Saville (eds), *Essays in Labour History, 1886–1923*, London, Macmillan, 1971.

Haseler, S., *The Gaitskellites: Revisionism in the Labour Party 1951–64*, London, Macmillan, 1969.

Hatfield, M., *The House the Left Built: Inside Labour Policy-Making 1970–75*, London, Gollancz, 1978.

Hattersley, R., *Choose Freedom: The Future for Democratic Socialism*, London, Penguin, 1987.
——, *Who Goes Home? Scenes from a Political Life*, London, Little, Brown & Co., 1995.
——, 'Tone of the Times', *The Guardian*, 27 April 1995.
Heffernan, M. and Marqusee, M., *Defeat from the Jaws of Victory*, London, Verso, 1992.
Hinden, R. 'The New Socialism', *Socialist Commentary*, November 1956.
——, 'Socialism by Half', *Socialist Commentary*, March 1962.
Hobsbawm, E., *Labouring Men: Studies in the History of Labour*, London, Weidenfeld & Nicolson, 1964.
——, 'The Forward March of Labour Halted', in M. Jacques and F. Mulhearn (eds), *The Forward March of Labour Halted?*, London, New Left Books, 1981.
——, 'Labour's Lost Millions', *Marxism Today*, October 1984.
——, 'The Face of Labour's Future', *Marxism Today*, October 1984.
Holland, S., *The Socialist Challenge*, London, Quartet, 1975.
Holmes, M., *The Labour Government 1974–79*, London, Macmillan, 1985.
Horner, D., 'The Road to Scarborough: Wilson, Labour and the Scientific Revolution', in R. Cooney, S. Fielding and N. Tiratsoo (eds), *The Wilson Governments, 1964–1970*, London, Pinter, 1993.
Howard, A., *Richard Crossman: The Pursuit of Power*, London, Pimlico, 1991.
Howell, D., *British Social Democracy*, London, Croom Helm, 1976; 2nd edn 1980.
Hughes, E., *Keir Hardie*, London, Allen & Unwin, 1956.
Hughes, C. and Wintour, P., *Labour Rebuilt: The New Model Party*, London, Fourth Estate, 1990.
Jacques, M. and Mulhearn, F. (eds), *The Forward March of Labour Halted?*, London, New Left Books, 1981.
Jay, D., *The Socialist Case*, London, Faber & Faber, 1937.
——, 'Beyond State Monopoly', in *Where? 5 Views on Labour's Future*, London, Fabian Society, 1959.
——, *Socialism in the New Society*, London, Longman, 1962.
——, *Change and Fortune: A Political Record*, London, Hutchinson, 1980.
Jefferys, K., *The Labour Party Since 1945*, London, Macmillan, 1993.
Jenkins, P., *Mrs Thatcher's Revolution: The End of the Socialist Era*, London, Cape, 1987.
Jenkins, R., 'Equality', in R. H. S. Crossman (ed.), *New Fabian Essays*, London, Turnstile Press, 1952.
——, *Pursuit of Progress*, London, Heinemann, 1953.
——, 'Hugh Gaitskell: A Political Memoir', *Encounter*, February 1964.
Jennings, J. R., *Georges Sorel*, London, Macmillan, 1985.
Jones, T., 'Labour Revisionism and Public Ownership, 1951–63', *Contemporary Record*, vol. 5, no. 3, Winter 1991.
——, 'Neil Kinnock's Socialist Journey: From Clause Four to the Policy Review', *Contemporary Record*, vol. 8, no. 3, Winter 1994.
Kelf-Cohen, R., *Twenty Years of Nationalisation*, London, Macmillan, 1969.
Kellner, P., 'Labour Learns to Love the Market', *The Independent*, 8 May 1989.

——, 'Labour Adaptions Since 1979', *Contemporary Record*, vol. 3, no. 2, November 1989.

Kinnock, N., *The Future of Socialism*, London, Fabian Society, 1985.

——, *Making Our Way: Investing in Britain's Future*, Oxford, Blackwell, 1986.

——, 'Reforming the Labour Party', *Contemporary Record*, vol. 8, no. 3, Winter 1994.

Labedz, L. (ed.), *Revisionism*, London, Allen & Unwin, 1962.

Labour Party, *Labour and the New Social Order*, London, 1918.

——, *Labour and the Nation*, London, 1928.

——, *Labour's Call to Action*, London, 1931.

——, *For Socialism and Peace*, London, 1934.

——, *The Labour Party's Call to Power*, London, 1935.

——, *Let Us Face the Future*, London, 1945.

——, *Labour and the New Society*, London, 1951.

——, *Facing the Facts*, London, 1952.

——, *Industry and Society*, London, 1957.

——, *Labour in the Sixties*, London, 1960.

——, *Labour's Aims*, London, 1960.

——, *Signposts for the Sixties*, London, 1961.

——, *Labour's Programme 1973*, London, 1973.

——, *Social Ownership*, London, 1986.

——, *Statement of Democratic Socialist Aims and Values*, London, 1988.

——, *Meet the Challenge, Make the Change*, London, 1989.

——, *Opportunity Britain*, London, 1991.

——, *Labour's Aims and Values*, London, 1995.

Lasswell, H. and Kaplan, A., *Power and Society*, New Haven, Connecticut, Yale University Press, 1946.

Leach, R., *Genesis as Myth and Other Essays*, London, Cape, 1969.

Lee, J., *My Life With Nye*, London, Cape, 1980.

Levy, B., 'The Double Image', *New Statesman*, 31 October 1959.

Lichtheim, G., 'New Right', *New Statesman*, 30 November 1962.

Luard, E., *Socialism Without the State*, London, Macmillan, 1979.

Mackintosh, J. P., 'Socialism or Social Democracy? The Choice for the Labour Party', *Political Quarterly*, vol. 43, no. 4, October–December 1972.

——, *John P. Mackintosh on Parliament and Social Democracy* (ed. D. Marquand), London, Longman, 1982.

McKenzie, R. T., *British Political Parties*, 2nd edn, London, Heinemann, 1963.

McKibbin, R., *The Evolution of the Labour Party, 1910–1924*, Oxford, Oxford University Press, 1974.

——, 'Homage to Wilson and Callaghan', *London Review of Books*, 24 October 1991.

Marquand, D., 'Clause Four Rides Again', *Times Literary Supplement*, 26 September 1975.

——, 'Inquest on a Movement', *Encounter*, July 1979.

——, *The Progressive Dilemma: From Lloyd George to Kinnock*, London, Heinemann, 1991.

Marr, A., 'He's Not One of Them – and it Shows', *The Independent*, 11 January 1995.

——, 'Welcome Back From the Wilderness', *The Independent*, 19 December 1995.

Middlemass, K., *The Politics of Industrial Society*, London, Deutsch, 1979.

Mikardo, I., 'Why Labour Can Attack', *Tribune*, 27 November 1959.

Miliband, R., 'The Labour Government and Beyond', in *The Socialist Register 1966*, London, Merlin Press, 1966.

——, *Parliamentary Socialism*, London, Merlin Press, 1961; 2nd edn 1972.

Minkin, L., *The Labour Party Conference*, Manchester, Manchester University Press, 1980.

——, *The Contentious Alliance*, Edinburgh, Edinburgh University Press, 1991.

Minkin, L. and Seyd, P., 'The British Labour Party', in W. Paterson and A. Thomas (eds) *Social Democratic Parties in Western Europe*, London, Croom Helm, 1977.

Morgan, K. O., 'The Rise and Fall of Public Ownership in Britain', in J. M. W. Bean (ed.), *The Political Culture of Modern Britain*, London, Hamish Hamilton, 1987.

——, 'The Labour Party Since 1945', in A. Seldon (ed.), *UK Political Parties Since 1945*, Hemel Hempstead, Philip Allan, 1990.

——, *Labour People, Leaders and Lieutenants: Hardie to Kinnock*, Oxford, Oxford University Press, 1987.

Morrison, H., *Socialisation and Transport*, London, Constable, 1933.

Nicholls, T., *Ownership, Control and Ideology*, London, Allen & Unwin, 1969.

Norman, W., 'Signposts for the Sixties', *New Left Review*, vol. 11, September–October 1961.

Oliver, F. S., *The Endless Adventure*, London, Macmillan, 1930.

Ovenden, K., *The Politics of Steel*, London, Macmillan, 1978.

Owen, D., Rodgers, W. and Williams, S., open letter to *The Guardian*, 1 August 1980.

Padgett, S. and Paterson, W. E., *A History of Social Democracy in Postwar Europe*, London, Longman, 1991.

Pease, E. R., *The History of the Fabian Society*, London, Frank Cass, 1918, 3rd edn 1963.

Pelling, H., *The Challenge of Socialism*, London, A. & C. Black, 1954.

——, *A Short History of the Labour Party*, London, Macmillan, 10th edn 1993.

Perkin, H., *The Rise of the Professional Society*, London, Routledge, 1989.

Pimlott, B., 'The Labour Left', in C. Cook and I. Taylor (eds) *The Labour Party*, London, Longman, 1980.

——, *Harold Wilson*, London, Harper Collins, 1992.

Ponting, C., *Breach of Promise: Labour in Power, 1964–1970*, London, Hamish Hamilton, 1989.

Punnett, R., *British Government and Politics*, 6th edn, Aldershot, Dartmouth, 1994.

Radice, G., *Labour's Path to Power: The New Revisionism*, London, Macmillan, 1989.

——, *Southern Discomfort*, London, Fabian Society, 1992.

Radice, G. and Pollard, S., *More Southern Discomfort*, London, Fabian Society, 1993.

Rentoul, J., *Tony Blair*, London, Little, Brown & Co., 1995.
Riddell, P., 'Theatrical Blow Struck in Battle to Banish the Old Dogma', *The Times*, 5 October 1994.
Rodgers, W. T. (ed.), *Hugh Gaitskell, 1906–63*, London, Thames & Hudson, 1964.
Rogow, A. and Shore, P., *The Labour Government and Industry, 1945–51*, Oxford, Blackwell, 1955.
Seyd, P., *The Rise and Fall of the Labour Left*, London, Macmillan, 1987.
Seyd, P. and Whiteley, P., *Labour's Grass Roots: The Politics of Party Membership*, Oxford, Oxford University Press, 1992.
——, 'Red in Tooth and Clause', *New Statesman and Society*, 9 December 1994.
Shaw, E., *The Labour Party Since 1979: Crisis and Transformation*, London, Routledge, 1994.
——, *The Labour Party Since 1945*, Oxford, Blackwell, 1996.
Shinwell, E., *I've Lived Through It All*, London, Gollancz, 1973.
Shore, P., 'Labour and Public Ownership', *New Statesman*, 21 September 1957.
——, 'In the Room at the Top', in N. Mackenzie (ed.), *Conviction*, London, MacGibbon & Kee, 1958.
——, *Leading the Left*, London, Weidenfeld & Nicolson, 1993.
Smith, J., Boateng, P., Holman, R., Vincent, J., Armstrong, H. and Smith, C., *Reclaiming the Ground* (ed. C. Bryant), London, Spire, 1993.
Smith, M. J., 'A Return to Revisionism? The Labour Party's Policy Review', in M. J. Smith and J. Spear (eds), *The Changing Labour Party*, London, Routledge, 1992.
Smith, M. J. and Spear, J. (eds), *The Changing Labour Party*, London, Routledge, 1992.
Smith, T., *The Politics of the Corporate Economy*, Oxford, Martin Robertson, 1979.
Socialist Union, *Socialism: A New Statement of Principles*, London, Socialist Commentary Publications, 1952.
——, *Twentieth Century Socialism*, London, Penguin, 1956.
Sopel, J., *Tony Blair: The Moderniser*, London, Michael Joseph, 1995.
Sorel, G., *Reflections on Violence*, Riviere, 1908; trans. by T. E. Hulme and J. Roth, Glencoe, Illinois, Free Press, 1950.
——, *From Georges Sorel* (ed. J. Stanley), New York, Oxford University Press, 1976.
Strachey, J., *Contemporary Capitalism*, London, Gollancz, 1956.
——, 'The New Revisionist', *New Statesman*, 6 October 1956.
Straw, J., 'Clause that Drew Blood', *The Guardian*, 24 February 1993.
——, *Policy and Ideology*, Blackburn, Blackburn Labour Party, March 1993.
Taverne, D., *The Future of the Left: Lincoln and After*, London, Cape, 1974.
Tawney, R. H., *The Acquisitive Society*, London, Bell & Sons, 1921.
——, *The Radical Tradition* (ed. R. Hinden), London, Penguin, 1966.
——, *The Attack and Other Papers*, Nottingham, Spokesman Books, 1981.
Taylor, I., 'Ideology and Policy', in C. Cook and I. Taylor (eds), *The Labour Party*, London, Longman, 1980.
Thomas, H., *John Strachey*, London, Eyre Methuen, 1973.

Thompson, A., *The Day Before Yesterday*, London, Sidgwick & Jackson, 1971.

Tomlinson, J., *The Unequal Struggle? British Socialism and the Capitalist Enterprise*, London, Methuen, 1982.

Tudor, H., *Political Myth*, London, Pall Mall, 1972.

Warde, A., *Consensus and Beyond*, Manchester, Manchester University Press, 1982.

Watson, S., 'Winning the Trade Unions', in W. T. Rodgers (ed.), *Hugh Gaitskell, 1906–63*, London, Thames & Hudson, 1964.

Webb, S., *Socialism: True and False*, London, Fabian Society, 1894.

Wertheimer, E., *Portrait of the Labour Party*, London, Putnam, 1929.

Whitehead, P., 'The Labour Governments, 1974–79', in A. Seldon and P. Hennessy (eds), *Ruling Performance*, Oxford, Blackwell, 1987.

Whiteley, P., *The Labour Party in Crisis*, London, Methuen, 1983.

Williams, P., *Hugh Gaitskell: A Political Biography*, London, Cape, 1979.

Williams, R. (ed.), *May Day Manifesto*, London, Penguin, 1968.

Wilson, H., 'A Four Year Plan for Britain', *New Statesman*, 24 March 1961.

——, *The New Britain*, London, Penguin, 1964.

——, *Purpose in Politics: Selected Speeches*, London, Weidenfeld & Nicolson, 1964.

——, *The Relevance of British Socialism*, London, Weidenfeld & Nicolson, 1964.

——, *Final Term: The Labour Government, 1974–76*, London, Weidenfeld & Nicolson, 1979.

——, 'Memories of Hugh Gaitskell', *The Guardian*, 8 September 1983.

Winter, J. M., *Socialism and the Challenge of War*, London, Routledge & Kegan Paul, 1974.

Wood, D., 'The Inheritance', in W. T. Rodgers (ed.), *Hugh Gaitskell, 1906–63*, London, Thames & Hudson, 1964.

Wright, A., *British Socialism*, London, Longman, 1983.

Young, H., 'Never Did a More Decent Man Rise to the Top in British Politics', *The Guardian*, 13 May 1994.

——, 'Why Blair is Now More than Mr Nice Guy', *The Guardian*, 6 October 1994.

——, 'The Crusade is Over for an Electorate of Deserters', *The Guardian*, 26 January 1995.

Index